CLARENDON LAW SERIES

Edited by

PETER BIRKS

CLARENDON LAW SERIES

PUBLIC LAW

ADAM TOMKINS

John Millar Professor of Public Law
University of Glasgow

OXFORD
UNIVERSITY PRESS

OXFORD

UNIVERSITY PRESS

Great Clarendon Street, Oxford OX2 6DP

Oxford University Press is a department of the University of Oxford.
It furthers the University's objective of excellence in research, scholarship,
and education by publishing worldwide in

Oxford New York

Auckland Bangkok Buenos Aires Cape Town Chennai
Dar es Salaam Delhi Hong Kong Istanbul Karachi Kolkata
Kuala Lumpur Madrid Melbourne Mexico City Mumbai Nairobi
São Paulo Shanghai Taipei Tokyo Toronto

Oxford is a registered trade mark of Oxford University Press
in the UK and in certain other countries

Published in the United States
by Oxford University Press Inc., New York

© Adam Tomkins 2003

The moral rights of the author have been asserted
Database right Oxford University Press (maker)

First published 2003

British Library Cataloguing in Publication Data

Data available

Library of Congress Cataloging in Publication Data

Data available

ISBN 0–19–926077–X

1 3 5 7 9 10 8 6 4 2

Typeset in Ehrhardt
by RefineCatch Limited, Bungay, Suffolk
Printed in Great Britain by
Biddles Ltd., Guildford and King's Lynn

for Lauren

'. . . the nature of every state depends on the character and will of its ruling body. So liberty has no home in any state except a democracy. Nothing can be sweeter than liberty. Yet if it isn't equal throughout, it isn't liberty at all. For how can liberty be equal throughout, I will not say in a monarchy, where slavery is evident and unmistakable, but in those states where everyone is free in name only?'

CICERO, *De Republica*, *c*.52 BC
(trans. N. Rudd)

Preface

This book offers an account of English public law that is designed to complement the treatment of the subject in the standard textbooks. The book has been written principally with students in mind, although I hope that teachers of public law and other interested readers may also benefit from it. I have not imagined that this book will be primarily used as a tool for learning the rules of public law: for that purpose there are already many fine text- and source-books on the market. This book does not aim to teach the rules of public law: rather, it offers an interpretation of what we might make of those rules. My aim has been to provide an argument about English public law that offers something of a counterblast to the assumptions contained in much of the existing literature.

Thus, I argue for example that the difference between written and unwritten constitutions is less important than that between legal and political constitutions; I set out and defend a new model of the separation of power, a model which has extensive consequences for the way in which I think we should understand our contemporary public law; I suggest that no account of public law can succeed unless the problems associated with the concept (and with the continuing power) of the Crown are fully dealt with; and I argue, against the prevailing orthodoxy, that political forms of accountability through doctrines such as ministerial responsibility to Parliament remain central to our system of public law. The book also contains a number of arguments about the sovereignty of Parliament, the law of judicial review, and human rights.

These are issues which are fundamental both to constitutional and to administrative law, and while it may be that it is to first-year law students, meeting public law for the first time, that this book primarily appeals, there is I hope something in it also for more experienced readers who are returning to the subject. In writing the book I have tried to keep footnotes to a minimum, but I have included a short bibliographical essay at the end of the book which may be used as a guide to further reading.

With a title as broad as *Public Law*, it will always be necessary to delimit the subject somehow. The argument in this book proceeds on the basis that public law does two things: it provides for the institutions that exercise political power, and it provides for mechanisms of holding the exercise of such power to some form of account. After an introductory chapter on constitutions, the first part of this book (chapters 2–4) is concerned with the first of these themes, 'power', and the second part (chapters 5–6) is concerned with the other, 'accountability'. One aspect of the law that might be considered important to public law, but which is not considered in depth here, is civil liberties and human rights law. While the impact of human rights law on our themes of power and accountability is considered (in chapters 4 and 6), the substance of civil liberties law is not otherwise dealt with here. This is for two reasons: first, because much of modern human rights law does not seem obviously 'public' in character—disputes concerning glossy magazines and the wedding photographs of film stars, for example, seem to be matters for tort or media lawyers, rather than for public lawyers. Secondly, human rights law has now become such a central component of the legal curriculum that squeezing its consideration into already over-crowded public law books is no longer appropriate, even if it ever was. Civil liberties and human rights law require books of their own, books which can discuss both the public law and private law dimensions of modern human rights.

By the time this book is published, I will have moved to Glasgow, but it was written while I was a Fellow and Tutor in Law at St Catherine's College, Oxford. I would like to thank the Master and Fellows of St Catherine's for granting me the sabbatical leave in early 2003 that enabled me to finish the book, and more generally (but no less importantly) for generating an atmosphere that was just about as conducive to research and writing as is possible nowadays in an undergraduate Oxford college. This is no mean achievement, and I am grateful for having been able to benefit from it.

I have been thinking about public law for more than fifteen years, and in that time I have accumulated a number of debts, intellectual and otherwise. In London I was extremely fortunate to have Carol Harlow, Rick Rawlings, Keith Ewing, and Conor Gearty as colleagues. In Oxford I have benefited from numerous insights gained from conversations with Paul Craig, Liz Fisher, Nicholas Bamforth, and Joshua Getzler. Martin Loughlin, Peter Oliver, Denis Baranger, and Nick Barber were all good enough to read several draft chapters, and their often critical comments are very much appreciated. I shall remember with particular fondness my many fights in North Oxford pubs with Nick Barber over questions of sovereignty, separation, the rule of law, and other matters. At OUP Jane Kavanagh has been an energetically supportive editor, and I am grateful to her. For football, beer, and other diversions I thank Mark and Lionel in London and Peter in Oxford. But most of all, for her extraordinary support, and for being the light in my life, I thank Lauren.

Contents

Part II: Accountability

Table of Legislation

Council of Europe

European Community

United States of America

Table of Cases

Canada

Council of Europe

European Community

United States of America

I

On Constitutions

ENGLISH PUBLIC LAW

This book is concerned with public law in England, and before we go any further it is as well to say something about what this means and why it is important. The principal unit in which and through which political power is exercised is the State. This is more clearly the case in some parts of the world than it is in others. The State of Australia, for example, currently looks a lot more stable and secure than does the State of Afghanistan. Closer to home, States in Western Europe are changing with remarkable speed. Individual States have internal tensions, with claims for varying degrees of secession, autonomy, or independence (Spain and the Basque country, and the United Kingdom and Northern Ireland are but the most obvious, and bloody, examples). Equally, all States in Europe which are, or which aspire to be, members of the European Union are learning new ways of pooling or sharing aspects of their sovereignty (or power) with each other, and with a complex central European authority based in Brussels. The State is a variable and changing commodity. In neither politics nor law is it any longer the sole player (if ever it was), and the varied challenges of regionalism, of internationalism, and of globalization have subjected the State to multiple and unprecedented pressures. Yet the State remains key to the constitutional worlds of both law and politics, and it is with public law as it operates in the context of the State that we are primarily concerned here.

The particular State which concerns us is the United Kingdom. The United Kingdom is a complicated State. It is an asymmetrical union of four component parts: England, Wales, Scotland, and Northern Ireland. The asymmetry of the union is dynamic, not static. The legal and political relationships between and indeed within the component parts are changing. The most recent change has had the effect of significantly augmenting the differences between the parts. By virtue of the Scotland Act 1998 Scotland now has its own Parliament and its own executive, headed by its own First Minister. But moreover, these Scottish institutions are not scaled-down versions of their UK counterparts. The Scottish Parliament is composed differently from the United Kingdom Parliament, its electoral system is different, its powers are different, and its internal organization and operation are different. The way in which the First Minister is appointed is different from the way in which the UK's Prime Minister is appointed, so that even though England and Scotland share a single monarch, her powers are different in the two territories. It is not just Scotland which is different—further differences are readily identifiable in the cases of Wales and of Northern Ireland.

This causes public lawyers a problem. The phrase 'public law' invites comparison with 'private law'. What is the distinction between the two? This is a difficult and contentious issue, to which we shall return, but for the past two centuries or more, one distinction between public and private law in the United Kingdom has been its jurisdictional scope. Private lawyers have tended to concern themselves with the *English* law of contract, or the *Scots* law of delict, whereas public lawyers have concerned themselves with the *British* constitution. This book does differently. While comparative examples will, where appropriate, be drawn from other jurisdictions (including other jurisdictions within the United Kingdom), our focus will be on England, and on English public law. This is for two main reasons. The first is modesty—with the growing changes in public law as between the component parts of the United Kingdom, English lawyers with no training in or direct experience of Scots law, or of devolved Welsh government, should be wary of continuing the lazy (not to say arrogant, even imperialist) assumption that the English can with authority equate themselves with and speak for the British.

But the second reason is, for this book, more pressing. Relative to its constituent parts, the United Kingdom is a young entity. It came into existence only in 1800, with the Act of Union between Britain and Ireland. Britain itself had been in existence at that point for less than a century, having been created only in 1707 with the Act of Union between England[1] and Scotland. Yet, as we shall see, many of the central and most

---

[1] 'England' here means England and Wales. Fitting Wales into the account is a problem. Wales was rather unceremoniously overtaken by England in 1536. Unlike Scotland, Wales has no separate legal system, and English law applies. However, since the Government of Wales Act 1998, Wales has enjoyed a form of administrative or executive devolution which may in time create a separate Welsh public law identity. For the time being though, Wales will continue to be regarded, however unsatisfactorily, as subsumed within English public law.

important pillars of the public law that we shall explore in this book were erected before 1707, and are in that historical sense, aspects of English public law, and not British. While this book is in no sense a work about the history of law, it is a principal contention of the argument here that English public law cannot be adequately understood without a sense of history.

WHAT ARE CONSTITUTIONS FOR?

We commence our inquiry into English public law with an examination of the nature of constitutions. The question, what are constitutions for, may be answered very simply. Constitutions perform three main tasks: they provide for the creation of the institutions of the State; they regulate the relations between those institutions and one another; and they regulate the relations between those institutions and the people (citizens) they govern. Each of these can briefly be considered in turn.

The institutions of the State normally include a legislature or series of legislatures to make the law; an array of executive agencies (government, Cabinet, civil service, local authorities, regulators) to administer the law; and a judiciary to determine authoritatively disputes about the meaning or implementation of the law. Additionally, a constitution may provide for there to be a Head of State (such as a monarch or president) and for there to be some form of defence of the State (armed forces, police service, secret intelligence and security services, and so forth). A constitution does not necessarily have to create or provide for the creation of all of the above institutions, but all constitutions make provision for at least some such institutions.

In addition to merely creating the institutions of State, a constitution will also make some provision for regulating the relations between the institutions. What if, for example, they all appear to disagree over a matter of public policy. Let us suppose that a State's government is elected on a manifesto commitment to reform abortion law such that abortions may be lawfully performed only during the first trimester of pregnancy. The legislature, however, rejects the government's proposal and passes a law which permits a woman to have an abortion at any time during her pregnancy. The State's highest court then declares that all abortions are contrary to what it proclaims to be the fundamental right to life and are therefore unlawful, no matter how far progressed the woman's pregnancy is. Which institution has the authority to have the last word in the event that they disagree? Constitutions answer this question in a variety of ways, but all constitutions answer it in some way. The constitutional order of the United States of America is such that it is the US Supreme Court which has the last word. In English law, however, it is the legislature—Parliament—which enjoys this status. The rule which confers this status on Parliament (which many would regard as the most important, or basic, legal rule of English public law) is known as the 'sovereignty of Parliament'. We will discuss this rule in more detail in chapter 4. In addition to the doctrine of the sovereignty of Parliament, English public law contains further principles which seek to regulate relations between the institutions of State. The doctrine known as the rule of law provides that the executive must have prior legal authority before it acts (the rule of law is discussed further in chapters 3 and 6). The principle of ministerial responsibility provides that the government's ministers are constitutionally responsible and accountable to Parliament (see chapter 5). The separation of powers and notions of federalism are further examples of the kinds of tools which constitutions may use to regulate the legal and political relations of the institutions of the State.

Finally, constitutions also say something about the people over whom these institutions rule. A constitution may provide for the legislature (or part of it) or for the executive (or its head) to be elected by the people (or some of the people) who live in (or are citizens of) the State. Similarly, a constitution may provide that there are certain things which the State may not do to its people, certain rights, sometimes called fundamental or civil or human rights, which the people enjoy as against the State, which act as limitations on what the State may lawfully do. So that, for example, the government may wish to govern free from criticism, but the law may provide that while certain forms of especially violent or racist speech may be moderately regulated, by and large the people have a 'right' to freedom of speech, especially political speech, such that the government is simply going to have to put up with the inconvenience of being criticized: no matter what the government's electoral or other mandate is, no law may be passed which eliminates free speech. Again, a constitution does not have to protect freedom of speech for it to be a constitution, but all constitutions will have something to say about citizenship, about the extent of democracy, and about the rights and freedoms which citizens can expect to enjoy.

What we have sketched out here is a perfectly adequate functional analysis of what constitutions are for, of what they do. But this analysis feels very flat and rather prosaic. There is something missing, it seems, from an account as dull as this. What is missing is the sense that constitutions, in addition to performing the three main functions outlined here, also embody something of a nation's values. Consider the following famous account of what a constitution is, which comes from the early eighteenth century Tory politician, Viscount Bolingbroke:

> By constitution we mean, whenever we speak with propriety and exactness, that assemblage of laws, institutions and customs, derived from certain fixed principles of reason, directed to certain fixed objects of public good, that compose the general system, according to which the community hath agreed to be governed.[2]

There are at least two elements present in this definition which are missing from the functional account offered above. The first is the notion that constitutional laws and institutions are *derived from certain fixed principles of reason* and are *directed to certain fixed objects of public good*. Leaving aside the now rather out-moded Enlightenment idea that principles of reason are fixed, what Bolingbroke is getting at here is that constitutions not only have functions, they also have goals. They are underpinned and indeed shaped by values, by certain visions of what is in the public good (or public interest), by political ideas. What he is suggesting is that you cannot understand what a constitution is for unless you first understand what values it is based on, and what policies it is seeking to promote. Constitutions are not value-neutral legal documents, dry as dust and dull as ditchwater: they are living representations of the politics which made them and which consume them. Lawyers can find this uncomfortable and embarrassing. It is as if our subject (public law) is somehow to be regarded as being above all this, that law is not only autonomous from but also superior to and purer than mere politics. Such lawyers need to lose their inhibitions. Let us not be ashamed of it: ours is inescapably and deeply a political subject.

The second arresting feature of Bolingbroke's account is contained in its final words: *according to which the community hath agreed to be governed*. Since the time of John Locke, who in the late seventeenth century wrote one of the most influential works on political philosophy ever composed in English—the *Two Treatises of Government*—constitutions have been thought of as higher-status contracts. The parties to the contract are the citizenry and the State: the governed and the

---

[2] Bolingbroke wrote these words in 1734: for a modern edition, see D. Armitage (ed.), *Bolingbroke's Political Writings* (Cambridge, 1997), at 88.

government. As with regular contracts, the process is one of bargaining, negotiation, and exchange. The parties agree to a future and binding course of action. You will deliver my milk if I pay you to do so. They will govern us according to these constitutional standards if we elect them to do so. There is a good deal of make-believe here, of course. Which one of us has been in a position of being able to insist on living under one form of government rather than another? The reality is that we inherit our system of government: we do not generally get the chance to construct it for ourselves. Yet under the fiction an important truth lurks: it is the idea that the constitution is somehow ours. We own it, or at least are stake-holders in it, and can change it, or at least can advocate that it should be changed. Constitutions are not to be regarded as 'out there', imposed from on high on us mere mortals below. Public law is not like banking law, a distant and anonymous external regulator. Its excitement is that it promises that we can all be part of it, if we want to. Whether the reality of contemporary public law lives up to this lofty Enlightenment dream will be a question to be asked throughout our inquiry.

There are numerous values which a constitution might seek to promote, or which a society might seek through its constitution to promote. Democracy is perhaps an obvious one: does a constitution allow for those who hold offices of political power to be democratically elected? Does it allow for the citizenry to participate in the processes of governmental decision-making? If so, does this occur only rarely, on election days, or are there ways in which the governed can make an input on a more frequent basis, through lobbying, or attending focus groups, or speaking at council meetings? Are processes and practices of government open and transparent, or closed and secret? Away from values of democracy, are there other ways in which the exercise of constitutional power can be rendered legitimate? Is heredity a constitutional value? Does the Punch and Judy show of party politics need to be tempered with cooler, more rational debate, which can come about only through non-democratic institutions such as the House of Lords? Is effectiveness a constitutional value? Does it matter that the political institutions are not especially democratic as long as they deliver? All of these questions are issues which can usefully be considered as we examine English public law in the pages that follow.

WRITTEN AND UNWRITTEN CONSTITUTIONS

The first thing anyone learns about English public law is that in England the constitution is unwritten. Almost every other country in the world has a written constitution save the United Kingdom.[3] Much agonizing goes on about whether, and if so why, this matters, but the issue is not as pressing as is generally made out. Indeed, the importance of the distinction between written and unwritten constitutions is greatly exaggerated. The distinction actually matters very little and, as we shall see, there are other constitutional distinctions (especially that between political and legal constitutions) which have rather more significant consequences. The first and most obvious thing to be said about this issue is that, notwithstanding its allegedly unwritten nature, much (indeed, nearly all) of the constitution *is* written, somewhere. The unhappily misleading phrase, 'written constitution' really means 'codified constitution'. Thus, a written, or codified, constitution is one in which all the principal constitutional rules are written down in a single document named 'The Constitution'.[4]

The reason the English constitution takes this unusual unwritten nature is simple. It is because of England's historical development. Written constitutions do not happen by accident. A country acquires a written constitution deliberately, and in direct consequence of a certain political event: either revolution (as in the United States in 1787, France in 1789, or Russia in 1993); acquiring independence from colonial rule (as in Canada in 1867, Australia in 1900, or Malaysia in 1957); or following defeat in war, when the victorious conquerors may impose a new constitution on the defeated enemy (as in West Germany in 1948). It would be an historical inaccuracy to suggest that these events have not occurred in England: there were successful invasions (or defeats at war) in 55 BC and in 1066, and there was a revolution in 1649. But written constitutions are creatures of political fashion. In their modern form they were invented in the radicalism of the political Enlightenment, in the late seventeenth and early eighteenth centuries. England experienced its moments of greatest

---

[3] Two other countries can be said to have unwritten constitutions: Israel and New Zealand. Israel, however, has a series of Basic Laws which now cover most of its constitutional ground, and New Zealand now has both a Constitution Act (1986) and a Bill of Rights Act (1990) which codify a significant proportion of its constitutional law.

[4] Because of their familiarity we will use the phrases 'written' and 'unwritten constitutions', rather than codified and uncodified constitutions, but on the understanding that the phrases are terms of art and are not to be construed literally.

political turmoil well before Enlightenment thinking took hold (indeed, the English political situation of the 1640s and subsequent reaction to it was one of the principal inspirations behind Enlightenment political philosophy), and was not therefore able to benefit from it. If there had been revolution in England, or in Britain, in the late 1700s rather than in the mid 1600s, our constitution would almost certainly look extremely different now.

The oldest and probably the most revered example in the western world of a written constitution is that of the United States of America, whose constitution dates from 1787 (although significant amendments were added both in 1791—the 'Bill of Rights'—and again after the American civil war in the 1860s as well as on other occasions). Yet even a cursory glance at the American constitutional text suffices to illustrate that notwithstanding its almost sacred status in the USA it does not contain a complete code of all America's constitutional rules, nor even of all the important ones. Take for example the impeachment proceedings against President Clinton in the mid 1990s: easily the most important constitutional event in recent American history.[5] The allegations against Clinton were that he had enjoyed extra-marital sexual relations with an office intern and had lied about it. What does the constitutional text tell us about presidential impeachment? To quote its terms in full, Article II §4 of the Constitution provides that: 'The President, Vice-President and all civil Officers of the United States, shall be removed from Office on Impeachment for, and Conviction of, Treason, Bribery, or other high Crimes and Misdemeanours'. This text poses more questions than it answers. What is a high crime or misdemeanour? Is having sex with an intern either of these? Were what Clinton and Monica Lewinsky did 'sexual relations' within the meaning of American constitutional law? If so, was stating that 'I did not have sexual relations with that woman', as Clinton famously declared, a lie? Is lying a high crime or misdemeanour? These are not small questions of detail. These are the most pressing and important questions that were asked of US constitutional law during the whole of the 1990s, and the constitutional text tells us nothing about

---

[5] It could be argued that the Supreme Court's decision in *Bush v Gore* 121 S Ct 525 (2000) to award the presidency to George W. Bush rather than to Al Gore following the apparently indecisive election of November 2000 has overtaken the Clinton impeachment proceedings as the most important constitutional event in recent American history. As it turns out, however, the same argument could be made of *Bush v Gore* as is here made of the Clinton impeachment: the text of the constitution was silent on the critical question of whether hanging chads were to be counted as lawful votes or not. As with the impeachment hearings in Congress, the text itself played only a minimal role in the decision of the Court.

how we may answer them. What this example shows is that written constitutions are not complete codes capable of answering all constitutional questions. Indeed no written constitution could ever be. Constitutional questions, which change over time, are too varied and too unpredictable for any single legal instrument to be capable of answering them all. Even countries with written or codified constitutions need to supplement those codes with unwritten, or more likely uncodified, rules. In this sense all constitutions are (at least in part) unwritten.

There is a lot of nonsense written about the unwritten constitution. In particular, two mistakes are often made. The first is to confuse constitutional content with constitutional form. The distinction between written and unwritten constitutions is one of form, not of substance. It speaks to the question of what the constitution looks like, not of what it actually tells us. No substantive consequences flow from the fact that the constitution is unwritten. As we have already seen, it is true that in English public law Parliament enjoys legislative supremacy (the doctrine of the sovereignty of Parliament). It is also true that the constitution is unwritten. But it is not true that Parliament is sovereign *because* the constitution is unwritten. You could have a written constitution which contained the clause 'Parliament may make or unmake any law whatsoever and nobody may overturn or set aside any Act of Parliament' just as you could have an unwritten constitution which conferred supremacy on a Supreme Court rather than on Parliament.

The second frequent mistake is to say that the unwritten nature of the constitution means that the constitution is flexible. This requires some careful explanation. If the constitution is not written, where is it to be found, and how do we know when we have found it? The answer is that the constitution is to be found in a variety of places: it is a constitution of multiple sources. There are constitutional statutes; there is constitutional secondary legislation; there are constitutional cases—some of which develop constitutional common law, while others interpret constitutional statutes. So far so unexceptional: all of what has been suggested here would be equally true of English criminal law, contract law, or family law. All areas of English law enjoy a multiplicity of sources: none of it is codified. However, in the constitutional context things become more complicated when the non-legal rules of the constitutional order are added. The constitution is not entirely legal. Public law is not exclusively about law (particularly if you define law narrowly to mean that it is concerned only with statutes and cases). As well as being based on ideas derived from political philosophy (as all constitutions are), the English constitution also relies on a number of political (that is, non-legal) sources. These we call 'constitutional conventions'.

A constitutional convention is a non-legal, but nonetheless binding, rule of constitutional behaviour. By non-legal is meant the notion that the rule is not enforceable by a court. Conventions may be recognized as existing, and may even be used by a judge as an aid to interpreting or developing the law, but no court will enforce a convention.[6] A convention is binding not because of the threat of judicial sanction but for one of two other reasons: either because of the political consequences which may follow from its non-observance, or because the person(s) bound by the convention simply feel this sense of being bound so strongly that they will not want to depart from it. Let us illustrate each with an example. It is a constitutional convention that ministers in the government are individually and collectively responsible to Parliament. The contours, strengths, and limitations of this convention will be fully explored in chapter 5, below. The convention of ministerial responsibility includes the rule that ministers must not knowingly mislead Parliament. Now, suppose a Minister does knowingly mislead (that is, lie to) Parliament. No-one could sue the Minister for such an act, nor could the Minister be judicially reviewed.[7] Lying to Parliament is not a legal wrong. But it is a constitutional wrong: it is an example of behaviour which is unconstitutional without being unlawful. While a Minister could not be taken to court over his or her lying to Parliament, however, this is not to say that there would be no reaction, no sanction, or no enforcement of the rule. On the contrary, Parliament would take action. Parliament would require the Minister to attend Parliament, to explain him- or herself, to apologize if the misleading had been inadvertent, or to resign from office if the misleading had been deliberate. Alternatively, the Prime Minister might sack any Minister who had lied to Parliament: the rule-book which the Prime Minister gives to each of his ministers upon appointment to office now provides that: 'Ministers who knowingly mislead Parliament will be expected to offer their resignation to the Prime Minister'.[8] The rule that ministers must not lie to Parliament is a good example of a convention which is politically enforced.[9]

---

[6] The leading case illustrative of the distinction between court-enforcement and court-recognition of constitutional conventions is *Attorney-General v Jonathan Cape* [1976] QB 752.

[7] Judicial review is the name given to the legal procedure by which actions and decisions of the government may be challenged in court. The law of judicial review is the subject of chapter 6.

[8] Ministerial Code (2001), para. 1(iii). This is discussed in more detail in chapter 5.

[9] It is also a good example, it should be noted, of a convention that is written down.

An example of a convention which is followed simply because of the weight of its own authority—that is to say, because people to whom it applies feel that it should apply to them—is the convention concerning the appointment of the Prime Minister. Legally, the Queen may appoint whomsoever she wishes to be her Prime Minister: absolutely anyone, whether a Member of Parliament or not, whether a Peer or not, whether a citizen or not. Indeed, legally, if the Queen so chooses she does not have to appoint anyone at all to the office. There is no legal requirement that there shall be a Prime Minister—the very office is the creation of convention, not law. Yet this legal position does not represent the contemporary reality. In practice the Queen appoints as Prime Minister the person who is the leader of the political party which commands an overall majority of seats in the House of Commons. She does not choose whom she wants. She always appoints someone, and that person is always the person who is the leader of the political party with an overall majority of seats in the Commons.[10] Yet why? It may be that the Queen fears the political consequences of not acting in this way. Perhaps she is jealous of her position and acts in accordance with convention because she does not want her status to be further diminished. But unlike the situation in which a Minister lies to Parliament, it is very unclear what the political reaction to the Queen acting unconventionally would be. It is more likely that the Queen acts conventionally simply because she considers it to be appropriate.

We should be slow to condemn this position. Lawyers frequently struggle to come to terms with the strength of rules which are not supported with judicial sanction. We like to imagine that to be observed rules need sanction and that the most effective form of sanction lies in the court-room. But consider for a moment all the conventional rules which you routinely and perfectly obey, yet which are neither legally binding on you nor enshrined in some form of written code. How many law lectures have you attended in fancy dress, or wearing nothing more than a swimming costume? How many law professors have you spat at? How many times have you picked your nose during tutorials? Every year I ask these questions of my lecture audiences, and never yet has anyone admitted to doing any of these things. Yet nowhere in my lecture theatre is it written

[10] This is true whenever such a person is available. If there is no party with an overall majority (as occurred in 1974), or if there is such a party but it has no clear leader (as occurred in 1957 and 1963), the position is inevitably more complicated. These complications are discussed in chapter 3. For now the important point is that it is not the conventional nature of the rule which gives rise to uncertainty: these complications would arise whether the rule we are considering were legal or conventional.

that students must wear appropriate clothing, must not spit at me, or must not pick their noses. We are all of us bound by convention and custom every day. We do not need to write rules down for them to be effective or for us to feel bound by them. Nor do we necessarily need to attach judicial sanction to them in order to ensure that they will be observed.

Having established what constitutional conventions are and having illustrated the reasons why they may be considered a binding part of the constitutional order, let us return now to the question of written and unwritten constitutions. It was suggested above that it is frequently asserted that the constitution, because unwritten, is flexible. A key part of this argument is that because the constitution is unwritten it relies more than written constitutions do on constitutional conventions, and that conventions, because they are mere political practices rather than legal rules, are flexible. Therefore, the constitution is flexible. This argument makes two assumptions, both of which may be challenged. The first is that the constitution relies so much on conventions because the constitution is unwritten. Does this claim withstand scrutiny? There does not seem to be any reason why this should necessarily be the case. It so happens that issues such as ministerial responsibility and the appointment of the Prime Minister are regulated by convention rather than by law, but there is no reason in principle why this should necessarily be so: it is an accident of history, not a logical requirement. We could easily have a Ministers Act or a Prime Minister Act in which the existing conventional rules could be written down in statutory form. We would still have an unwritten constitution, but it would now be one in which conventions played a lesser role. Equally we could draft a written constitution which provided for a doctrine of ministerial responsibility, but which did not spell out in detail what the obligation of constitutional responsibility would require in various different circumstances. Here we would have a written constitution which, notwithstanding its codified status, continued to rely on conventions to flesh out the basic structure laid down in the text. The extent to which a constitution relies on conventions as a source of authority does not appear therefore to be dependent on whether the constitution is written or unwritten.

The second assumption is that because conventions are political rather than legal they are flexible. To evaluate this claim we have to consider how a rule becomes a convention. There is no authoritative list of constitutional conventions. Equally, however, it is not the case that all political practices would qualify as binding constitutional conventions. Some political practices are merely descriptive of what *does* happen, rather than binding rules setting out what *should* happen, and ought therefore not properly to be regarded as constitutional conventions at all. But how can we tell whether a practice is a binding rule or a mere description? Jennings, a constitutional lawyer writing in the 1930s, considered that a three-pronged test should be applied: to decide whether something is a mere political practice or a binding conventional rule you should ask first, what are the precedents—how long has the thing happened? How long is it since the monarch last appointed someone as Prime Minister who was not the leader of the majority political party in the House of Commons? For how long have ministers been responsible to Parliament? The longer the period of unbroken observance of the rule, Jennings posited, the more likely the thing was to be a constitutional convention. Secondly, Jennings suggested, you should ask whether the people concerned—the leading actors on the constitutional stage—feel bound by the rule. Do they consider it to be a mere practice which could be changed on a whim, or is there a sense that there is an obligation to follow? And finally, Jennings stated, you have to consider whether there is a good constitutional reason for the rule. Is the rule connected to what the constitution is about? In other words, is the thing concerned with the institutions of State, with the regulation of relations between them, or with the regulation of the relationship between the individual and the State?[11]

Thus, a convention is a practice which enjoys a long history of unbroken observance, in respect of which there is a strong sense of obligation, and which forms an integral part of the constitutional order. This does not sound much like a recipe for flexibility! Conventions are traditions—they are things which traditionally happen, over and over again.[12] Tradition is a force for conservatism, for doing the same thing as was

---

[11] See Sir Ivor Jennings, *The Law and the Constitution* [1933] (5th edn., London, 1959), at 136. For a more recent statement to similar effect, see J. Jaconelli, 'The Nature of Constitutional Convention' (1999) 19 *Legal Studies* 24.

[12] Two examples suffice to illustrate the point. As a matter of law a Bill cannot become an Act of Parliament until it is passed by both Houses of Parliament and also receives the royal assent (the only exception, immaterial here, concerns the House of Lords and is considered in chapters 3 and 4, below). However, it is a convention (not a law) that the monarch will not refuse her royal assent to legislation which has been passed by the Houses of Parliament: the last time the royal assent was refused was in 1708 during the reign of Queen Anne. Similarly, as a matter of law the monarch may dismiss the government at any time for any reason or for none. However, it is a convention (not a law) that this power will not be exercised unless the government first suffers a vote of no confidence in the House of Commons: the last time the dismissal power was used without there having been a prior vote of no confidence was in 1834 during the reign of William IV.

done in the past, not a force for change. In this sense reliance on conventions makes the constitution more rigid and more fixed, not more flexible. We should guard against making lazy assumptions about what the source of flexibility is. To the extent that the constitution is flexible, such flexibility does not exist *because* the constitution is unwritten or *because* it relies particularly on conventions. It is true that the constitution is unwritten, and it is true that conventions remain an integral source of constitutional authority, but neither of these facts is itself capable of explaining why the constitution is flexible.

THE CHARACTER OF THE CONSTITUTION

This being the case, is it sustainable to claim that the constitution is flexible at all? In one sense, yes it is: there is a relatively straightforward, indeed rather obvious, way of arguing that the constitution is flexible. A decade ago there was no Scottish Parliament, no Welsh Assembly, no London mayor, and no Human Rights Act. Now we have all these things. The fact that we have recently witnessed extensive constitutional reform is itself evidence of the inherent flexibility of the constitutional order, it seems. Yet there is something troublingly superficial about this argument. Simply because the constitution may from time to time be reformed does not necessarily mean that the constitution must therefore be flexible. As it turns out, many of the changes we have recently seen were exceptionally difficult to make. The processes of devolving power to Scotland and to Wales, for example, can be seen to have comprised several stages, taking many years: first, during the earlier 1990s there were numerous think-tanks looking at the arguments in favour of devolution and then at the detailed mechanics of how it might work;[13] then the Labour government came into office following the 1997 general election; then Parliament passed the Referendums (Scotland and Wales) Act 1997 which created the legal power for the government to conduct referendums in Scotland and in Wales to determine whether there was sufficient popular will in support of devolution; then the government published its White Papers (formal policy documents) outlining the different models of devolution which would be on offer in Scotland and in Wales; then the referendums were held; then the Scotland Act 1998 and the Government of Wales Act 1998 were introduced in, debated in, and eventually passed by,

---

[13] Much of this work built on the earlier experience of the unsuccessful attempts at devolution in the 1970s.

Parliament; then elections were held to elect the Scottish Parliament and the Welsh Assembly; and only then was power devolved, with effect from July 1999. Thus, the process involved, among other things, three rounds of popular voting, and two rounds of legislation in the Westminster Parliament. Change was achieved at the end of the process, but it did not come about easily, nor especially quickly.

An equally straightforward, and indeed equally rather obvious, argument could be made that far from exhibiting great flexibility, the constitution manifests remarkable continuity. Considering the fact that public law in England can be traced back over 800 years to Magna Carta in 1215, the continuities are perhaps unique in the western world. With one short hiatus in the middle of the seventeenth century, there has been an otherwise continuous monarchy for over eight centuries; the House of Lords can be traced back to the early fourteenth century; the powers of the House of Commons have not vastly changed in over 400 years. The relationship between the two Houses of Parliament was significantly reformed in 1911, but has remained broadly constant since then; the balance of power between Parliament on the one hand and the Crown on the other gradually shifted (from the Crown to Parliament) over the eighteenth and nineteenth centuries, but, again, has remained broadly constant since the reign of George V (that is, since the 1930s). But again, this argument too is troublingly superficial. Amid this apparent institutional continuity there has been momentous change: the emergence of democracy, the rise and fall of local government, and the growing power and influence of the judiciary are but three examples. These changes may not have required a new constitutional settlement to be drawn up, but they have clearly radically altered the dynamics of the existing constitution.

Thus, it can readily be seen that both change and continuity are abiding features of the English constitution. Indeed, as with all successful constitutions, a key ingredient of its success is that it has managed to achieve a certain balance between continuity and change. The balance is not fixed but is dynamic, and is open to renegotiation. Some periods will experience rather little reform, and others will witness more. Taking the last twenty years as an example, it might be thought that the period of Conservative government (1979–1997) was a period of relative stability and consolidation, whereas the period since 1997 has been one of rapid and radical reform. Yet, again, both views would be overly simplistic. There was in fact substantial constitutional change during the 1980s and early 1990s: in terms of the relationship between central and local government (with the former taking more control over and even abolishing aspects of the latter); in terms of the constitution and role of the civil service (with senior civil servants becoming more politicized, in a number of senses);[14] and in terms of civil liberties law, with the powers of the police and of the security and secret intelligence services being extended throughout the period. Similarly, notwithstanding the well-known reforms which we have seen since 1997 there have been considerable and significant continuities: the powers and composition of the House of Commons, and the powers and influence of the monarch being among the most notable examples.

As focusing overly narrowly on questions of flexibility and continuity leads only to what might be regarded as rather banal conclusions, perhaps we would do better to change the terms of debate a little. Consider the following observation: the 'constitution is marked by three striking features: it is indeterminate, indistinct, and unentrenched'.[15] This is a much more acute (as well as more interesting) observation than merely asserting that the constitution is flexible. The constitution is said to be indeterminate because not all of its rules are clear: some are vague. The question of whom the monarch should appoint as Prime Minister in the event of a hung Parliament, or in the event that the party with an overall majority of seats has no clear leader, for example, is notoriously unclear. The constitution is said to be indistinct because constitutional law is not sharply demarcated from other areas of law. Is the Police and Criminal Evidence Act 1984 a 'constitutional' statute or one which properly belongs to criminal law? Is freedom of information legislation constitutional in character, or administrative? The questions are without legal significance in the English legal system because there is no special significance attached to the adjective 'constitutional'. It makes no legal difference whether a rule is described as constitutional or not.[16] Thus, the definition we adopted above of what a constitution is carries no authoritative weight in law—as a definition it was not derived from law, but from scholarly analysis. The two should not be confused! Finally, the constitution is said to be unentrenched because there is nothing in it that cannot be changed. The key to entrenchment lies in the power of Parliament. We have already noted the doctrine of the sovereignty of Parliament. This doctrine (which will be discussed more fully in chapter 4) provides that Parliament has

---

[14] This is discussed further in chapters 3 and 5.

[15] S. Finer, V. Bogdanor, and B. Rudden, *Comparing Constitutions* (Oxford, 1995), at 40.

[16] For a contrary view, see Laws LJ in *Thoburn v Sunderland City Council* [2002] 3 WLR 247. This case is discussed in chapter 4.

legislative omni-competence. In short, Parliament may make or un-make any law whatsoever, and nobody has the power to override or to set aside Parliament's legislation. The consequence of this doctrine is that nothing is entrenched: there is nothing which cannot be undone; no law which cannot be unmade.[17] The Scotland Act 1998 could be repealed, as could the Human Rights Act 1998, the Representation of the People Acts, or the European Communities Act 1972. As has been demonstrated, however, the fact that everything can be changed does not mean that everything will be changed. It does not even mean that anything will be changed. As we have seen, neither conventions nor laws are necessarily easily amended: indeed, experience suggests that embarking on constitutional reform entails considerable challenges in practice, notwithstanding the lack of entrenchment in theory.

Would any of this necessarily be different if the constitution were codified? Let us take each feature in turn. First determinacy. Would the constitution necessarily be any less indeterminate if it were written down? Of course not. There is nothing necessarily clearer about a rule which appears as part of a codified text than one which does not. Merely writing down the *existing* rules governing the appointment of the Prime Minister, for example, would not make any clearer what the monarch should do in the event of a hung Parliament. Now, it might be that if we decided to codify our constitution we would simultaneously decide to clarify some of the aspects of the constitutional order which we know to be currently indeterminate. We might, for example, want to make clearer what the monarch should do as regards appointing a Prime Minister in the event of a hung Parliament. But in this case the enterprise would not be one of writing down or codifying the existing constitution, but of writing down new rules. The mere process of writing things down does not of itself make rules less indeterminate.

The second feature was the indistinct nature of the constitution. Unlike the issue of determinacy, this question does appear to be more directly related to the constitution being unwritten. Under a written

---

[17] It could therefore be argued that in a sense it is the law of the constitution which is more flexible than are the conventions of the constitution, and not the other way around. While, as we saw above, conventions are based on traditions, on things which routinely happen, the doctrine of parliamentary sovereignty means that law is relatively difficult to safeguard from future reform. Of course, Parliament could pass a law which replaced a convention (where the two overlap it is the law which prevails), but this rarely happens in practice: conventions are conventions for good reason, and Parliament rarely sees the need to alter them. This may be counter-intuitive to many lawyers, but perhaps the constitution would be *more* flexible if conventions were replaced by laws.

constitution, constitutional law would be that law relating to the written constitutional code and thus a rather easy distinction could be made between constitutional law and other law, if that were felt to be important. This feature of the constitution would be altered by writing the constitution down.

The final feature was the unentrenched nature of the constitution. Would the constitution necessarily become entrenched if it were written down or codified? Again, as with the indeterminacy point above, the answer here is no. Written constitutions do not have to be entrenched, even though they frequently are (at least partially so). A written constitution could contain a clause which provided that legislative power included the power to amend the constitution. Equally, an unwritten constitution could contain entrenched rules. An unwritten constitution could for example contain the following rules: 'the legislature may make or unmake any law save that no law shall infringe the fundamental right to freedom of expression' and 'nobody may override or set aside legislation save that legislation which infringes the fundamental right to freedom of expression may be set aside by the supreme court'. There is no necessary connection between the constitution being unwritten and it being unentrenched.

POLITICAL AND LEGAL CONSTITUTIONS[18]

A constitutional distinction which is of rather more significance than the familiar distinction between written and unwritten constitutions is that between political and legal constitutions. It is a central theme of this book that public law does two things: it provides for the institutions which exercise political power, and it seeks to hold those institutions to some form of account. Thus, public law regulates the enterprise of government. One way of putting this is to say that the purpose of a constitution is to find ways of allowing the government to get away with less. Now, there are essentially two ways in which this may be achieved: politically, or legally. A political constitution is one in which those who exercise political power (let us say the government) are held to constitutional account through political means, and through political institutions (for example, Parliament). Thus, government ministers and senior civil

---

[18] This section is introductory: it does no more than sketch out, in the most rudimentary terms, the models of the political and the legal constitution. We return to these issues and consider them fully in chapters 5 and 6.

servants might be subjected to regular scrutiny in Parliament. The scrutiny may consist of taking part in debates, answering questions, participating in and responding to the investigations of committees of inquiry, and so forth. A legal constitution, on the other hand, is one which imagines that the principal means, and the principal institution, through which the government is held to account is the law and the court-room. If you dislike something which the government has done or is proposing to do, instead of lobbying for parliamentary scrutiny, you simply sue the government in court or seek some form of judicial review.

How may we evaluate the respective merits and limitations of each of these basic models? Two methods suggest themselves: one would be to examine their effectiveness, and the other would be to consider the values which they represent—which is the more democratic, or open, or accessible? Let us briefly consider each of these methods. To be effective a political constitution would clearly require strong and vibrant politics; it would require those performing the scrutiny function to take that function seriously, and to have a relatively high degree of independence from the government of the day. If these conditions were met, it can readily be seen that the model promises much. Governments in a democracy are entirely dependent on politics—it is through the political act of election that they attain much of their legitimacy (as well as their power) and democratic governments continue to possess such power for only as long as they continue to enjoy the support of the majority. This is an exceptionally difficult task for governments to achieve: governments are subject to endless press and media scrutiny, as well as to political opposition from opponent political parties. Thus, politics looks at first sight to be potentially an extraordinarily potent source of accountability: governments will not do things which they cannot politically get away with, as they will lose power. Therefore, imposing on governments systems which allow them politically to get away with less seems to make good constitutional sense.

For a legal constitution to be effective the same initial criteria of seriousness and independence are equally as important as in the political constitution model. Legal systems, courts, and judges will require independence from the government of the day, and will be required to take seriously the idea that law can and ought to be used as a technique of holding the government to account. This may seem axiomatic, but it cannot be taken for granted, as we shall see. Even if these ingredients can be secured, the potential effectiveness of the legal constitution does not seem as obvious as it does for the political constitution. Suing is notoriously expensive, and access to the courts is limited to the well-resourced. Once over that hurdle, suppose that a court does find that a government Minister has acted unlawfully. What then? What is there to ensure that in implementing the judgment of the court the government does as the court wished?

Suppose, for example, that in a case brought by the Equal Opportunities Commission a court rules that the government has acted unlawfully in discriminating against women: that the treatment of women in a certain respect has been worse than that of men. The government could remove the discrimination (and hence comply with the judgment) not by improving the position of women, as the court might have hoped, but by making the position of men worse. The discrimination would be removed (and the judgment of the court therefore technically complied with) but the position of women would not have been improved, and the position of men would have been made worse. This might be the reverse of what the court intended or expected to happen. It would certainly be the reverse of what the EOC, which brought the case, would have wanted. Yet it would be perfectly compatible with what the court had ruled. It is very difficult for courts to have any follow-up to ensure that their judgments are implemented in a particular way. Law and legal institutions lack the continuity and follow-up that politics and political institutions enjoy. We shall see in chapter 6 when we consider matters of legal accountability more fully that there are in English public law a number of instances of courts making what look like effective and powerful—even progressive—judgments but which turn out to be rather weak, as the government finds it so easy (for a variety of reasons) to evade or to dilute the strictures which the court had endeavoured to lay down. This is not to say that legal enforcement can never be effective, nor that political enforcement always will be, but as lawyers we should be very careful about making assumptions that legal means and institutions will necessarily be preferable to political.

What of the values which the two models embody? The political constitution relies on the rigour and the vigour of the political process. The more open, transparent, participatory, representative and deliberative politics is, the better the model will work in practice. These are commendable values, but there are two problems with them: first, these values are far easier to articulate than they are to follow in practice, and most, if not all, political systems fail to live up to them. Secondly, there is the inescapable problem of what a democracy (based on majority rule) does with its minorities. This is the strength, perhaps, of the legal model of constitutionalism. Suing may be expensive, but it is at least equally expensive whether you form part of the political majority or not—unlike the political constitution model, there is no inherent discrimination in favour of the majority. The down-side, however, is that, unlike those who in a democracy hold political office, judges are neither democratically elected, accountable, nor representative. In England they remain over-whelmingly male, white, old, upper-middle class lawyers. The greater their constitutional and political role, the more this matters. We shall return to these issues in chapters 5 and 6.

Having set out, in rather basic terms, the political and the legal models of constitutionalism, we can now begin to apply those models to English public law. Which of these models does English public law more closely resemble? The answer to this question is changing. Traditionally, English public law has been based on the political constitution, but over the past thirty years the tradition of the political constitution has come under increasing pressure from the rival theory of legal constitutionalism. This pressure, while present since the early 1970s, has only intensified in the past decade. By 'traditional' English public law I am referring (loosely) to the century between about 1870 and 1970. During the course of this period the relationship between the courts on the one hand and the institutions of parliamentary government on the other was broadly stable. The abiding influence over English public law throughout this period was that of Dicey. Dicey was an Oxford law professor in the late nineteenth century whose most famous book, first published in 1885, was *An Intro-duction to the Study of the Law of the Constitution*. Dicey's view was that the courts should play only a limited role in public law. This needs to be carefully explained. Dicey's argument was that the law of the constitution was composed of two cardinal rules, which he labelled the sovereignty of Parliament and the rule of law. We have already encountered the first of these, and we need not say anything further on it just here. It is on the rule of law that we now need to focus.

Dicey placed great weight on the importance of the rule of law as a central concept of English constitutional (or public) law, and it might be thought from this that it would follow that he would have been an advo-cate of the legal constitution, the rule of law being the conceptual vehicle through which the legal constitution would manifest itself. However, while he considered the rule of law to be central, Dicey gave it a minimal content—he defined it not only precisely, but narrowly. For Dicey, the rule of law meant three things: first, the absence of arbitrariness—that government should govern by known rules rather than by whim or discretion; secondly, that there should be equality before the law in the sense that there should be no separate code or system of law which applied only to the public sector, to the government, or to the administration; and thirdly, that civil liberties were best protected by the ordinary courts determining questions of the ordinary common law and required no separate or special code or bill of rights. Dicey's is a contentious account of the rule of law, and it should not be thought that his view is the only, or even the best one. Dicey's views are important not because of their intrinsic merit, but because of the influence they had in the period we are considering.[19]

It is the second of Dicey's three statements about the rule of law which is of significance here. Dicey was passionate about the common law. One feature of the common law is that it applies both to the public and to the private. In France, Dicey saw that instead of common law there were separate laws: civil law for private citizens and administrative law for the State and for disputes between the individual and the State. Dicey assumed that any separate administrative or public law would benefit the State, as it would act as an immunity by which the State could avoid being subjected to the full rigours of the common law. In order to seek to prevent this from happening in England, Dicey argued that it was part of the constitutional rule of law that there should be no public/private divide, and that the same common law should apply equally to government and governed. The problem with this is that the State exercises unique power, and if a legal system is to be effective in regulating the power of the State, the law is going to need unique laws to apply to the State. Thus, I may decide after years of buying my morning paper from one particular newsagent that I am going to change to a different vendor. I have no contract with the newsagent: I am in the habit of buying my paper from him, but I am not obliged to do so. Thus, no legal action can be taken against me. Suppose now that a local authority runs a day-centre for the elderly or disabled, and decides to close it and to spend the money it will save on subsidizing bus fares for teenagers. It might be thought that such a decision should be subject to legal action even if an analogous decision which was wholly private would not be. It might be thought that, even in the absence of a contract, or of express reliance, the courts ought to be able judicially to review the fairness and the legality of what the local authority is proposing to do.

---

[19] Further consideration of what the rule of law means in contemporary public law is given in chapters 3 and 6.

Yet, such a procedure, which would apply to the local authority's decision to close the day-centre, but not to the private citizen's decision to
buy his paper from a different newsagent, would apparently violate
Dicey's understanding of the rule of law, which insisted that there
should be commonality, rather than distinction, between public and
private.

Because Dicey's views were so influential as a statement of English
public law, courts in England were exceptionally slow to develop principles of administrative law, that is to say, principles which apply to public
administration (or government) but not to private individuals. As a consequence, the legal constitution struggled to take hold as the animating
idea of English public law. The onus of seeking ways to hold the government (whether local or central) to constitutional account rested not with
the courts, but with the political institutions, with Parliament, and with
the ballot box.

This remained broadly the position until the early 1970s. Since then
the public law role of the courts has grown remarkably. Neither the extent
nor the significance of this development should be under-estimated.
Indeed, the move witnessed in England since 1970, and even more markedly since 1990, from the political to the legal constitution represents one
of the most fundamental realignments of the constitutional order since
the end of the seventeenth century. Even the emergence of democracy
in the early twentieth century—significant though that was—did not
rewrite the unwritten constitution to such an extent. The word is much
over-used but a revolution is happening. The constitution is up for grabs,
and it is the judges who are grabbing it.

There are three causes underpinning the collapse of the Diceyan
constitutional order. The first is Europe. Since 1973, when the United
Kingdom belatedly acceded to the European Economic Community, as it
then was, EC law has had a considerable impact on domestic public law, as
later chapters will spell out in more detail. Legally, there is not one
Europe but two. The second Europe is that of the European Convention
on Human Rights (ECHR). Formally, this Europe has nothing to do with
the EC. The ECHR is a treaty established under the auspices of the
Council of Europe, an international body with forty-one members (the
EC currently has fifteen). Whereas EC law is enforced under the supervision of the European Court of Justice (ECJ) in Luxembourg, the
ECHR is enforced by the European Court of Human Rights (ECtHR)
in Strasbourg. The UK has been a signatory of the ECHR since it was
first drawn up in 1950, but has only relatively recently incorporated the

principal terms of the Convention into domestic law (by virtue of the Human Rights Act 1998). That said, both Europes—the EC and the ECHR—have made a profound contribution to the reshaping of English public law since the early 1970s. One such contribution has been to encourage the judiciary to play a greater constitutional role. We will explore this in greater detail in later chapters.

The second cause of the shift from the political to the legal constitution is that the political constitution has come to be widely seen as having broken down. Ministers, it is felt, are rarely held to account by Parliament. Parliament is no longer able to do its constitutional job—the executive has grown too strong and the domination of political party has effectively undermined the independence from government which non-governmental, backbench, politicians had formerly regarded themselves as having. Were it not for the courts coming to the rescue, the government would have spun out of control, and the first task of the constitution—to hold the politically powerful to account—would be performed by nobody: constitutional government would have ended.[20]

The third cause was that the judges changed. Dicey's influence waned in the academy long before it withered in the court-room, and by the 1970s lawyers were being appointed to the bench who had been educated in law schools which no longer incanted Dicey's views uncritically. As the academic interpretation of public law developed, so too gradually did the judges begin to move out from under the Diceyan shadow. Even the law, eventually, managed to pull itself out of the nineteenth century.

FROM POLITICS TO LAW: *FIRE BRIGADES* AS A CASE-STUDY

This issue, namely the changing relationship between the politics and the law of the constitution, forms a major theme of this book, to which we shall return in many of the chapters that follow. For the remainder of this chapter, we shall consider in detail a single case, decided by the House of Lords in 1995, taking it as a case-study of the contemporary shift in focus from political to legal accountability. Our case is called *R v Secretary of State for the Home Department, ex parte Fire Brigades Union*.[21] In it the House of Lords held that the Home Secretary, Michael Howard, had

---

[20] The argument that the political constitution has broken down, and that party has contributed to the breakdown, is considered at greater length in chapter 5.

[21] [1995] 2 AC 513.

acted unlawfully in attempting to use his prerogative powers[22] to effect changes in the system of compensating victims of criminal injuries. A scheme for this purpose had been in existence since 1964. This scheme operated under the prerogative power of making *ex gratia* payments. In 1988 Parliament passed the Criminal Justice Act, sections 108–117 of which were to introduce a new, statutory, system to replace the old prerogative scheme. The Act received its royal assent in July 1988, but the relevant sections of the Act did not come immediately into force. The commencement provision, section 171 of the Act, provided that the relevant provisions 'shall come into force on such day as the Secretary of State may . . . appoint'.[23]

By 1993 the statutory scheme had still not been brought into effect. In December of that year Michael Howard (the Secretary of State responsible) published a White Paper[24] on *Compensating Victims of Violent Crime: Changes to the Criminal Injuries Compensation Scheme* in which a new (third) system was outlined, whereby awards would be based on a tariff according to the injuries received without any separate or additional payments being made for loss of earnings or other past or future expenses. This so-called 'tariff' scheme would be cheaper and more efficient. The White Paper stated that even though 'provision was made in the Criminal Justice Act 1988 for the scheme to be placed on a statutory footing . . . with the impending demise of the current scheme *the provisions in the 1988 Act will not now be implemented. They will accordingly be repealed* when a suitable legislative opportunity occurs'.[25] The tariff scheme came into force in April 1994. The Fire Brigades Union sought judicial review of the Home Secretary's continuing decision not to bring the relevant provisions of the Act into force and of his decision to implement the tariff scheme. The House of Lords held by a majority of three to two that the Home Secretary had acted unlawfully. Lords Browne-Wilkinson, Lloyd, and Nicholls constituted the majority; Lords Keith

---

[22] Prerogative powers are considered in more detail in chapter 3, below. Prerogative powers are common law powers which are enjoyed by the Crown—that is to say, by the monarch or by her Ministers.

[23] There is nothing unusual in this. Merely because an Act has been passed by Parliament and has received the royal assent does not mean that it is necessarily in force. Most Acts empower the government, in the form of a Secretary of State, to decide when the provisions of the Act should come into force. The Human Rights Act 1998, for example, did not come fully into force until October 2000, and the Freedom of Information Act 2000 is not scheduled to come fully into force until 2005.

[24] A White Paper is a document setting out government policy. White Papers usually, but do not have to, precede legislation.

[25] Cm. 2434, para. 38, emphasis added.

and Mustill dissented. The speeches in the majority focused on the statutory language of section 171. But this is no ordinary case of statutory interpretation: this is a case where the majority of their Lordships significantly moved forward the frontiers of judicial review. As Lord Mustill stated, 'this appeal turns on certain important . . . constitutional issues, which form part of a wider debate on the relationship between Parliament, ministers, the courts and the private citizen'.[26]

We will come to consider the views of Lords Keith and Mustill shortly, but first we must outline the position of the majority. Lord Browne-Wilkinson held that the various aspects of the Home Secretary's actions were 'inextricably inter-linked and the legality of the decision to introduce the new tariff scheme must depend' on the legality of the resolution 'not to exercise either immediately or in the future the power or duty conferred on him by section 171'.[27] The first question to consider, therefore, was whether section 171 conferred a power or a duty on the Secretary of State. Lord Browne-Wilkinson ruled that section 171 did not impose a 'legally enforceable statutory duty on the Secretary of State' but continued by stating that:

it does not follow that, because the Secretary of State is not under any duty to bring the section into effect, he has an absolute and unfettered discretion whether or not to do so. So to hold would lead to the conclusion that both Houses of Parliament had passed the Bill through all its stages and the Act received the Royal Assent merely to confer an enabling power on the executive to decide at will whether or not to make the parliamentary provisions a part of the law. Such a conclusion . . . flies in the face of common sense. . . . The plain intention of Parliament in conferring on the Secretary of State the power to bring certain sections into force is that such power is to be exercised so as to bring those sections into force when it is appropriate and unless there is a subsequent change of circumstances which would render it inappropriate to do so.[28]

In Lord Browne-Wilkinson's view, this reading of section 171 meant first that 'the Secretary of State comes under a clear duty to keep under consideration from time to time the question whether to bring' the relevant sections into force, and secondly that 'the Secretary of State cannot himself procure events to take place and rely on the occurrence of those events as the ground for not bringing the statutory scheme into force'. Thus, the decision to give effect to the statement in the White Paper that 'the provisions in the Act of 1988 will not now be implemented' was

---

[26] [1995] 2 AC 513, at 555.　　[27] Ibid., at 549.　　[28] Ibid., at 550–551.

unlawful.[29] The speeches of Lords Lloyd and Nicholls were to similar effect, Lord Lloyd ruling that he would 'construe section 171 so as to give effect to, rather than frustrate, the legislative policy' of the Act, and that he would therefore 'read section 171 as providing that sections 108–117 *shall* come into force *when* the Home Secretary chooses, and not that they *may* come into force *if* he chooses. In other words, section 171 confers a power to say when, but not whether.'[30]

In dissent, Lord Keith stated that to his mind there were four reasons why the court should not intervene in the case: first, that Parliament had evinced no 'intention to confer upon the courts an ability to oversee and control the exercise by the Secretary of State' of his powers; secondly that the terms of section 171 were 'not apt to create any duty in the Secretary of State owed to members of the public'; thirdly that the Home Secretary's decision was of an essentially 'political and administrative character quite unsuitable to be the subject of review by a court of law'; and finally that 'any interference by a court of law would be a most improper intrusion into a field which lies peculiarly within the province of Parliament'.[31]

Lord Mustill ruled in similar terms to Lord Keith, but at greater length. Lord Mustill's speech was the only one of the five which was from the beginning firmly rooted in the context of an overtly stated understanding of the proper constitutional relationship between Parliament, the executive, and the courts. In direct contradiction of Lord Browne-Wilkinson, Lord Mustill expressly stated that the courts have no 'competence to express any opinion on the relationship between the executive and Parliament'.[32] He gave by way of example the passage from the White Paper (to the effect that the provisions in the 1988 Act 'will accordingly be repealed') which Lord Browne-Wilkinson had focused on and stated that such a passage may illustrate a certain degree of forgetfulness that it is Parliament and not the Secretary of State which decides whether to repeal legislation, but this 'is of no consequence here. If the attitude of the Secretary of State is out of tune with the proper respect due to parliamentary processes this is a matter to which Parliament must attend.'[33] In analysing the meaning of section 171, Lord Mustill stated that:

parliamentary government is a matter of practical politics. Parliament cannot be taken to have legislated on the assumption that the general state of affairs in which it was thought desirable and feasible to create the power to bring a new

---

[29] Ibid., at 551.   [30] Ibid., at 570–571; emphasis in the original.
[31] Ibid., at 544.   [32] Ibid., at 560.   [33] Ibid.

regime in effect will necessarily persist in the future . . . I cannot attribute to
Parliament an intention that all the provisions of this Act falling within section
171(1) . . . will be brought inexorably into effect as soon as it is physically possible
to do so, even if the country can no longer afford them.[34]

Consequently Lord Mustill rejected the Fire Brigades Union's argument
that the continuing omission to implement the statutory scheme was a
breach of any duty arising from section 171: 'if there is no duty to bring
the relevant provisions into force, there can be no breach of duty simply
by announcing in advance that the non-existent duty will not be performed'.[35] Lord Mustill further remarked that 'for the courts to grant
relief of this kind would involve a penetration into Parliament's exclusive
field of legislative activity far greater than any that has been contemplated
even during the rapid expansion of judicial intervention during the past
twenty years.'[36] Lord Mustill concluded by stating that the courts have
intervened more and more over the past thirty years where Parliament
has 'been perceived of falling short, and sometimes well short, of what
was needed in order to bring the performance of the executive into
line with the law' and that while he was 'quite satisfied that this
unprecedented judicial role has been greatly to the public benefit', on the
other hand he felt that 'ideally' it is to Parliament that we should turn 'to
check executive errors and excesses; for it is the task of Parliament and the
executive in tandem, not of the courts, to govern the country'.[37]

This is a powerful dissent, and graphically illustrates precisely the
argument that is ongoing in the contemporary English polity: namely,
should we abandon the tradition of relying primarily on Parliament to
hold the executive branch to account and turn instead to the courts, or
should we keep the courts in their traditional—secondary—place, and
continue to allow the political institution of Parliament to play the lead
role in checking excessive government? While the speeches of the three
judges in the majority are framed as if *ex parte Fire Brigades Union* were
merely a straightforward and uncontroversial case of statutory interpretation (a traditional judicial task), Lord Mustill is absolutely right to point
to the constitutional significance of the case. The fact that the judges in
the majority do not deign to discuss the broader constitutional ramifica-
tions of their decision should not mislead us into thinking that there are
none. Indeed, the speeches of the judges in the majority are notable not
only for their apparent constitutional silence, but also for the lack of case
law cited in support of the conclusions which they reach. This lack is

[34] Ibid., at 561–562.   [35] Ibid., at 563.   [36] Ibid., at 562.   [37] Ibid., at 567.

unusual in the common law (which relies heavily on precedent—on the weight of past authority) but in this instance is easily explained. No authority was cited because there was no authority to cite: what was being done in this case was novel.

Lord Nicholls based his judgment, for example, on the notion that, as he expressed it, 'Parliament enacts legislation in the expectation that it will come into operation'.[38] There are two oddities about this: first, if this were true, why does Parliament include in its legislation commencement provisions which do not on their face appear to compel ministers to bring legislation into force? From reading the commencement provision in section 171—which, let us not forget, is wholly unexceptional—would it not appear, *contra* Lord Nicholls, that Parliament enacts its legislation on the understanding that it will not necessarily be brought into force: rather, legislation is enacted on the understanding that the Secretary of State *may* bring it into force? Even if Lord Nicholls is correct, however, a second and more serious oddity remains. Even if the expectation which Lord Nicholls identifies does exist, on what authority is it an expectation which is to be judicially enforced? If Parliament is unhappy that a Secretary of State has not brought legislation into operation, Parliament can do something about it. Parliament does not need the judiciary to step in on its behalf. The Secretary of State is constitutionally responsible and accountable to Parliament, and Parliament can easily put pressure on the Secretary of State so as to compel him to act as Parliament desires. In the last resort, Parliament could pass legislation amending section 171 of the 1988 Act, removing the Secretary of State's discretion and imposing on him a clear duty.

As Lord Mustill implies, this would have been precisely what a court would have ruled under the Diceyan or political constitution model. This would not have been because the court would have been in favour of the Secretary of State's delaying tactics—it is clear from his speech that Lord Mustill thinks that Mr Howard behaved badly. But it would have been because the remedy against the Secretary of State abusing his powers would have been perceived as residing in Parliament, and not in the courts. This being the case, why did the majority of the House of Lords intervene? What has caused the change of approach? The clue, again, lies in Lord Mustill's speech, where he talks of Parliament having been perceived of falling short of what is needed in order to bring the executive into line. The majority do not say this (Lord Mustill states it for them),

[38] Ibid., at 574.

but their intervention was fuelled by their belief that Parliament should have stopped Mr Howard from behaving as he did, but that Parliament had failed to do so.[39]

If the diagnosis of the majority in the *Fire Brigades Union* case is correct, that is, if the political constitution is broken, this leaves us with a stark choice. Either we can do as the majority judges did and give up on it, and hand over to the courts the job of keeping the executive in line, or we can seek to repair it. This is the question which should be borne in mind throughout the chapters that follow, as this is the crucial question which faces us: not do we want to replace our unwritten constitution with a written one, but do we want to replace our political constitution with a legal one?

---

[39] Parliament had tried, as it happens, but it had been unsuccessful. In the longer term, the court also failed to stop Mr Howard. After the judgment of the House of Lords was handed down Mr Howard introduced into Parliament a Bill, which Parliament passed, which put his tariff scheme on a statutory basis, and which repealed the relevant provisions of the 1988 Act: see the Criminal Injuries Compensation Act 1995.

Part I

Power

'since the king ... holds his authority of the people, both originally and naturally for their good in the first place, and not his own, then may the people, as oft as they shall judge it for the best, either choose him or reject him, retain or depose him'

MILTON, *The Tenure of Kings and Magistrates*, 1649

2

The Separation of Power

HISTORY AND PRINCIPLE

Having introduced in the previous chapter some background constitutional issues against which the substance of English public law should be considered, we can now move on to commence our inquiry into the first of our two public law themes: power. There are two ways in which a task such as this may be approached. We may adopt either a principled approach or an historical approach. Under the former we would ask questions such as, what are the principles on which political power is exercised? What makes the exercise of political power just or unjust? Which institutions require to be democratic, which require to be transparent, which require to be representative, and which should be required to encourage or facilitate participation? We would have to spend some time thinking about where such principles might come from—how they might be grounded or justified—but there is more than enough political philosophy to choose from, much of which considers just these questions. Leading political theorists in both the United States and Europe have devoted, and are continuing to devote, a great deal of effort to addressing questions such as these.[1] Having identified our principles, we could then apply them to contemporary public law and use them to explain it.

This would be a perfectly legitimate approach to take, but if it is to be adopted it must be done properly. It is no good simply asserting that public law can be satisfactorily explained by reference to principles of (say) legitimacy, justice, liberalism, and democracy. Such an approach begs two questions: why pick these principles, and what do these principles actually mean—what do they require in practice? A good example of the principled approach being done badly can be found in the decision of the Supreme Court of Canada in the *Quebec Secession Reference* case in 1998.[2] The case concerned the issue of whether Quebec possessed a

---

[1] Some suggestions for further reading along these lines are included in the bibliographical essay.

[2] (1998) 161 DLR (4th) 385.

constitutional right unilaterally to secede from Canada. In giving its answer (which was that there was no such right) the Supreme Court ruled that the Canadian constitution, which dates from 1867, is based on four fundamental principles, namely: federalism, democracy, constitutionalism and the rule of law, and respect for minorities. Now, where do these come from, as a matter of law? For sure, we can see that there are many people who would like their constitution to be based on principles as modern and progressive as these, but that is a different issue. Would it not (sadly) be more accurate to say that a constitution dating from 1867 is more likely to be based on principles of elitism, racism, sexism, and imperialism than on the four good things the Supreme Court identified? We can all pluck principles out of the air and optimistically declare that they form the basis of our constitution, but it is a temptation which should be resisted.[3]

Under the historical approach, we would ask rather different questions. We would think less about how power should be exercised in the abstract, and more about how power actually is exercised in practice. We would consider the development of the roles of the various institutions we have (Crown, Parliament, government, judiciary) and examine the ways in which the power and authority of the institutions have evolved. We would seek to explain the nature of English public law not by the application to it of abstract principles of constitutionalism and the like, but through an understanding of its historical development. Given that, as we saw in the previous chapter, English public law extends back over several centuries and has developed gradually and incrementally, and is not founded on a special document drawn up at a particular time and inspired by particular political principles, it would seem to make good sense to adopt an historical, rather than a principled, method of analysis when considering the peculiarities of public law in England.

This is an approach very much in accordance with the way that public law has traditionally been presented in England. All the great late-nineteenth and early-twentieth century public lawyers had an acute sense of the historical dimension of their subject. This was true not only of Dicey and Jennings, but also of such authors as Erskine May, Anson, Keir, Wheare, and so on. In more recent times this historical sense has been lost somewhat, as writers have tried to adopt a more principled

---

[3] Principles may play a valuable role in evaluating what a constitution *should* do, but evaluating what ought to happen, and explaining what does happen, are different enterprises that need to be kept sharply distinct.

approach, neglecting the historical dimension of the subject. As was suggested above, there is nothing necessarily wrong with this, as long as it is done properly. If public lawyers engage fully with the intricacies and debates of contemporary political philosophy, then there will be much to be gained from thinking about public law from a position of principle. A public law text, or course, which sought to present public law from the perspective of liberalism, for example, would be extremely valuable. But to do it well, considerable time would have to be spent not only on the complexities of modern liberalism itself, which are many, but also on the various criticisms to which it has been subjected from republicans, feminists, Marxists, communitarians, and deliberative democrats, among others.

We are not going to attempt this task here. This book will not argue that English public law can be understood by the application to it of abstract principles of constitutionalism, liberal or otherwise. Rather, this book will take an historical approach. Indeed, one of the main overall arguments of this book is that if we are to understand our contemporary public law properly, we must recover a sense of its history. Now, this is nothing to be frightened of, or worried about. You do not need to be an expert in English constitutional history in order to understand public law. Nor do you have to have studied history to any advanced level before you can thrive as a public lawyer. All that is being asserted here is the much more modest claim that when you read about public law, it is important to remember the temporal dimension of the subject-matter. Remember that public law did not arrive, ready-made, from nowhere. Rather, it has grown out of, and is continuing to grow out of, political events, some of which (such as joining the European Union) are relatively recent, but others of which (such as limiting the powers of the Crown) have been happening for centuries. Exactly what is meant by remembering the historical dimension will become clearer during the course of this chapter.

POWER AND ITS SEPARATION

Our consideration of the theme of power starts with a discussion of its separation. It is clear that not all political power is exercised by the same persons or institutions. The monarch has the power to appoint the Prime Minister; the Prime Minister has the power to request that the monarch dissolve Parliament; Parliament has the power to pass legislation; the courts have the power to ensure that in exercising their statutory functions government Ministers and local government officials act lawfully

and do not abuse their powers, and so on. There are multiple constitutional actors, each with a distinctive role to play. The roles may overlap—and indeed frequently do, as we shall see—but nonetheless we may
with confidence assert that English public law separates power. It divides
it up and shares it out among a variety of persons and institutions.

So far so simple. The more difficult issue comes in considering how
power is separated. In answering this question the contrast between those
who would adopt a principled approach and those who would take an
historical approach is stark. There is a well-known and important constitutional principle which concerns exactly this issue: rather helpfully, the
principle is known simply as 'the separation of powers'. The principle as
it is classically understood emanates from an interpretation of Montesquieu,[4] a mid-eighteenth century French political theorist, combined
with Madison, one of the authors of the *Federalist*, written in America in
1787–1788 in order to generate support for the ratification of what
became the US Constitution. The principle of the separation of powers
supposes that the business of the State can be divided into three functions: legislative, executive, and judicial, and that each function ought to be
carried out by a different institution, each institution being separated
from the other two. The legislature should make the laws; the executive
or government should be responsible for the administration of the laws;
and the judiciary should determine disputes arising out of the interpretation or application of the laws. Each institution should stick to its
prescribed function, and should ensure that it does not trespass onto the
territory of the other two.

These three agencies (legislature, executive, and judiciary) should be
separate in two senses: both as regards their function and as regards their
personnel. Not only should they be responsible for performing different
tasks, but they should be staffed by different people. If you are a member
of the legislature you should not simultaneously also be a judge. If you are
a member of the government you should not also be a legislator, and so
on. An additional ingredient of the principle of the separation of powers,
at least in some accounts, is that the three agencies should be not only
separate from each other but also equal to one another. Further, they
should each be entrusted with the tasks of checking and balancing the

---

[4] See Montesquieu, *The Spirit of the Laws* [1748] (eds. A. Cohler, B. Miller, and H. Stone,
Cambridge, 1989), especially book 11, ch. 6. Montesquieu did not invent the doctrine, but
the interpretation of his work played a pivotal role in developing it in its modern form. For
the history of the separation of powers, see W. Gwyn, *The Meaning of the Separation of
Powers* (The Hague, 1965).

other two. All this is for the purpose, it is said, of safeguarding liberty: as Madison insisted in *Federalist* 47: 'The accumulation of all powers, legislative, executive and judiciary, in the same hands, whether of one, a few, or many, and whether hereditary, self-appointed, or elective, may justly be pronounced the very definition of tyranny'. Montesquieu and Madison were among the eighteenth century's most influential political thinkers, and their work was nowhere more instrumental than in the United States, whose constitution is clearly and firmly based on the separation of powers. It is a very powerful idea.

What about English public law, however? What has been the contribution of the separation of powers here?[5] For most of the twentieth century constitutional commentators took the same basic approach in answering this question. After a brief description of the doctrine, they would assess the extent to which the constitution fitted the model, concluding 'almost with one voice in denying that the separation of powers is a feature of the constitution'.[6] This is not surprising. The numerous instances of fusions, rather than separations, of powers in English public law are well known. The Lord Chancellor, for example, is not only England's highest judge, but also a key member of the House of Lords as a legislative chamber (he is the loose equivalent in the Lords of the Speaker of the House of Commons), and also a senior member of the Cabinet. The monarch has a legislative role (the royal assent), several executive roles (from appointing the Prime Minister down), and remains, at least formally if not in practice, the fount of justice. The nation's highest court is the judicial committee of the House of Lords, the House of Lords also being, of course, the upper house of the legislature. The judges who compose the judicial committee still have a legislative voice (and a vote) in the Lords, even if they now choose to exercise it only rarely.[7] Finally, and perhaps most significantly, every single Minister in the executive is also a member of

---

[5] Understanding the role of the separation of powers in England is complicated by the fact that Montesquieu is often taken to have based his theory on what he had seen on a visit to England in 1729. However, eighteenth century English practice did not in fact reflect Montesquieu's portrayal of the separation of powers. Two explanations are possible: either Montesquieu simply misunderstood what he thought he had seen in England, or in his passage on English government he was writing about an idealized England and not the real one. The latter interpretation is favoured by M. Vile, *Constitutionalism and the Separation of Powers* (2nd edn., Indianapolis, 1998), ch. 4.

[6] C. Munro, *Studies in Constitutional Law* (2nd edn., London, 1999), at 304, citing Emden, Robson, Holdsworth, Griffith and Street, Hood Phillips, and de Smith.

[7] This self-denying ordinance is relatively new. Even 15 years ago the law lords were still actively engaged in the legislative process: witness for example the extensive judicial contributions during the passage of the Bill that became the Courts and Legal Services Act 1990.

either one of the Houses of Parliament: in this sense there is complete
fusion between the legislative and executive branches.

These are overlaps in terms of personnel. But there are also many
functional overlaps: the parliamentary enforcement of parliamentary
privilege appears to be a judicial function carried out by Parliament; the
role in criminal sentencing of the Home Secretary appears to be a judicial
function exercised by a member of the executive;[8] the making of delegated legislation is an example of law-making by the executive rather than
by the legislature; the making of procedural rules governing judicial process is an example of law-making by the judiciary rather than by the
legislature; the extensive use of senior judges to chair public inquiries
involves the judiciary in delicate and often acutely sensitive executive
processes, and so forth. All of these and many more examples besides
could be cited as evidence for what might be called the traditional view:
that English public law is based not on the separation of powers but on
their fusion, the 'efficient secret' of the constitution, as Bagehot famously
expressed it.[9] While we can as a matter of practice identify a distinct
legislature, executive, and judiciary, that is to say, we can say descriptively
that there exist in England a Parliament, a government, and a court
structure, we cannot argue that the constitution prescribes that such a
division should exist. To the limited extent that there is some separation
along these lines, it is merely descriptive and not normative.

More recently, however, the dominance of this view has been challenged. A revisionism has been attempted, led perhaps by three constitutional authors: Colin Munro, T. R. S. Allan, and Eric Barendt. Instead
of dismissing the doctrine as irrelevant in the English context, such
commentators have attempted to portray the constitution as one which
does reflect at least the spirit, if not the letter, of the separation of powers.
Munro, for example, traces as we have just done the overlaps which exist
in contemporary constitutional practice between the legislature and the
judiciary, between the executive and the judiciary, and between the legislature and the executive. But in his survey he lays at least as much
emphasis on the restrictions placed on those overlaps as he does on the
overlaps themselves. Munro places weight, for example, on the fact that
while the law lords possess legislative powers they do not freely use
them; that while the Houses of Parliament possess penal powers, they do

---

[8] On this issue, see now *R (Anderson) v Secretary of State for the Home Department* [2002]
4 All ER 1089.
[9] W. Bagehot, *The English Constitution* [1867] (ed. P. Smith, Cambridge, 2001), at 8.

not generally use them; and that while all Ministers must be members of
one of the Houses of Parliament, there is a statutory cap on the number of
Ministers in the House of Commons. Thus, Munro's conclusion is that
while 'we must grant . . . that there is no absolute separation of powers in
this country . . . in a variety of important ways, ideas of the separation of
powers have shaped constitutional arrangements and influenced our constitutional thinking, and continue to do so'.[10] Allan has taken this view
further: he has relied heavily on the importance of the separation of
powers in relation to establishing a variety of arguments about the constitutional independence of the judiciary.[11] But the scholar who has gone
furthest along the revisionist road is surely Barendt, who in his book
An Introduction to Constitutional Law[12] structures his entire account of
British constitutional law around the separation of powers.

THE SEPARATION OF POWER IN
HISTORICAL PERSPECTIVE

All of these authors exemplify, to varying degrees, what was described
above as the principled approach to public law. They have taken a principle—the separation of powers—and have sought to explain aspects of
English public law by reference to it. How would an account of English
public law that adopted a more historical perspective treat the question of
separating power?

In England power started with the Crown. Power was not conferred
through the force of a revolutionary constitutional document on three
institutions separate but equal, as happened in the United States at its
founding at the end of the eighteenth century. Rather, power emerged. By
the beginning of what historians refer to as the early modern period,
power vested in the Crown. In the Tudor period (1485–1603) great monarchs ruled England. This was the grand, flamboyant, and self-confident
time of Henry VIII and Elizabeth I. England was proud, protestant, and
powerful. For England, it was a time of intellectual and cultural development, of commercial success, and of military domination. At the centre of
everything—the social, the religious, the legal, and the political—was the

---

[10] Munro, n. 6 above, at 328–332.

[11] See his essays, 'Law, Liberty, and the Separation of Powers' and 'The Separation of
Powers and Judicial Review', both in his *Law, Liberty, and Justice: the Legal Foundations
of British Constitutionalism* (Oxford, 1993).

[12] (Oxford, 1998). See also E. Barendt, 'Separation of Powers and Constitutional
Government' [1995] *Public Law* 599.

Crown. This was an age when the Crown did not merely reign: it ruled. Parliaments were summoned, and dissolved, at the Crown's will. When they met their task was not so much to make the law as to offer guidance and support, and especially financial support, to the sovereign. The administration of justice likewise fell under the authority, and the control, of the Crown.

Even by this early stage, however, the Crown's power was not absolute. Three hundred years before the Tudors came to power King John had been required by his barons to accede to the terms and conditions of Magna Carta. This document, first drawn up in 1215 and reconfirmed on numerous occasions since, marked the first great attempt to limit the power of the Crown, which had grown steadily since the Norman conquest of 1066. Magna Carta provided for a series of liberties to be enjoyed by English freemen: rights which the people would hold as against the Crown. A small number of Magna Carta's provisions remain on the statute book to this day, and are indeed still relied on from time to time in modern day case law.[13] The most important of these is contained in cap. 29, which provides that 'no freeman shall be taken or imprisoned . . . or exiled . . . but by . . . the law of the land'. More significantly for present purposes, however, Magna Carta also contained a number of provisions limiting the powers of the Crown to raise various forms of revenue, both through its powers over land and through taxation. While the great fame of Magna Carta, both in England and perhaps even more so in the United States, derives from its somewhat mythological status as the source of such basic rights as trial by jury and habeas corpus, from the sense that it was the first great Bill of Rights, its constitutional significance actually lies less in what it says about liberty and more in what it says about the Crown.

Magna Carta was not alone. Similar charters were drawn up elsewhere in Europe during the thirteenth century. In two respects, however, Magna Carta was special. First, consider its target. Whereas the continental charters were aimed at safeguarding municipal independence or the privileged position of the aristocracy, Magna Carta was aimed instead at the control and subjection of the Crown. It was based on the emerging political theory of 'monarchical responsibility and communal participation in government'.[14] Secondly, its drafting was such that Magna Carta was framed not as a document of force, but as one of law. Even though the

---

[13] An important recent example is *R (Bancoult) v Secretary of State for Foreign and Commonwealth Affairs* [2001] QB 1067.

[14] See J. Holt, *Magna Carta* (2nd edn., Cambridge, 1992), at 29.

political circumstances in which Magna Carta was drawn up were of political crisis and indeed civil war, both the King and the baronage appeared eager to conceal this. The reality was that Magna Carta represented a series of concessions and promises which had to be squeezed out of the King by force and might—it was not until after King John lost effective control of London that he eventually agreed, at Runnymede, to its terms. But the presentation was that Magna Carta was a freely given grant in perpetuity of the liberties of freemen.[15] Legally, Magna Carta was a mix of the old, the new, and the wishful: 'sometimes Magna Carta stated law. Sometimes it stated what its supporters hoped would become law. Sometimes it stated what they pretended was law.'[16] Constitutionally, however, what turned out to be its central claim was its extension and reinforcement of the notion that the Crown is not to levy certain forms of taxation 'except by the common counsel of our realm'.[17]

Who would give this common counsel or consent? At the time of Magna Carta there was no Parliament. The Crown ruled through the *Curia Regis*, the members of which were supplied from among the baronage. Parliament emerged during the course of the thirteenth century out of these medieval institutions, the greater barons forming what became the House of Lords, with the lesser barons emerging as the House of Commons slightly later. Only by the middle of the fourteenth century had a settled bicameral Parliament been established. The constitutional role of this Parliament was to be the vehicle through which the Crown would consult. If the Crown needed revenue, as frequently it did—the process of governing is expensive enough in peacetime but is exorbitant in war—it was to Parliament that it would turn. The Crown ruled, but Parliament held the purse strings.

Magna Carta did not establish this doctrine, but it rapidly became and long remained the most important constitutional document in which the doctrine was set out. On the basis of the terms laid down by Magna Carta, Parliament during the fourteenth and fifteenth centuries established three principles: first, that all taxation without the consent of Parliament is illegal; secondly, that the consent of both Houses of Parliament is required for the passage of legislation; and thirdly, that the Commons has the right to inquire into and to amend the abuses of the Crown's administration.[18] These are the principles of what has become

---

[15] Ibid., chapters 6–7.   [16] Ibid., at 300.   [17] Magna Carta 1215, cap. 12.
[18] See Taswell-Langmead, *English Constitutional History* [1875] (6th edn. by P. Ashworth, London, 1905), at 217.

known as the ancient constitution. Under the ancient constitution power started with the Crown, but its power was checked by Parliament. Now, this division of power, with the Crown on one side and Parliament on the other, clearly looks rather different from the principle of the separation of powers which was considered above. Here there is no division into legislative, executive, and judicial, with each function neatly distinguished from the others and each being performed by separate constitutional actors. Instead, the separation of power in the ancient constitution is an institutional divide. Power resides in the authority of the Crown, save for that which has been specifically forced from it by Parliament.

The doctrines of the ancient constitution have not gone unchallenged since medieval times. The most significant threat to them was posed by the Stuart kings in the seventeenth century. The Tudor line came to an end with the death of Elizabeth I in 1603. The throne passed to James Stuart, King James VI of Scotland, who became James I of England. Neither James nor his son and successor, Charles I (1625–1649), found it at all easy to accommodate themselves to the doctrines of the ancient constitution. The Stuarts were advocates of an altogether different theory of kingship, the divine right theory. This view supposed that kings were God's representatives, and were accountable only to God, and not to such earthly authorities as Parliament. Under the ancient constitution, not all of the powers of the Crown had to be shared with Parliament: in areas such as foreign affairs, the army and navy, and coinage, the Crown reigned supreme. James and Charles sought to extend these limited spheres of absolute power to embrace also areas of domestic policy. James fixed new, higher, levels of forms of indirect taxation such as import duties (known as impositions) without parliamentary assent. Charles could not make do with the levels of revenue available to him through indirect taxation, and imposed a forced loan, again, without parliamentary assent. When faced with opposition in the House of Commons Charles had his opponent MPs arrested and they were incarcerated in the Tower of London. After dissolving Parliament in 1629 Charles ruled without it for eleven years—the period known as the personal rule. But the Crown was short of revenue throughout the 1630s and was required to impose ever more imaginative forms of taxation on its subjects—always without parliamentary sanction, of course—the most notorious form of which was the ship-money. All of these royal acts were challenged in court, but in every case unsuccessfully. In a series of controversial, and critical, cases, the judges offered support to the Crown, even when the weight of precedents was against them.[19]

By the 1640s the ancient constitution could take the strain no longer, and it collapsed as England descended into civil war. The constitutional disagreements between the parliamentarians and the royalists were not the only causes of the English civil war—religion too played a significant role—but they were a central aspect of it. War engulfed England, and spread to Scotland and Ireland, between 1642 and 1648. The war was won by the parliamentarians, led by the end of the decade by Oliver Cromwell. In 1649 Charles I was executed, and between 1649 and 1660 England was, for the only time in its history, a nation without a Crown. Together with the monarchy the House of Lords was also abolished, leaving the House of Commons, along with Cromwell's new model army, to rule. But the republic did not last. Cromwell died in 1658, and within two years of his death the Stuart dynasty had been restored to the throne, Charles II becoming king. However, while the Stuarts were returned, this was no restoration of divine right or of absolutist monarchy. Parliament allowed Charles II to enjoy neither the religious, the military, nor the political powers which his father had assumed.

The restoration, however, settled the constitutional disagreements of the seventeenth century only temporarily. On the death of Charles II in 1685 the throne passed to his (Catholic) brother, James II, and, once again, England rapidly descended into political and religious crisis as the new king, 'with a fixed design to make himself an absolute monarch',[20] attempted to subvert the established church; radically augmented the size of the standing army; procured a judgment from the courts affirming his prerogative power to dispense with the observance of the law;[21] and generally made it clear that 'constitutional limitations would no longer be suffered to stand in the way of his despotic designs'.[22] Three years after having come to power James was overthrown, as Parliament offered the Crown to William of Orange, the protestant husband of James' daughter Mary. In 1688–1689, unlike in 1660, Parliament took no chances, and

---

[19] On impositions, see *Bate's Case* (1606) 2 St Tr 371; on the forced loan, see *Darnel's Case* (1627) 3 St Tr 1; on the imprisonment of the MPs, see *Eliot's Case* (1630) 3 St Tr 293; and on ship-money, see *R v Hampden* (1637) 3 St Tr 825. Extracts from these cases are conveniently collected in J. Kenyon (ed.), *The Stuart Constitution 1603–1688: Documents and Commentary* (2nd edn., Cambridge, 1986).

[20] Taswell-Langmead, n. 18 above, at 499.

[21] *Godden v Hales* (1686) 11 St Tr 1166.

[22] Taswell-Langmead, n. 18 above, at 503–504.

passed into law arguably the most important single document of England's unwritten constitution, the Bill of Rights.

The Bill of Rights 1689 lays down the circumstances under which the Crown may exercise its power. The 'rights' of the Bill of Rights are those enjoyed by Parliament. It is thus a document which governs the constitutional relationship between Parliament and the Crown. Its central provisions are still in force, and it forms a key pillar of the contemporary constitution. Its effects include the following: the prerogative power of dispensing with the law is abolished (Article 1); 'levying money for or to the use of the Crown by pretence of prerogative, without grant of Parliament . . . is illegal' (Article 4); no standing army may be kept in peacetime other than with the consent of Parliament (Article 6); and the 'freedom of speech, and debates or proceedings in Parliament, ought not to be impeached or questioned in any court or place out of Parliament' (Article 9). If the Bill of Rights established that Parliament could lay down the terms and conditions on which England was to continue as a monarchy, the Act of Settlement, which followed in 1701, established that Parliament could also control the very identity of the monarch, by altering, if it wished, the line of succession. The combined effect of these constitutional statutes is that monarchs reign in England not because they have a divine right to do so, but because Parliament has permitted it. Power started with the Crown, but it continues to vest in the Crown only because, and for only as long as, Parliament continues to wish it.

THE CONTEMPORARY POSITION

Why does any of this matter to us? Of what relevance is seventeenth century political history to twenty-first century public law? On one view, it could be argued that while it is an interesting diversion, it does not help us understand contemporary public law: that as long as we have a reasonable grasp of the principles on which our public law is based, the story of how we arrived at our contemporary position is mere background. A better view, however, is that we cannot grasp what those public law principles are without an understanding of where they came from. What the brief history sketched out in the previous section suggests is that, far from being based on a separation of powers between legislature, executive, and judiciary, to the extent that there is a separation of powers in English public law it is a separation between the Crown on the one hand, and Parliament on the other.

This is an interpretation of English public law quite different from both the early twentieth century view that the constitution was not based on the separation of powers at all, and from the more recent revisionism of Munro, Allan, and Barendt. From an historical perspective, the revisionist position looks to be very odd. Surely the earlier commentators were right to argue that the traditional account of the separation of powers plays no real role in English public law. After all, how could it? To suggest that it does is simply ahistorical. As we have seen, the traditional account of the separation of powers was formulated by eighteenth century theorists in France and in America. What the revisionists overlook is that the English constitution was already formed by this time. The structure of the English constitution, at least as far as the legal relationship between the institutions of State is concerned, was already largely in place by the end of the seventeenth century, secured by the Bill of Rights and the Act of Settlement. How could a seventeenth century construct (such as the English constitution) be based on an eighteenth century theory? It is a nonsense to suggest that it could be.[23]

But—and this is where the present argument differs from the early twentieth century writers—this is *not* to say that English public law is not based on a notion of the separation of powers at all. It is just that that notion must be a seventeenth century one. The seventeenth century was the formative period of the English constitution—our foundational moment. The English constitution was forged in the blood of civil war and its aftermath, not in the political idealism of the Enlightenment. Civil war; regicide; interregnum, commonwealth and protectorate; restoration; and the so-called 'glorious' revolution of 1689 were the core components of English constitution-making. By the close of the seventeenth century the foundations of the English constitutional order had been laid. The institutions of State, and the constitutional relations between the institutions of State and each other, were already in place in England by 1700, laid down in the bed-rock of the Bill of Rights and the Act of Settlement. It is hardly surprising, therefore, that an eighteenth century political philosophy cannot explain the English constitution. Sadly for British liberal constitutionalists, the English constitutional order had already emerged before the radical genius of Montesquieu, Tom Paine, and James Madison had become available.

[23] This is not to say, of course, that nothing has changed since 1700. Such an argument would be absurd. The constitution has developed considerably since 1700, particularly in terms of the relationship between the individual and the State. But, at least in terms of the relationship between the institutions of State and each other, such development as there has been since 1700 is based on the foundations which were laid in the seventeenth century.

The Civil War, of course, was fought not between three powers separate but equal, but between two. On the one side there was the Crown, and on the other stood Parliament. Just as the war was fought between parliamentarians and royalists, so too were the peace settlements of 1660–1662 and 1689–1700 negotiations between the forces of Parliament on the one hand and of the Crown on the other. Now, it is one thing to sketch an historical argument to the effect that seventeenth century constitutionalism was based on a separation of power between the Crown and Parliament; it is quite another to take the argument further and to suggest that contemporary public law continues to reflect this historical division. But such is precisely the issue that we will now explore: in what sense may it be argued that contemporary English public law is based on a separation of power between the Crown and Parliament, a separation derived from England's political history?[24]

The argument presented here will be that the separation of power in today's English public law does indeed continue to reflect its seventeenth century heritage. The separation of power English-style, it will be argued, is and remains a confrontational, bi-partisan, bi-polar separation, between the only two powers the constitution has ever recognized as enjoying any degree of sovereign authority, namely the Crown, and Parliament.[25] Every constitutional actor falls on one side or the other of this great divide, in that all constitutional actors ultimately draw their power from either the Crown or from Parliament. This is a separation of power which is designed to facilitate accountability—our second great theme of public law, and the subject of the second half of this book. As with Magna Carta so too with the Bill of Rights and the Act of Settlement: the purpose of these instruments is to find ways of holding the power of the Crown to some form of constitutional or parliamentary account. This stands in some contrast to the classical, eighteenth century understanding of the separation of powers, which, as Madison made clear, was designed not to facilitate constitutional accountability, but to safeguard liberty.

---

[24] I refer to the 'Crown versus Parliament' thesis as a separation of power rather than a separation of powers deliberately. In English public law it is not so much that discrete functions or powers are allocated to separate bodies, but that constitutional authority—power—is divided between the Crown and Parliament.

[25] By describing the Crown and Parliament as the two 'sovereign' authorities of England what is meant is that within their respective domains the Crown and Parliament possess ultimate power—that is, neither is legally dependent on any further source of authority—their power is immanent, not derived. Of course, it may be that their continued ability to *exercise* their power is ultimately dependent on the continued will of the people, but this is a political point about the legitimation of power, not a legal point about its existence.

We shall now explore this thesis in more detail. But rather than continuing to discuss this matter in these somewhat general terms, we shall seek to illustrate the argument with practical examples. Three central aspects of contemporary public law will now be considered, all of which are illustrative of the 'Crown versus Parliament' thesis: that is to say, of the argument that English public law is based on a separation of power not between legislature, executive, and judiciary, but between the Crown and Parliament.

(A) THE SOVEREIGNTY OF PARLIAMENT

In chapter 1 we encountered the rule that in English law there is nothing higher than an Act of Parliament. Usually known as 'the sovereignty of Parliament' this rule governing the hierarchy of legal norms would be more accurately portrayed by the phrase, 'the legal supremacy of Acts of Parliament'. The sovereignty of Parliament was the phrase that Dicey used. Dicey wrote that the rule has two aspects: first, and positively, it means that Parliament may make or unmake any law whatsoever. Secondly, and negatively, it means also that no-one may override or set aside the properly enacted legislation of Parliament. Case law in the century following Dicey supported these propositions, but in the last thirty years a number of legal developments have occurred which threaten, in some senses at least, the Diceyan understanding of the sovereignty of Parliament. These include the United Kingdom's accession to the European Community in 1972, its partial incorporation of the European Convention on Human Rights by virtue of the Human Rights Act 1998, and devolution, particularly Scottish devolution. Both the traditional Diceyan position and the legal effects of the more recent developments will be considered in depth in chapter 4.

Notwithstanding the recent challenges to parliamentary sovereignty, however, (and as we shall see academic legal opinion is divided on whether these developments constitute merely a change to, or a demolition of, traditional understandings of sovereignty) the point to be made here about sovereignty is completely unaffected by the European Community, by human rights, or by devolution. The point here is this: it is important to understand what it is about Parliament that is sovereign, to appreciate what it is about Parliament that enjoys legislative supremacy. It is not the case that everything which Parliament does is sovereign. If a backbench MP stands up in the Commons and makes a speech, there is nothing sovereign about what he or she says. Equally, if a government Minister makes a statement in Parliament, there is nothing sovereign about that, either. The sovereignty of Parliament is a rule which applies only to the legislation which Parliament makes. But it is not even the case that all parliamentary legislation is sovereign: the rule of the sovereignty of Parliament applies only to primary legislation, that is, to Acts of Parliament, to statutes (these three terms are synonymous), and not to delegated or secondary legislation.

Now, how is primary legislation made? Primary legislation is made by three bodies coming together to agree to the terms of a proposal, called a Bill. Those three bodies are the House of Commons, the House of Lords, and the Queen. Acts of Parliament are properly called, in law, Acts of the Queen-in-Parliament. Technically, in law the legislature is not Parliament, but the Queen-in-Parliament. No Bill can become an Act unless it is passed in the requisite way by both the House of Commons and the House of Lords, and then goes on to receive the royal assent. There are exceptional circumstances in which the House of Lords can be effectively by-passed where it is unable to come to an agreement with the Commons,[26] and the Queen retains a legal discretion as to whether or not to grant her assent, although by convention she will not withhold her assent to a Bill which has been properly passed by the Houses of Parliament unless she is advised by her Ministers (presumably that means the Prime Minister) so to do. The last time that the royal assent was withheld was by Queen Anne in 1708. Again, however, these exceptional situations, while important, do not affect the argument here.

The question here is *why*? Oddly, perhaps, this is a rarely asked question. Why does the constitution provide that Acts of the Queen-in-Parliament should have a legal status higher than any other known in English law? The answer is connected to the seventeenth century notion of the separation of power (the 'Crown versus Parliament' thesis) out-lined above. An Act of Parliament represents the legal moment when the two sovereign authorities of England come together and agree: Parliament on the one hand, and the Crown on the other. What could be a higher authority in this scheme of dual sovereignty than the formal agreement of England's two sovereigns? Parliament has never legislated to confer legislative supremacy on itself. The source of law, which pro-vides authority for the propositions that Parliament may make or unmake any law whatsoever and that no-one may over-ride or set aside the prop-erly enacted legislation of Parliament, is not statute. Rather, its source lies in judicial recognition of the historical fact that England has two

---

[26] These procedures are governed by the Parliament Acts 1911 and 1949.

sovereigns, who share power, and that there is no higher authority than these two sovereign authorities coming together formally to agree a measure. In this sense, the doctrine of the sovereignty of Parliament—that is to say, the doctrine of the legislative supremacy of Acts of the Queen-in-Parliament—is a contemporary manifestation of the 'Crown versus Parliament' thesis.

(B) MINISTERIAL RESPONSIBILITY TO PARLIAMENT

A second well-known and prominent feature of the contemporary constitution is that Ministers are accountable to Parliament. Prime Minister's Question Time is but the most dramatic (and televisual) tip of this constitutional iceberg. The doctrine of ministerial responsibility is far more profoundly important—and more effective—than this deceptive tip would credit. It provides that all Ministers are both collectively and individually responsible to their House of Parliament (as we saw above, all Ministers must be members of either the House of Commons or the House of Lords: in most administrations there are about ninety from the Commons and twenty from the Lords).[27] This means that they must give account to Parliament for, and be responsible for, the development and operation of government policy, administration, and expenditure. The obligations of responsibility and accountability are owed both to the chambers of the Houses (the floor) and to the various select committees, especially of the House of Commons, which have grown in importance and power since they were reorganized in 1979. The doctrine of ministerial responsibility was introduced in chapter 1 as being a central feature of the political constitution. Its strengths and limitations will be considered in detail in chapter 5. Our concern here is not to explore the workings of ministerial responsibility at any length but rather to ask the same question as was asked above in relation to the sovereignty of Parliament: namely, why? Why are Ministers constitutionally accountable to Parliament, rather than to each other, to the Prime Minister,[28] to the people, or to the Lord Chief Justice?

Ministers are Ministers of the Crown. They are the monarch's

---

[27] These figures are not binding, although the House of Commons Disqualification Act 1975, s. 2 provides that there may not be more than 95 Ministers in the House of Commons at any one time.

[28] It may be that in current practice the doctrine of ministerial responsibility turns on Ministers' rapport with the Prime Minister, or popularity with their party, as well as on their relationship with Parliament—but our focus here is not on the question of how ministerial responsibility works in practice, but on how the constitution imagines that it should work. See further on this issue chapter 5, below.

advisers. Their oath of allegiance is to the Crown, and they may exercise considerable royal prerogative power on behalf of the Crown. Whenever the Foreign Secretary signs an international treaty, he is exercising prerogative power. Whenever the Home Secretary (or more likely a civil servant in the passport office, an executive agency of the Home Office) issues a passport he is exercising prerogative power. There has not always been a Prime Minister in England, and there have not always been Cabinet Ministers. As we saw above, in the sixteenth and seventeenth centuries the government was carried out not merely in the king's name, but by the king himself. In the early eighteenth century, however, this changed, as the early Hanoverian kings (George I and George II) relied more heavily on advisers than had their Stuart predecessors. The Crown's principal advisers are the Prime Minister and his senior Cabinet colleagues, positions which emerged in the early eighteenth century and which have continued to evolve ever since. However, this development— the shift in the location of Crown power from the king himself to his advisers and Ministers—did not change the fundamental principle won in the constitutional battles of the seventeenth century: namely that there is a royal government in England for one reason and for one reason only, and that is because Parliament says so. Ministers are responsible to Parliament, then, because they are the Crown's servants. The Prime Minister and his senior Cabinet colleagues remain, constitutionally, the Crown's principal advisers, and as such they are the vehicles through which Parliament holds the Crown to constitutional account, keeping the exercise of the Crown's administrative and executive authority within parliamentary terms.

Earlier we saw that the orthodox, eighteenth century version of the separation of powers would view the fusion of legislative and executive personnel in the Houses of Parliament as a breach of the doctrine of the separation of powers. Now, almost the reverse is being argued: namely, that the English vision of the separation of power *requires* that Ministers simultaneously be parliamentarians. If Ministers operated outwith or beyond Parliament, how would Parliament go about its fundamental constitutional task of holding the Crown's government to account? English government is no longer carried out principally by the monarch herself (although the Queen does retain extraordinary personal powers, as we shall discuss in more detail in the next chapter). But that does not mean to say that we no longer have royal government in England. On the contrary, we do, but it is in the main indirectly royal, carried out by the Crown's Ministers, rather than directly royal, carried out by the monarch herself. Ministerial membership of Parliament in this way facilitates, rather than violates, the separation of power. That is to say, ministerial membership of Parliament is the device that enables Parliament to perform its constitutional function of checking the Crown's government. In this sense, the doctrine of ministerial responsibility to Parliament is a second contemporary manifestation of the 'Crown versus Parliament' thesis.

(C) THE LAW AND THE CROWN

Our third example of the contemporary importance of the 'Crown versus Parliament' thesis of the separation of power concerns the tortured relationship of the law to the Crown. The modern case which most clearly illustrates this is *M v Home Office*, decided by the House of Lords in 1993.[29] As with the *Fire Brigades Union* case in the previous chapter, it is useful to consider *M v Home Office* in some detail here. This tragic case involved an asylum-seeker, M, from Zaire (as it then was). He was refused asylum. He sought judicial review of this decision, but his application for judicial review failed. He changed his lawyers, who advised him to seek judicial review a second time, on grounds substantially different from—and stronger than—those on which his first application had been based.

His second application for judicial review was heard in court on the very day that M was due to be deported and repatriated. It occurred late on that day, in the late afternoon, about half an hour before M was due to be flown out from Heathrow. By this time of the day most of the judges have gone home. They leave behind, however, one judge whose task it is to hear emergency applications which cannot be deferred until the morning. That night the judge was Garland J. He heard M's emergency application and sought, and received, an undertaking from the Home Office's barrister that M would not be deported until the application could be fully heard (the following morning); Garland J consequently adjourned the proceedings. The barrister involved later denied that he had ever understood that this is what Garland J had required. Half an hour later M's plane took off, with M on it. M's flight was to Paris, where, after being on the tarmac for three hours, he would be put on a connecting flight to Kinshasa. One might have thought that three hours was ample time for Home Office officials in London to contact Home Office representatives in Paris to prevent M

[29] [1994] 1 AC 377.

from being flown out to Zaire. But apparently not. M was flown to Zaire. On hearing this, M's lawyers in London contacted Garland J seeking from him (this in the middle of the night) a mandatory interim injunction against the Home Secretary ordering him 'by himself, his servants, or his agents' immediately to return M to the United Kingdom. Garland J granted the order of the court which M's lawyers had sought.

The following afternoon the Home Secretary himself became involved, for the first time, in the proceedings. He was advised by his junior Minister that the underlying asylum decision had been the correct one, and by his lawyer that the order made the previous night by Garland J could safely be ignored, as it had been made without jurisdiction. The Home Secretary decided on the basis of this advice that M's return flight to the United Kingdom should be cancelled. M went into hiding and we do not know what became of him, although the government subsequently changed its mind and stated that if he were still alive, and could find his way to the United Kingdom, he would be granted political asylum after all. The day after the Home Secretary made his decision, his lawyers went into court to argue that Garland J's midnight order should be set aside, as it had been made in want of jurisdiction. This argument was successful, and the order was annulled.[30]

M's lawyers, however, were furious, and rightly so. The Home Secretary had ignored an order of the court. Ignoring an order of the court made against you is an offence: it is contempt of court. Even if another court subsequently rules that the court order has been made in want of jurisdiction, only a court can annul an order of the court, and until it is annulled it remains in force. It is not for us, whether we are private citizens or Secretaries of State, to take it upon ourselves to decide which court orders we shall follow and which we shall ignore. M's lawyers brought contempt proceedings against the Home Secretary. Never before in English legal history had a court found that a Cabinet Minister had acted in contempt of court. The question arose whether the courts had the jurisdiction to find that a Minister of the Crown had acted in contempt of court. At first instance, Simon Brown J held that they did not. Commenting on this ruling, the judge stated that:

---

[30] The Crown Proceedings Act 1947, s. 21(2) provides that 'the court shall not in any civil proceedings grant any injunction or make any order against an officer of the Crown . . .'. As the law then stood applications for judicial review were included in the definition of 'civil proceedings' for the purpose of this section, although this ruling has subsequently been changed.

reluctant though any court must be to proclaim the Crown beyond the reach of its ultimate coercive jurisdiction, it is, I believe, difficult to regard this as a black day for the rule of law or for the liberty of the subject. The court is not abrogating an historic responsibility for the control of executive government. Rather, it is recognising that when it comes to the enforcement of its decisions the relationship between the executive and the judiciary must, in the end, be one of trust.[31]

So much for the rule of law then! For Simon Brown J, the relationship between the executive and judiciary is one which is based not on law, on force, on coercion, but on trust, grace, goodwill, and a spirit of co-operation. Both the Court of Appeal (by a majority) and the House of Lords (unanimously) subsequently overturned this verdict. The leading speech in the House of Lords was given by Lord Woolf. It is not an easy read. It is over thirty pages long. Why does a senior and well-respected public lawyer take thirty pages of convoluted constitutional interpretation to arrive at what might seem the fantastically banal conclusion that the courts do indeed have the power to find a government Minister in contempt of court?

If we put this question in more constitutionally sensitive terms, the difficulties which Lord Woolf faced become rather clearer. In the 'Crown versus Parliament' thesis of the separation of power, from where do the courts derive their constitutional authority? Is judicial power sourced ultimately from the parliamentary well or from the Crown? The answer is surely that the courts derive their constitutional authority not from Parliament but from the Crown. The High Court and the Court of Appeal are housed in a cathedral-like building on the Strand in London called the *Royal* Courts of Justice. This name is not an accident. The judicial oath of allegiance is to the Crown—not to the constitution, not to the people, and certainly not to Parliament—but to the Crown. Senior judges, like Cabinet Ministers, are privy counsellors. With this in mind, Lord Woolf's question can be reformulated as follows: can the Crown's courts find the Crown's Ministers in contempt of the Crown's courts? Can one branch of the Crown find that another branch of the Crown is in contempt of the Crown? Clearly, when phrased like this, the question becomes rather more problematic: perhaps this explains Lord Woolf's difficulties.

The House of Lords in *M v Home Office* resolved the case by severing the Crown. By this I do not mean that the court severed itself from its

---

[31] The first instance judgment of Simon Brown J is unreported, but is cited extensively in the judgment in the Court of Appeal of Lord Donaldson MR: see [1992] QB 270, at 284.

font of royal authority, but that it severed the Minister (against whom the proceedings were brought) as a servant of the Crown from the Crown itself. The House of Lords came to the conclusion that while it has no jurisdiction to find the Crown itself in contempt of court, it does have the power to find a mere servant of the Crown in contempt. The decision was hailed as a great victory for the rule of law. But before we prematurely run into the sunlight celebrating the case as a vindication of the rule of law, we should do well to remember three aspects of the Lords' decision which are sometimes overlooked. The first concerns the interpretation given by the House of Lords to the old maxim that 'the Crown can do no wrong'. This maxim was interpreted to mean that whatever the Crown does cannot in law be held to be wrong. This is, however, not the only way in which the maxim could have been interpreted: it could have been interpreted to mean that the Crown has no immune power to authorize wrong-doing. This interpretation had been favoured in an 1865 case called *Feather v The Queen* but in *M v Home Office* the House of Lords chose to adopt an interpretation much more favourable to the Crown, and rather less resounding in its defence of the rule of law. The second aspect of the decision of the House of Lords which should give us pause for thought lies in its ruling that it had no power to find that the Crown (that is to say, the Crown itself, as opposed to a servant of the Crown) could be in contempt of court, thus confirming the essence of Simon Brown J's statement that the relationship between the Crown and the law is one of mere trust: as Lord Woolf expressed it, 'the Crown's relationship with the courts does not depend on coercion'.[32] The final aspect of the decision which should not be overlooked is that the Lords ruled that in the case of Ministers of the Crown, while the courts have the power to find them to be in contempt of court, they have no power to punish them for it: a mere finding 'should suffice' as Lord Woolf stated it.[33]

What this case shows, then, is that even as recently as the 1990s the courts in England have found it exceptionally difficult to subject the Crown and its sovereign authority to the rule of law.

A WORD ON THE COURTS

The aspect of the 'Crown versus Parliament' thesis that will be most controversial among lawyers is likely to be the argument that the courts are in some sense part of, or dependent upon, the Crown, and are not

---

[32] [1994] 1 AC, at 425.　　[33] Ibid.

independent of it. A few words of clarification on this important point are called for here. First, it should be made clear what the argument is *not* saying. It is no part of the present argument to claim that individual judges can be removed from office by mere royal whim, as James I and Charles I thought 400 years ago. The Act of Settlement put a stop to that in 1701.[34] Neither is it being argued here that in disputes involving the Crown the courts will always or necessarily hold for the Crown. Such a thesis would be bound to fail, as both the *Fire Brigades Union* case considered in chapter 1 and *M v Home Office* illustrate. What the argument here *is* suggesting, however, is that the judiciary derives its constitutional power ultimately from that of the Crown. Unlike the position under Article III of the US Constitution, or under Article 220 (formerly Article 164) of the EC Treaty, for example, in English law there is no independent source of judicial authority. The English judiciary is not the third branch of the State, separate yet equal, as is the case in the United States. In England the judiciary is, properly conceived, neither entirely separate nor entirely equal: it is not fully separated (even now) from the Crown, and it remains subservient to it as a source of authority. This is a controversial analysis, but it can be illustrated by examining two lines of authority: one historical and the other contemporary.

Let us take the historical line first. To do this we shall have to return one last time to the all-important seventeenth century. We have already seen how in a series of cases in the early seventeenth century the courts notoriously failed to support Parliament in its constitutional and fiscal battles with the Crown: *Bate's Case*, *Darnel's Case*, *Eliot's Case*, and the *Case of Ship-Money, R v Hampden*, are among the leading examples.[35] In all of these cases the judges, or at least a majority of them, found in favour of Crown practices which were at best of dubious legality, and which were more often than not unambiguously contrary to established doctrine. This is an exceptionally important point: Parliament won the constitutional battles of the seventeenth century by force and by the blood of war, and not through litigation. The courts had the chance of showing their support for Parliament, but it was a chance they chose to let slip.

---

[34] Actually, the Act of Settlement did not entirely stop all aspects of this practice. It was only after 1760 (when George II died and was succeeded by George III) that the death of the reigning monarch no longer put an end to all judicial patents. Before that, even after the Act of Settlement became effective, in 1714 (Anne to George I) and 1727 (George I to George II), a number of judges failed to be reappointed on accession of the new monarch: see C. McIlwain, 'The Tenure of English Judges', in his *Constitutionalism and the Changing World: Collected Papers* (Cambridge, 1939), at 302.

[35] See n. 19 above.

Despite these authorities, however, the period is remembered by many constitutional lawyers not as one of judicial compliance with illicit Crown activities, but as one in which the courts rather magnificently stood up to the power of the Crown, defied it, and sought to subject it to the superior rule of law. Two cases, in particular, are generally cited in support of this view, both decisions of the much-celebrated Lord Coke: first, *Prohibitions del Roy* in 1607[36] and, secondly, the *Case of Proclamations* in 1611.[37] Any argument against the position taken here (that under the 'Crown versus Parliament' thesis the courts fall on the Crown's side) would be likely to rely heavily on these two authorities. It is therefore important to ensure that what Coke decided in these seminal cases is not misunderstood.

The dispute in the first of these cases, *Prohibitions del Roy*, arose out of two related uncertainties: what was the scope of the authority of the ecclesiastical judges, and how should such judges interpret statutes? The King, James I, had in 1605 been advised by his Archbishop of Canterbury, Bancroft, that as to either of the uncertainties 'the king may decide . . . in his royal person'. When the issue came to court, however, Coke stood Bancroft's advice on its head. Coke's famous words on this matter are frequently quoted:

His Majesty was not learned in the laws of his realm of England, and causes which concern the life, or inheritance, or goods, or fortunes of his subjects, are not to be decided by natural reason but by the artificial reason and judgment of law, which law is an act which requires long study and experience, before that a man can attain to the cognizance of it.

Coke's judgment in this case is generally taken to be a striking constitutional defence of the autonomy of the courts from the power of the Crown, Coke insisting that the interpretation of statutes was a task which only the judges, and not the king himself, could authoritatively perform. Is this interpretation of the case correct? When he gave judgment in this case Coke was Chief Justice of the Court of Common Pleas. During the reign of James I, the Church was in the process of launching a determined attempt to shake off the control of the common law courts, of which the Court of Common Pleas was one. What seems to have motivated Coke, as a common lawyer, was a concern to consolidate the power and position of the common law courts over the Church. As the great legal and constitutional historian Maitland argued, Coke was in fact much less interested in *Prohibitions* in limiting the powers of the Crown

---

[36] (1607) 12 Co Rep 63; 77 ER 1342.   [37] (1611) 12 Co Rep 74; 77 ER 1352.

than he was in seeking to justify the controversial intrusion of the common law into ecclesiastical fields.[38] This is the context in which Coke's famous words need to be read: Coke's judgment in *Prohibitions del Roy* is no defence of the common law courts against the power of the Crown. Rather, this is a common lawyer's attack on the power of the seventeenth century Church.

If *Prohibitions del Roy* has been regarded as important for what it has been taken to say about the divide between executive (that is to say, royal) and judicial power, the *Case of Proclamations* has been regarded as central to the establishment of a constitutional distinction between executive (royal) and legislative power. But, as with the former case, here too we need to be careful how we approach this decision. The *Case of Proclamations* concerned the legality of two proclamations made by James I. The first sought to prohibit new buildings in and about London, and the second sought to prohibit the making of starch from wheat. Coke held that the king cannot by his proclamation change any part of the common law. Nor could the king create any new offence by way of proclamation, as that would be to change the law. Coke summarized his judgment with the following well-known words: the king, he said, 'hath no prerogative but that which the law of the land allows him'. In an important recent analysis of this case, Paul Craig has argued that Coke's decision in *Proclamations* has a three-fold significance: first, it 'clearly established that the prerogative was bounded and not unlimited'; secondly, it established that such boundaries were to be determined by the courts, and not by the Crown itself; and thirdly, that 'the principal beneficiary of the court's judgment was, of course, Parliament'.[39] However, as with *Prohibitions*, we ought to treat such analysis with caution. This is for two reasons: first, any protection which Parliament did gain from Coke's decision in *Proclamations* was purely incidental and, secondly, Coke's decision was not based on grand constitutional theory, on seeking to subject the power of the Crown to the rule of law, but on something far more mundane: it was based simply on economics.

Let us briefly examine each of these points in turn. It is always important when reading cases not to stop at the end of the judgment, but to consider what happened next. This is not usually easy: the law reports fall silent once judgment is reached. But what happened next, after

---

[38] See F. Maitland, *The Constitutional History of England* (Cambridge, 1908), at 265–268.
[39] See P. Craig, 'Prerogative, Precedent, and Power', in C. Forsyth and I. Hare (eds.), *The Golden Metwand and the Crooked Cord* (Oxford, 1998), at 68.

Proclamations? The answer is that despite having the opinion of the court against him James I continued to issue proclamations, and his son Charles I went on to issue them in ever greater volume. Such proclamations were enforced by one of the prerogative courts—the Court of Star Chamber. This court was eventually abolished in 1641 by Act of Parliament (note: by Parliament, not by the common law courts) but until that point, and despite Coke's judgment, Parliament did not benefit. In the end it had to act for itself and abolish the authority (Star Chamber) through which proclamations were issued and enforced: it could not rely on the common law courts to act on its behalf. The more important point, perhaps, is Coke's motivation. Just as in *Prohibitions* so too here Coke did not have the high constitutional ideals he is now (mis-)remembered for. His concern in *Proclamations* was not so much to stop the power of the Crown, as it was to protect a certain form of economic liberalism: for Coke 'the ruling principle at common law was freedom of enterprise' and it was the promotion of exactly this freedom which was Coke's motivation in *Proclamations*, not some grand constitutional design.[40]

This brief analysis shows, then, that if public lawyers want to argue, contrary to the 'Crown versus Parliament' thesis presented here, that the courts do possess a fully independent source of constitutional authority, they will be unlikely to be successful if they seek to rely on these famous decisions in support of their argument.

In addition to this historical argument, there is also a more contemporary argument that can be made in support of the notion that the courts are dependent on the Crown for their constitutional authority. As *M v Home Office* illustrates, the courts even in very recent times have struggled to find ways of holding the Crown and its Ministers to constitutional account through extending to them the principles of the rule of law. It might be thought that this does not matter very much, as the constitution imagines that the principal vehicle through which the Crown and its Ministers are held to account is not the court-room, but Parliament. But leaving this point to one side for the moment, we can see that the House of Lords managed to bring the Home Secretary within the jurisdiction of the law of contempt of court only by engaging in the most flagrant of

---

[40] See D. Wagner, 'Coke and the Rise of Economic Liberalism' (1935) 6 *Economic History Review* 30, at 44. Coke ceased to be a judge in 1616 and became a leading parliamentarian in the 1628 Parliament. It may be from his parliamentary career that he has acquired his reputation as a scourge of the Crown: but his parliamentary career and his prior judicial career need to be kept separate from one another when considering Coke's contribution to English constitutional law. This has not always been done.

constitutional fictions: that is to say, only by distinguishing the Crown as monarch (who even after *M v Home Office* remains beyond the reach of the rule of law) from the Crown as executive (which after *M v Home Office* falls partially within the rule of law, in that a court may find a Minister in contempt even though it may not punish a Minister for being in contempt).

In struggling to bring the Crown (whether as monarch or as executive) within the rule of law, *M v Home Office* is quite typical. While the courts have over the past forty years rapidly expanded the law of judicial review of administrative action to bring the executive exercise of discretionary powers more and more fully within the scope of judicial review (and therefore within the rule of law), there remains one major area of executive discretion in which such judicial expansionism has been far more cautiously attempted, and with regard to which far less has consequently been achieved. This area is the prerogative. Now, most judicial review cases concern the exercise by government of statutory powers, rather than of prerogative powers—we shall consider this growing area of law in more detail in chapter 6. The standard example is where Parliament passes an Act which confers on a Minister a statutory power (that is, a discretion) to act in a certain way if he sees fit. The Minister acts, using his statutory discretion, and it is the task of the court to ensure that in doing so the Minister has acted fairly, legally, reasonably, proportionately, or whatever. This is what is known as judicial review of administrative action.

But what of the situation where, instead of seeking to rely on statutory discretion, the Minister is seeking to rely on his prerogative powers—that is to say, on the legal powers he derives from the Crown in his capacity as a Minister of the Crown. The full extent and importance of prerogative power is a topic considered in the next chapter. Here, all that needs to be said is that in contradistinction to the situation regarding the exercise of statutory powers, the courts have over the past forty years struggled to bring the exercise of prerogative powers fully within the scope of judicial review law. There has been the odd breakthrough, in which first the existence, then the extent, and finally the exercise of prerogative power have been subjected to judicial review, but the growth of the law here has been slow and difficult, once again reflecting the sense that the courts are not fully independent of the authority of the Crown.

This is an important topic, and we shall return to it on a number of occasions in the chapters that follow. All that has been done in this chapter, and in particular in this last section of it, is to introduce the thesis of the 'Crown versus Parliament' idea of the separation of power, and to begin to think about where that thesis, if correct, leaves the judges. We shall have more to say about the relationship between the courts and the Crown in the next chapter, and about the courts and Parliament in chapter 4.

3

The Crown

This chapter will consider the public law powers of the Crown. The analysis will be divided into five sections. First, we shall consider the position of the monarch herself. Secondly, we shall discuss the institutions of central government—Prime Minister, Cabinet, civil service, and so forth. The following two sections then address questions of the nature and exercise of royal prerogative power, and of the compatibility of the prerogative with the constitutional doctrine of the rule of law. In the final section of the chapter we shall step back a little from the more detailed discussion of the preceding sections and consider the broader question of what problems are caused for modern public law by its continuing reliance on the power and authority of the Crown.

Before we proceed, a word of clarification is called for on the meaning of the term 'the Crown'. Clearly, when public lawyers talk of the powers of the Crown they are talking metaphorically. The actual Crown is nothing more than a piece of somewhat garish jewellery that is kept securely locked up in the Tower of London.[1] The legal metaphor of the Crown has two meanings: it refers first to the person who is entitled to wear the Crown—that is to say, the monarch. Secondly, it also refers to those who may by virtue of their public office exercise powers on behalf of the monarch, powers which emanate from the authority of the monarch, powers which in former times would have been exercised by the monarch him- or herself, but which have now passed to Ministers and civil servants. The first legal sense of the Crown is sometimes referred to as the Crown-as-monarch, and the second as the Crown-as-executive. This distinction is a relatively recent innovation in the law, dating only from the mid-twentieth century, and it is one that is fraught with difficulty. Sir William Wade, one of the twentieth century's foremost public lawyers, has described it as 'highly artificial'.[2] We shall see as this chapter unfolds

---

[1] See F. Maitland, *The Constitutional History of England* (Cambridge, 1908), at 418.

[2] Sir William Wade, 'The Crown, Ministers and Officials: Legal Status and Liability', in M. Sunkin and S. Payne (eds.), *The Nature of the Crown: A Legal and Political Analysis* (Oxford, 1999), at 26.

that contemporary English public law does not always keep to the distinction between Crown-as-monarch and Crown-as-executive as sharply as perhaps it ought to. We shall return to this issue in the final section of the chapter.

THE MONARCH

The monarch is no mere figurehead. As Queen, Elizabeth II has extraordinary power. We have seen in the previous chapters how the exercise of monarchic power is now constrained in practice, both by constitutional convention and by Act of Parliament. But notwithstanding these constraints the Queen remains immensely powerful. Her power can be analysed as falling into two categories: first there are the specific prerogative powers which continue to be exercisable only by the monarch herself and not by her Ministers; and, secondly, there are the constitutionally significant spheres of influence which remain open to the monarch. Of these, two are especially important: her unique relationship with the Prime Minister and her roles with regard to the Commonwealth. We shall come to these spheres of influence a little later. First, let us consider the prerogative powers which remain personal to the monarch.

The royal prerogative is, as we saw in chapter 1, a source of English public law. Prerogative powers are legal, not conventional, although their exercise in practice may be regulated or limited by convention. Prerogative powers may be exercised either by the monarch herself or on her behalf by her Ministers. Prerogative powers concerning issues such as the ratification of treaties, the defence of the realm, making *ex gratia* payments, issuing passports, and the prerogative of mercy, among others, are now exercised by Ministers rather than by the monarch. However, there remain four major prerogative powers which continue to be exercised by the monarch herself, and not by her Ministers. These are: the appointment of the Prime Minister, the dissolution of Parliament, the dismissal of the government, and the granting of royal assent to legislation.

The law with regard to each of these four powers is relatively simple. The formal legal position is that the monarch may appoint whomsoever she wishes to be her Prime Minister and, if she so desires, she does not have to appoint anyone to the office. As regards the dissolution of Parliament, the monarch may dissolve Parliament at any time, for any reason, or for none, save that the maximum duration of a Parliament is set by statute at five years,[3] which means that if there is no dissolution of Parliament within five years of that Parliament having been summoned it will in any event lapse.[4] The monarch may in law dismiss her government at any time, for any reason, or for none. Similarly, with regard to the royal assent, no Bill may become an Act unless and until it receives the royal assent, and the monarch has in law a complete discretion as to which Bills passed by the Houses of Parliament she assents to. To repeat, from a legal point of view, even the twenty-first century monarch is an extraordinarily powerful person.

This is, however, an area of public law that is heavily regulated by constitutional convention. The conventions are not always as easy to identify as are the formal legal powers. The conventions concerning the dismissal of Ministers and the royal assent to legislation are perhaps more straightforward than are those with regard to the appointment of the Prime Minister and the dissolution of Parliament. We can deal with the more straightforward cases relatively easily. With regard to the dismissal of the government, it might appear that the convention is that this is a power which the monarch will no longer exercise. After all, the last time that a monarch used this power was in 1834, when William IV dismissed a Whig administration led by Melbourne. However, the mere fact that a power has not been exercised for some time is not necessarily conclusive evidence that the power is no longer available. Indeed, the prerogative power of dismissal was—very controversially—exercised as recently as 1975, in Australia, where the Governor-General (the representative of the Crown in Australia) dismissed Prime Minister Gough Whitlam and his government.

A similar argument can be made with regard to the royal assent: while the monarch retains the power to refuse assent, this is a power which, it might be thought, ought no longer to be exercised. The last time that a monarch used this power was in 1708 when Queen Anne refused her assent to the Scottish Militia Bill. However, two caveats should be entered at this point. First, it is highly likely that there is an exception to this rule. If the monarch were given clear and firm Prime Ministerial advice that

---

[3] Parliament Act 1911, s. 7, amending the Septennial Act 1715.

[4] The maximum duration of a Parliament may be extended by Act of Parliament. This occurred during the Second World War: the 1935 Parliament survived until 1945. In addition to its power to dissolve Parliament, the Crown also enjoys a prerogative power to summon Parliaments. The exercise of this power has been controlled by statute since the first Triennial Act (of 1641) provided that Parliament must be called to meet at least every third year, a rule which remains in effect: see now the Meeting of Parliament Act 1694.

she should withhold her royal assent to a Bill which had passed through the Houses of Parliament, it seems to be the case that the monarch should follow that advice. We will consider the issue of Prime Ministerial advice to the monarch further, below. Secondly, we should not be deceived by the longevity of the practice that the royal assent is not withheld into thinking that this is a power the exercise of which is now entirely beyond comprehension. George V came very close to withholding his assent to the Irish Home Rule Bill in 1914, and was arguably prevented from doing so only by the outbreak of the First World War.

When we turn to the appointment of the Prime Minister, the conventional position becomes rather more complicated. Here the convention is easy to state, but not always possible to apply. The convention is that the person appointed Prime Minister is the leader of the political party that commands an overall majority of seats in the House of Commons. The difficulty arises either when there is no such person, or when there is no such party. What if the party with an overall majority of seats in the Commons has no clear leader? This situation is now very unlikely to occur, as all the major political parties have settled rules governing leadership elections. This is a relatively recent development in the evolution of political parties, however, and twice during the reign of the present monarch the Queen has been called upon to appoint a Prime Minister when the party with a Commons majority (in both instances the Conservative Party) had no clear leader.

The first time was in 1957, and the second in 1963. In 1957 Eden resigned as Prime Minister due to illness. It was apparent that there were two possible successors: Macmillan and Butler. In order to decide which of these should be invited to form an administration, the Queen consulted with senior Conservative parliamentarians, who themselves had consulted with various Cabinet Ministers. From such consultations it had become clear that Macmillan had the greater parliamentary support, and accordingly he was called to become Prime Minister. By 1963 Macmillan had himself become too ill to carry on but, concerned to influence his succession, unlike Eden in 1957 he did not resign as Prime Minister. Instead, he announced that his resignation was imminent. This triggered widespread consultations throughout the parliamentary Conservative party, consultations which (again unlike in 1957) were conducted largely by the Prime Minister himself and by junior whips, not by senior parliamentarians. In 1963 there were at least five apparent contenders, not just two. The most popular choice would have been Butler, but for personal political reasons Macmillan was anxious that Butler be stopped.

Macmillan concluded at the end of the process that Lord Home should be called to form the next administration. Only at this point did Macmillan resign. Within an hour of his resigning Macmillan was visited in hospital by the Queen. She asked him for his advice, and he responded that she should call Home. Both of them knew that this advice would be contentious. But despite this, and despite the fact that the advice was not constitutionally binding on the Queen (as Macmillan had ceased to be Prime Minister), the Queen followed the advice, and Home became Prime Minister.

In so doing, did the Queen act improperly? Certainly she acted unwisely. The result of the events of 1963 was that the Conservative party changed its rules, so that its leader would be chosen internally, by party members in Parliament, a rule change the effect of which was to eliminate the monarch's role in the selection process. By allowing herself to be 'duped by' Macmillan,[5] a scheming and clever politician with concerns of his own, the monarchy was effectively deprived of one of its principal prerogative powers. For her own role in co-operating with Macmillan's scheme, and for the appointment of a Prime Minister who was widely felt to have been an inferior choice to Butler, 'the Queen and her Palace advisers were partly culpable. Her decision to opt for passivity, and in effect to collude with Macmillan's scheme for blocking [Butler] must be counted as the biggest political misjudgement of her reign.'[6] Regardless of how the events of 1963 should be assessed, their consequence is clear: all the major political parties now have detailed rules in their party constitutions governing leadership elections, so that whichever party is in office the monarchy will play no role in determining who the Prime Minister should be.

One situation that party rule-books cannot deal with, however, is a hung Parliament. A hung Parliament is one in which no single party enjoys an overall majority of seats in the House of Commons. Because of the 'first past the post' electoral system used for elections to the Commons a hung Parliament is returned only very rarely:[7] since the Second

[5] This is the verdict of the Queen's (unofficial) biographer: see B. Pimlott, *The Queen: Elizabeth II and the Monarchy* (2nd edn., London, 2002), at 335.

[6] Ibid.

[7] To explain: under the 'first past the post' system the country is divided into 659 roughly equal electoral districts known as constituencies. To win a general election (and thereby form the government) a party must win 330 seats—that is, 330 constituencies. This would give that party an overall majority of seats in the Commons. Obviously, the further over the 330 target a party scores, the bigger that party's majority. There is one MP (Member of the House of Commons) elected for each constituency. To become elected, the candidate simply

World War the only election to result in such a Parliament was in February 1974. In such a situation it may be argued that the monarch has a choice as to whom to ask to form an administration. The monarch could choose the leader of the party which was in office before the election, on the ground that that party has not clearly lost, and it is in the interests of continuity (something dear to the hearts of hereditary rulers, it might be thought) for that government to carry on. Alternatively, the monarch could choose the leader of the party with the largest number of seats even though that party did not have an overall majority, on the ground that this is the party which has come closest to winning. A further alternative might be that the monarch should choose the leader of the party which in the monarch's view is most likely to be able to form a stable administration.

On the results of the February 1974 election, each of these options might have led to a different politician being asked by the Queen to form a government. Before the election the Conservatives had been in office, with Edward Heath as Prime Minister. But the largest party in the Commons was Labour, led by Harold Wilson. However, the party with the balance of power—the party which could decide to go into coalition with either the Conservatives or with Labour—was the party in the middle, the Liberals, led by Jeremy Thorpe. In the event, the politicians played their roles in such a way as to prevent the Queen from having to make a choice. Heath initially refused to resign as Prime Minister, instead going into coalition negotiations with Thorpe. Only when these broke down, two or three days after the election, did Heath resign. At that point the Queen had no alternative but to call for Wilson, which she did. He

---

needs more votes in his or her constituency than any other candidate. Thus, suppose in one constituency the Labour candidate receives 34% of the votes cast, the Liberal Democrat candidate receives 33% of the votes cast, and the Conservative candidate receives 32% of the votes cast, the Labour candidate is elected even though he or she polled fewer than half the votes cast: the rule is that you must poll more than any other single candidate, not that you must poll more than all the others put together. In the last two general elections (1997 and 2001) the Labour party polled approximately 40% of the national vote, the Conservatives approximately 33%, and the Liberal Democrats approximately 17%. Yet Labour's majority since 1997 has been around the 170 seat mark, meaning that its 40% of the vote has been translated into over 60% of the seats. If instead of the 'first past the post' system a system of proportional representation or PR were adopted for elections to the Commons, this would mean that the share of the parties' seats in the Commons would reflect the national share of the vote, so that 40% of the vote would translate into 40% of the seats. This form of PR would mean, in the UK, permanent coalition government, as no party commands the support of more than 50% of the electorate. Thus, under this form of PR every Parliament would be a hung Parliament. Further consideration is given to elections to the House of Commons in chapter 4, below.

formed a minority administration, which survived until the autumn, at which point a second election was called, in October, which Labour won with a small overall majority. Labour then continued in office until 1979, the year of Mrs Thatcher's first election triumph.

In the days immediately following the February 1974 election, before Heath resigned, Wilson kept quiet, biding his time. He could have jumped up and down, demanding to be called to the Palace, and making life difficult for Heath and for the Queen. But he did not. Equally, Heath could have resisted resignation for longer, despite the collapse of his coalition negotiations, in the vain hope that Parliament might support him. But again, he did not. Both played their hands like statesmen, rather than careerist party hacks, deliberately keeping the monarchy away from having to intervene. Even if Heath and Wilson had acted less honourably, however, it is likely that the constitution would have operated so as to continue to insulate the Queen. If Heath had not resigned, Parliament would have met, a vote of no confidence would have been moved by the Labour opposition, the vote would have been carried (as the Conservatives no longer had the numbers—they had lost their majority) and Heath would have had no choice but to resign. The most basic of constitutional rules (again, this is a convention, not a rule of law) is that the Prime Minister and the Cabinet remain in office only for as long as they continue to enjoy the support of a majority in the House of Commons: we saw this in the previous chapter when we considered questions of the relation of the Crown and its Ministers to Parliament.

Unlike the House of Commons, the Scottish Parliament is elected under a system that includes a substantial element of proportional representation, greatly increasing the likelihood of a hung Parliament being returned. The terms of the Scotland Act make it clear that the Queen has no discretion as to whom to appoint as First Minister in Scotland: she is compelled to accept the recommendation of the Presiding Officer of the Scottish Parliament, whatever that recommendation may be.[8]

So much for the monarch's prerogative power of appointment of the Prime Minister. Let us turn now to the prerogative of the dissolution of Parliament. The convention here is that the timing of a dissolution is a matter for the Prime Minister. While statute provides that each Parliament has a maximum life of five years, Parliament is not elected for a fixed term. Formally, the monarch may dissolve Parliament at any time—and in the seventeenth century this was an effective weapon in the Stuart

---

[8] Scotland Act 1998, s. 46.

kings' armoury against the parliamentarians. Now, however, the convention is that the monarch will dissolve Parliament only on the advice of the Prime Minister. It will be a key part of the political strategy of most Prime Ministers to decide early in their term of office when to plan for the next election—that is to say, when to request a dissolution. The most successful Prime Ministers seem now to plan on a four-year cycle: Mrs Thatcher requested a dissolution in 1983 (four years after coming into office) and again four years later in 1987. The Conservative party won both elections convincingly. Similarly, Tony Blair requested a dissolution in 2001, four years after coming into power in 1997. However, politics is not always so smooth, of course. There were, as we saw, two elections in 1974. Conversely, there was no election between 1987 and 1992, or between 1992 and 1997, John Major deciding in both 1992 and 1997 to wait the full five years.

The question here is, what is the role of the monarch in these decisions? Is dissolution entirely a matter now for the Prime Minister, or are there any circumstances in which the monarch could constitutionally insist on there being a dissolution even where the Prime Minister did not want one, or, conversely, could the monarch constitutionally refuse a prime ministerial request for a dissolution? No such request was refused by a monarch in the United Kingdom in the twentieth century, although there are two examples from the Commonwealth of Governors-General refusing requests, one in Canada in 1926 and the other in South Africa in 1939.[9] There is, however, an important example of royal insistence on a dissolution even where the Prime Minister did not want one. This occurred during the constitutional crisis of 1909–1911. These were, constitutionally, the most difficult years of the twentieth century, and the story of the 1909–1911 crisis should not be forgotten.

In 1906 the Liberal party was elected to government with a landslide majority. By 1909 Asquith had become Prime Minister, and David Lloyd George was Chancellor of the Exchequer. Lloyd George's 1909 budget reflected his Welsh radicalism.[10] In a brazen attack on vested English landed interests, the budget included proposals to increase death duties; to establish duties on undeveloped land, on coal and mineral royalties,

---

[9] See E. Forsey, *The Royal Power of Dissolution of Parliament in the British Commonwealth* (Toronto, 1943).

[10] In his magnificent study of the period 1910–1914, George Dangerfield wrote that Lloyd George was 'less a Liberal than a Welshman on the loose. He wanted the poor to inherit the earth, particularly if it was the earth of rich English landlords'. See G. Dangerfield, *The Strange Death of Liberal England* (New York, 1935), at 29.

and on reversion of leases; and to impose a super-tax on all incomes over £5,000 a year. While the Commons with its large Liberal majority passed the budget, the Tory-dominated House of Lords hated it, and refused to pass it. The Liberal Cabinet resigned and an election was called—this in January 1910. The election campaign was dominated by the constitutional issue that the budget crisis had brought about: namely, whether the unelected House of Lords should have the power to veto legislation passed by the Commons, and if so whether such power should include the power to veto the budget, the cornerstone of any government's programme. In the event the Liberals were returned, but they lost their majority. From this point on their continuation in office was dependent on the support in the Commons of the Irish nationalists.

Once back in office, the issue became whether the Lords would again reject the budget proposals. Asquith asked the King, Edward VII, to exercise his prerogative power to create between 400 and 500 new Liberal peers to wipe out the inbuilt Conservative majority in the Upper House. The King refused Asquith's request, however, and informed him through his private secretary that he regarded 'the policy of the government as tantamount to the destruction of the House of Lords' and that consequently he would not feel justified in creating peers unless Asquith first called a further general election.[11] Here, then, we have our example of a monarch insisting on a dissolution and subsequent election where the Prime Minister did not want one. As it turned out, Asquith did not need his new Liberal peers, as the House of Lords reluctantly allowed the budget to pass—the Tory majority preferring to vote for a budget they loathed rather than having to live with 400 new Liberals invading their beloved club.

The story does not end here, however. The experience over the budget had persuaded the Liberal government that the powers of the House of Lords needed to be curtailed. Before 1909 there had been an informal understanding that the Lords would not veto money bills which had passed through the Commons. The events of 1909–1910 had shown that something more solid than an informal understanding was now needed if the government was going to be able to conduct its business efficiently. Thus the government introduced legislative proposals to limit the powers of the Lords. To become law, of course, the proposals would have to be passed not only by the Commons but also by the Lords. Would the House of Lords allow its powers to be reduced? Within weeks of the budget eventually passing into law, it looked as if a further constitutional crisis

---

[11] See V. Bogdanor, *The Monarchy and the Constitution* (Oxford, 1995), at 114.

loomed. The crisis was averted by the King's death: Edward VII died in May 1910. Neither Liberals nor Conservatives wanted to welcome the new King, George V, by plunging him into immediate constitutional difficulty, so they agreed that over the course of the summer a closed constitutional conference would be held, at Lansdowne House, at which four leading Liberals and four leading Conservatives would endeavour to negotiate a new settlement, resolving the differences between them over the respective legislative powers of the two Houses of Parliament. The attempt at a negotiated compromise, however, was ultimately unsuccessful, as by the autumn the talks had collapsed.

If the grandees could not decide, then the country would have to, and a further general election was called—this in December 1910. Before the election Asquith sought from the new King an undertaking similar to the one he had earlier sought from Edward VII: namely, that if the Liberals were once again returned to power, and if the House of Lords refused to accede to the terms of the Parliament Bill (the legislation which would reduce the powers of the Lords), then the King would exercise his prerogative to create new Liberal peers to enable the legislation to pass. George V, unlike his father, indicated (albeit reluctantly) that he would be prepared to use his prerogative in this way. The agreement he reached with Asquith was kept secret. In the election the Liberals were again returned. Much to the King's displeasure Asquith then disclosed to the Conservative opposition in Parliament the nature of the undertaking he had received from the King, and the House of Lords, as it had done with regard to the budget, gave way and allowed the Parliament Act 1911 to pass. The Act removed the power of the Lords to veto primary legislation and replaced it with a power to delay legislation. Money bills could be delayed by one month, and other legislation by two years.[12]

What this analysis of the monarch's various constitutional roles shows is that the monarchy, far from being a mere figurehead, remains a powerful force, central to government. Even though conventions have reduced the monarch's room for manoeuvre they have not eliminated the personal discretion which the monarch continues to enjoy over a range of key constitutional activities. In the nineteenth century Bagehot famously opined that the monarch had three constitutional rights: 'the right to be consulted, the right to encourage, [and] the right to warn'.[13]

---

[12] The Parliament Act 1949 reduced the period for which the House of Lords could delay non-money bills from two years to one year.

[13] W. Bagehot, *The English Constitution* [1867] (ed. P. Smith, Cambridge, 2001), at 60.

Notwithstanding the fame of this sentiment, it vastly under-rates the ongoing significance of the monarchy. Clearly the monarch does possess the rights to encourage and to warn, and to be consulted by, the Prime Minister of the day, but to imagine that this accurately captures the extent of the monarchic input into contemporary constitutional government would be misguided.

We have considered in this section the prerogative powers which are exercised by the monarch. Before we leave the monarchy to consider other institutions of central government, there are two further points which should be made. These concern not the powers of the monarch but the more general influence of the monarch. It is clear from a number of the episodes discussed in the previous paragraphs (from Asquith in 1909–1911 to Macmillan in 1963) that the monarch and Prime Minister will have a particularly close working relationship. Indeed, the Prime Minister and the monarch have weekly audiences when they are both in London. In the mid 1980s rumours spread that the incumbent Prime Minister, Mrs Thatcher, and the Queen had fallen out and were at loggerheads over a range of policy issues, including the matter of sanctions and South Africa, an issue over which there were at the time furious disagreements between various heads of government in the Commonwealth. The rumours were compounded when the *Sunday Times* published a major story, written by senior and widely respected journalists, that the Queen was despairing at the policies of her Prime Minister. She was reported to be dismayed at the 'uncaring, confrontational and socially divisive' policies of the government.[14] The row which followed the publication of the story led the Queen's private secretary, William Heseltine, to write a letter to *The Times* re-stating the constitutional orthodoxy: namely, that while the Queen has the right to be consulted by, to encourage and to warn the Prime Minister, and therefore has the right to hold opinions on government policy, whatever her personal views, as monarch she is bound to accept and to act on the advice of her Ministers; and that both she and the Prime Minister are obliged to treat their communications with one another in the strictest confidence.[15]

The notion that the monarch is bound to accept and to act on the advice of her Ministers (advice which would ordinarily be that of the Prime Minister) is perhaps the most fundamental doctrine, or convention, regulating the exercise by the monarch of her prerogative powers.

[14] See Pimlott, n. 5 above, at 507.
[15] See G. Marshall, 'The Queen's Press Relations' [1986] *Public Law* 505.

Yet, as we have seen, it would be simplistic and inaccurate to think that it always applies. Clearly the monarch does not always act on ministerial advice, for all that Heseltine insisted to the contrary. The political area in which the present Queen has perhaps most frequently acted independently of ministerial advice is in relation to the Commonwealth. Since the beginning of her reign Elizabeth II has identified herself closely with the Commonwealth, and in relation to it she acts sometimes on the advice of Ministers from Commonwealth jurisdictions other than the United Kingdom, and sometimes apparently without ministerial advice at all.[16]

THE INSTITUTIONS OF CENTRAL GOVERNMENT

We have already discussed the question of how the Prime Minister is appointed. Once installed his (or, once, her) powers are vast. The Prime Minister has complete powers of hire and fire over all other Ministers. The Prime Minister decides which positions to appoint to, and which people to appoint to them. Aside from internal political considerations (to the effect that there may be some senior politicians whom the Prime Minister does not dare omit from his government) the only limitation is that those appointed must be either MPs in the House of Commons or peers in the House of Lords, but, seeing that the Prime Minister may advise the monarch to create new peers, even this limitation does not have to restrain the Prime Minister for long. Usually about 120 Ministers will be appointed, between twenty and twenty-five of whom will be Cabinet Ministers; the remainder junior Ministers. The Cabinet was formerly of great significance in British politics, constituting in its nineteenth and early twentieth century heyday something akin to a seminar where policy and priorities were argued over and ultimately decided. But under recent Prime Ministers—Thatcher and Blair especially—it has declined in importance, as matters of government policy are decided more and more in small groups of Ministers (called Cabinet committees, but comprising Ministers both from inside the Cabinet and outside) from related government departments. Thus, for example, constitutional policy may be decided in a Cabinet committee of the Prime Minister, the Lord Chancellor and his junior Minister, the Home Secretary, and perhaps one or two others. Once agreed in committee, the policy may be taken to full Cabinet for formal ratification, and where there are insurmountable differences of

---

[16] This is a recurring theme of Pimlott's biography of the Queen: see in particular at 463–469.

view within a committee the matter may have to be referred to the full Cabinet for resolution, but these are generally swift tasks. Under Mr Blair Cabinet has frequently met for little more than half an hour a week.

There is much argument about whether the apparent decline in Cabinet signifies a shift from collective government to government by prime ministerial *diktat*. Although this is an argument which public lawyers have engaged in, it actually raises no questions of public law.[17] The Cabinet has no formal legal authority over government departments. The very existence of the Cabinet is a matter of constitutional convention, rather than of law: thus it may be thought by some to be unwise, but it would not be unlawful, for the Cabinet to disappear altogether.

In law as well as in contemporary political practice, it is the government department rather than the Cabinet that is the locus of executive power. British government is organized into a series of departments, such as the Treasury, the Foreign Office, the Home Office, and the big-spending departments—Social Security, Health, Education, Transport, and so forth. Each department is headed by a Secretary of State, who sits in the Cabinet. In addition, each department has a team of three or four junior (non-Cabinet) Ministers. Even this feature of government, however, is not constitutionally fixed: the Prime Minister enjoys under the prerogative the power to decide which departments his government will have, as well as which individuals will serve in them. Thus, recent Prime Ministers have abolished the Department of Energy; established the Department of Media, Culture, and Sport; split the Department of Health and Social Security into two; and merged the Departments of the Environment and of Transport into one giant department. These alterations notwithstanding, the abiding image of ministerial government in the United Kingdom is one of continuity, not change. Government departments have similar names and similar relations with one another now as they did at the end of the reign of Queen Victoria, more than 100 years ago.

The same is not true, however, of the civil service. Working under the Ministers of the day are about half a million permanent civil servants.

[17] It is however a question which is central to understanding contemporary British politics and political science. Despite the appearance of Cabinet decline, care should be taken not to exaggerate its extent. It should not be forgotten that Mrs Thatcher, one of the twentieth century's most domineering (and successful) Prime Ministers, lost power not because of the electorate or because of Parliament, but because the majority of her Cabinet Ministers had lost confidence in her ability to lead the Conservative party into a fourth successive election victory.

Over the past twenty years the civil service has been the subject of vast changes. Not only has the overall number of civil servants been reduced (by over one third: from about 750,000 in the late 1970s to 460,000 by the late 1990s), but significant reforms have also been made to the organization of the civil service, many of which have had considerable constitutional and public law consequences. The modern civil service was formed in the middle of the nineteenth century along lines proposed in an influential report known as the Northcote–Trevelyan report, of 1854. Its essential features were that the civil service was permanent, politically neutral, objective, independent, and anonymous. Civil servants would be appointed (and promoted) on merit on the basis of fair and open competition. They would not be political appointees, loyal to the party in power: rather, they would serve equally under Whigs and Tories, under Conservatives, Liberals, and Socialists, loyal to the State (that is, in law, to the Crown). Ministers would be responsible for deciding what the policy of the government would be (a task in which the civil service would be in a position to offer advice) and Ministers would be the ones who would have to defend such policy in Parliament and before the electorate. Civil servants would offer advice—always in the strictest confidence—and, under ministerial supervision, would implement their Ministers' policies. Such remained the basic position from the 1850s until the 1980s.

Over the course of the last twenty years a series of major changes has been brought about, changes which have resulted in a number of the Northcote–Trevelyan values being placed under considerable strain. One of the best-known features of Conservative party policy under the Thatcher administration was privatization. Not only did the government sell off formerly publicly-owned enterprises (such as British Telecom, British Gas, British Rail, and an array of electricity and water companies), but, in addition, the government sought to reduce the size and scope of itself. A number of formerly public or governmental activities were contracted out to the private sector. That is to say, a number of activities formerly performed by the civil service, or within the National Health Service, or by local government officers, were transferred, usually through processes of compulsory competitive tendering, to the commercial sector. Techniques of contracting out require statutory authority: that for central government is found in the Deregulation and Contracting Out Act 1994. All of these various aspects of the privatization programme had knock-on consequences for the civil service.

The aspect of Conservative government policy in the 1980s and 1990s with the most direct consequences for the civil service was the advent of 'next steps agencies'. The philosophy underpinning next steps agencies is closely related to that which underpinned the privatization programme. In both cases the central idea is efficiency. Conservative ideology posited that the market is the best instrument for maximizing efficiency. Companies will not be successful, and will not make profits, if they waste resources. Thus, in order to maximize efficiency in the public sector, it was felt that it ought more keenly to learn from, and more closely to resemble, the private sector. An influential government report in 1988 suggested that the best way of reforming the civil service to make it more closely resemble the private sector would be to 'hive off' those parts of the civil service that are engaged in service delivery from those that are engaged in policy advice. As the report was entitled *Improving Management in Government: the Next Steps*, the hived-off agencies that undertook service delivery became known as 'next steps agencies', and the name has stuck. By the time the Conservatives left office, in 1997, 75 per cent of civil servants were employed in about 135 next steps agencies. Prominent examples include the Prison Service, a next steps agency in the Home Office, and the Benefits Agency, a next steps agency in the Department of Social Security. The reform constitutes the biggest shake-up of the civil service since the emergence of the modern professional civil service in the 1850s. A next steps agency remains part of the parent department, but under a 'framework document' negotiated with the parent department it is given a chief executive, a budget, a designated staff, and a set of performance targets of its own.

What is the significance of the next steps reform for public law? Three consequences for public law can readily be identified. The first concerns accountability: as next steps agencies have a chief executive, a budget, and a set of performance targets of their own, to what extent do the Ministers of the parent department remain constitutionally accountable (to Parliament) for the actions of next steps agencies within their departments? Does the establishment of a next steps agency break the link in the chain of responsibility of Ministers to Parliament? This is an important—and not straightforward—matter, and is considered in chapter 5, below. The second concerns the values that the next steps reform embodies. We saw above that the modern civil service was founded on values of permanence, independence, and neutrality. The managerialist reforms of the 1980s and 1990s were inspired, however, by values of the promotion of economy, effectiveness, and efficiency. The framework documents that establish next steps agencies make it clear that it is these values that agencies are to prioritize. Are the foundational values of nineteenth century public service and the reformist values imported from the private sector necessarily compatible? There are clear signs, from debacles involving agencies such as the Child Support Agency, that the values of new public management (the so-called three Es, of economy, effectiveness, and efficiency) have begun to supplant, and not merely to supplement, those on which the civil service was founded.[18]

The danger with this is that once the Northcote–Trevelyan principles are diluted, the integrity of government suffers. Between the 1950s and the 1970s the perception was that the civil service was something of an unregulated beast, and that, far from being the neutral servants of the elected politicians, civil servants used their permanence and consequent experience to obstruct the policy of the elected government. The permanent yet faceless bureaucracy was taking over, pulling the strings of the old boys' network. This fear manifested itself in places as diverse as the House of Commons,[19] in Tony Benn's diaries,[20] and through the magnificent comedy series, *Yes, Minister*, still the apogee of British television. Now, however, this fear has been turned on its head, and the concern is that the civil service is being manipulated by the spin-obsessed government of the day. Rather than being above the fray, the civil service is being caught in the fray, a tool of government presentation, a slave to government–media relations rather than a servant to the people.[21] One reason these perceptions pose more problems than perhaps they need to, and indeed one reason they come about in the first place, is that the formal constitutional position of the civil service is unclear and precarious. This is the third of our public law concerns. Next steps agencies are not the cause of the precariousness, but they constitute a telling illustration of it.

This issue takes us back to the Crown. Civil servants are employed under the authority of the prerogative. There is no Civil Service Act (although before coming into office in 1997 the Labour party did promise that it would introduce one). Instead there is a plethora of legal instruments and non-legal documents which set out, not always consistently, the various powers and responsibilities, and the various limitations to

---

[18] See C. Harlow, 'Accountability, New Public Management, and the Problems of the Child Support Agency' (1999) 26 *Journal of Law and Society* 150.

[19] See e.g. the reaction in the Commons to the Crichel Down affair in 1954: this is discussed in chapter 5, below.

[20] Tony Benn was a Cabinet Minister in the Wilson and Callaghan (Labour) governments of the 1960s and 1970s.

[21] See T. Daintith, 'A Very Good Day to Get Out Anything we want to Bury' [2002] *Public Law* 13.

those powers and responsibilities, of civil servants. The formal legal regulation vests in the Civil Service Order in Council, an instrument made under the delegated authority of the royal prerogative, and the Civil Service Management Code, an instrument made under the further delegated authority of the Order in Council. In addition, the non-legal Armstrong Memorandum, Ministerial Code, and Civil Service Code augment and amplify the basic legal position. What is noteworthy about this complex net of codes and memoranda, however, is that both Parliament and the courts are effectively excluded from the entire process. The rules are not made by Parliament—there is no legislation here, the Order in Council being made within the executive, and not in consultation with Parliament. Equally, there is neither parliamentary nor judicial oversight here—Parliament holds Ministers to constitutional account, but not civil servants, and the courts can review the legality of executive decisions and actions only against a framework of law, and not against a framework of informal, non-binding codes.

In this sense the civil service is a manifestation of what could be termed the self-regulation of the Crown. In the absence of both political and legal oversight and accountability, the Crown-as-executive is left free to develop and to transform itself, unsupervised and unconstrained. The great eighteenth century radical, Thomas Paine, wrote in his celebrated book, *Rights of Man*, that 'a constitution is something antecedent to a government'.[22] A constitution is something that is supposed to constitute the government, so that the government is accountable, politically and legally, within the framework of, and in accordance with, the principles that the constitution sets out. In England, the reverse is the case. Here, government is antecedent to the constitution. It is the government itself that lays down the way in which it will be structured, and the constitution simply has to adjust accordingly. This is true as much in the context of the changing power and importance of the Cabinet as it is in the context of the shaping and the values of the civil service. Paine argued that this form of government—that is to say, government under the Crown—is incompatible with the principles of constitutionalism. A constitutional government would not possess the powers of self-regulation which under the legal umbrella of the Crown the executive branch in England continues to enjoy.

Even now, 200 years on, we remain a considerable distance from being able to subject the Crown's government to fully effective scrutiny. We explore some of the reasons why this is so in the following sections.

---

[22] T. Paine, *Rights of Man* [1792] (ed. G. Claeys, Indianapolis, Ind.,1992), at 42.

THE EXECUTIVE AND PUBLIC LAW

In the previous section we outlined the nature of the central executive. We saw that in terms of both our themes of public law—power and accountability—there were a number of problems, particularly with regard to the civil service. Neither the powers of central government actors, nor the systems of accountability with regard to those powers, seem to be especially clearly articulated or demarcated. Two causes of these problems were suggested: first, the fact that so much of the executive's power stems not from legislation but from the reservoir of vague prerogative (Crown) authority; and, secondly, the fact that non-legal documents play such a prominent role in the public regulation of executive power. We shall return to this second issue in chapter 5 below, which offers a detailed examination of political forms of accountability. For the remainder of the present chapter we shall focus on the first of these two causes: namely, the nature of prerogative power. Clearly, in this context, while we are still discussing questions relating to the Crown, we are concerned here less with the monarch herself than with the use made of the legal authority of the Crown by the government of the day.

The doctrine of public law that is designed to regulate and to limit the powers of the executive is known as the 'rule of law'. The bad news is that there has been a great deal of confusion surrounding the use of this term, but the good news is that almost all the confusion is unnecessary, at least as far as public law is concerned. It is in legal philosophy that the confusion arises, not in public law. In English public law the rule of law has at its core a single, simple, and clear meaning. It is a rule that concerns the powers of the executive, of government (and not of Parliament or other legislatures), and it governs the relationship of the executive to the law. The rule of law provides that *the executive may do nothing without clear legal authority first permitting its actions*. Now, we shall see in chapter 6 that over the past forty years or more the courts have expanded this core idea into a series of what might be termed legal principles of judicial review and human rights. We shall consider these principles in chapter 6. For now, let us focus only on the core idea—the more recent expansion can come later.

The rule of law is a common law rule: that is to say, it is judge-made. It is the opposite of the common law's approach to private individuals. Whereas the rule of law provides that the executive may do nothing without clear legal authority, individuals may conversely do anything unless expressly prohibited by law. In this rule lay the foundations of the common law's approach to the protection of individual liberty, an approach that has now been superseded by the Human Rights Act 1998. Under the common law approach, instead of having a list of rights that individuals positively enjoyed (such as, for example, the right to freedom of expression), the common law provided simply that individuals enjoyed freedom (including freedom of expression) as long as it was not curtailed by law: no individual could be liable in respect of anything he or she said unless such liability was provided in law.

Authority for these propositions is contained in the seminal common law case, *Entick v Carrington*.[23] John Entick was a pamphleteer: a political commentator who wrote a series of pamphlets critical of government policy. The government wanted him silenced. To this end, the Earl of Halifax, a government Minister, summoned Carrington and three other messengers to go to Entick's house, to enter his house, to search his house, to seize his papers, and to arrest him. This they did, and Entick was imprisoned in the Tower of London for eleven days. Upon his release he sued Carrington and the other messengers for trespass. Carrington's defence was that he was acting on the basis of a warrant sealed under the authority of a Secretary of State. The court rejected this defence, and held for Entick. The court ruled that an Englishman's property could be interfered with by the State only on the authority of law, and not on the putative authority of the Secretary of State's warrant. As there was no legal authority for Halifax's warrant, it could not justify Carrington's actions: only law could permit Carrington to act in the way he had, not the mere word of a Secretary of State. Lord Camden CJ famously ruled that 'If it is law, it will be found in our books. If it is not to be found there, it is not law'.[24] This may strike us as an odd thing to say in the context of an unwritten constitution, but what Lord Camden meant was that for the executive to act it must have legal authority that permits its actions. If no such authority can be found, the executive may not so act.

This core idea of the rule of law can be regarded as a formal constraint on government rather than a substantive constraint. A substantive constraint on government would hold that there are some substantive things which are so important to us that government simply must not be allowed to threaten them. For example, we might consider that, say, privacy was such a fundamental part of our individuality, or humanness, that the government should not be permitted to interfere with it. Bills of Rights,

[23] (1765) 19 St Tr 1029.   [24] Ibid., at 1066.

such as the Human Rights Act 1998, might be regarded as constituting substantive notions of the rule of law. By contrast, the common law's core idea of the rule of law, encapsulated in the court's judgment in *Entick v Carrington*, does not lay down substantive restrictions on what the government may do. Under the rule in *Entick v Carrington* the government *may* (to continue the example) interfere with privacy, but it may do so only where it has the legal authority to do so. Thus, the critical question becomes: does the government have the legal authority and, if not, how can it get it? This is where the common law notion of the rule of law begins to lose its bite. This is because it is spectacularly easy for the government to find or otherwise to acquire legal authority for its actions even where it did not initially have any. There are two ways in which this may happen: the first is through Parliament, and the second through the courts.

If the Home Secretary (the contemporary equivalent of the Earl of Halifax) wants new powers to act against what he perceives to be subversive activists (modern-day John Enticks—let us say, anti road-building environmentalist protesters), all he has to do if he does not already possess the powers he desires, is draft a Bill, present it to Parliament, and watch while Parliament obediently passes it into law. As the government of the day is composed from the political party with an overall majority of seats in the House of Commons, and as most politicians are generally loyal to their party, government does not find it difficult to persuade Parliament to confer on it even the most draconian and illiberal powers, as both Conservative and Labour Ministers have found.[25] Once the Act is passed and brought into force, the government will have the powers it sought, and the rule of law will be satisfied.[26] The second way in which the rule of law may relatively easily be circumvented is not by legislation through Parliament, but through the courts. This issue is the subject of the next section.

[25] Among a frighteningly large number of recent examples, see the Official Secrets Act 1989, the Criminal Justice and Public Order Act 1994, the Regulation of Investigatory Powers Act 2000, and the Anti-terrorism, Crime and Security Act 2001.

[26] Those who thought that the Human Rights Act 1998 would make a difference here will have been disappointed by the decision of the House of Lords in *R v Shayler* [2002] 2 WLR 754 in which the Lords unanimously dismissed a challenge to the compatibility with Convention rights of the Official Secrets Act 1989.

THE NATURE OF THE PREROGATIVE

As we have just seen, the constitutional doctrine of the rule of law provides that the executive may do nothing without clear legal authority first permitting its actions. There are two sources of law which may provide the executive with such authority. The first is statute and the second is the prerogative.[27] Thus, even if the executive lacks the statutory power to act in a certain way, it will nonetheless be able lawfully so to act if its actions can be justified under the prerogative. For example, there is no statute that empowers the government to enter into or to ratify treaties that bind the United Kingdom in international law. Yet it is no violation of the rule of law for the government to do this, as there is a prerogative power that covers treaty-making. It is therefore self-evident that for the rule of law to be effective as a check on the executive the courts must be able (and willing) not only to police rigorously the boundaries of the executive's statutory authority, but also to ensure that the government does not misuse or abuse its prerogative authority. Unfortunately for those who celebrate the value of the rule of law, the courts have struggled to find ways of giving it real bite in the context of the prerogative.

There are a number of overlapping reasons for this. The first and most general concerns the nature of the prerogative. In his *Commentaries* in the eighteenth century Blackstone offered a relatively narrow definition of prerogative power, when he wrote that the prerogative is 'in its nature singular and eccentrical [in] that it can only be applied to those rights and capacities which the king enjoys alone . . . and not to those which he enjoys in common with any of his subjects'.[28] The important point of Blackstone's definition is that prerogative powers are unique to the Crown. For Blackstone, the prerogative is not a *carte blanche*, coming to the government's rescue whenever statutory authority runs out. Rather, the prerogative is a closed list of identifiable and discrete powers covering areas of government which are its especial province. Thus, individuals may not issue passports or ratify treaties (and neither for that matter may local authorities): these are tasks uniquely for the State, and are in English public law tasks that are the unique responsibility of the Crown and its Ministers, both being governed by the prerogative.

---

[27] This is true of central government but not of devolved regional government nor of local government, both of which are creatures entirely of statute. Unlike central government, local authorities have no reservoir of prerogative power to draw on when their statutory authority runs out.

[28] Sir William Blackstone, *Commentaries on the Laws of England* (London, 1765), i, at 232.

Dicey, however, granted to the prerogative a far broader meaning. He wrote that the prerogative consists of the 'residue of discretionary or arbitrary authority which at any given time is legally left in the hands of the Crown'.[29] It is this more expansive definition that has found judicial favour, Dicey's view having been expressly approved and followed in the leading House of Lords decision *Attorney-General v De Keyser's Royal Hotel*.[30] Dicey's view of the prerogative is not only more expansive than Blackstone's: it is also considerably vaguer. What precisely is this residue of discretionary authority that is left in the hands of the Crown? Answering this question has not proved easy. Two cases illustrate the problem. The first concerns taxation. As a matter of law, the Crown is not obliged to pay tax. In a case in 1965 the British Broadcasting Corporation argued that it was entitled to Crown immunity from taxation. The BBC's argument was put on the basis that it had been created under Royal Charter and that it broadcast under terms and conditions set out in a licence and agreement with the relevant Minister of the Crown. The Court of Appeal had little difficulty in rejecting this argument, Diplock LJ proclaiming rather grandly that it was '350 years and a civil war too late for the Queen's courts to broaden the prerogative. The limits within which the executive government may impose obligations or restraints on citizens of the United Kingdom without any statutory authority are now well settled and incapable of extension.'[31]

If only it were so simple. Our second case shows that it is not. In *R v Secretary of State for the Home Department, ex parte Northumbria Police Authority*,[32] a police authority challenged the legality of a decision made by the Home Secretary to allow police chief constables access to CS gas and to plastic baton rounds (plastic bullets) in some cases without the consent of and despite the objections of the local police authority. At first instance the Divisional Court held that even though the Home Secretary had no statutory power to act in this way, he did have prerogative authority to do so. On appeal the Court of Appeal held that the Home Secretary's decision could be justified under both statute and the prerogative. The case is a classic public law tussle between local and central government, and between the political left and right. The police authority, composed in principal part of representatives of the (elected) local authority did not want the local police force using CS gas against protesters such as

---

[29] A. Dicey, *Introduction to the Study of the Law of the Constitution* [1885] (10th edn., London, 1959), at 424.
[30] [1920] AC 508.
[31] *British Broadcasting Corporation v Johns* [1965] Ch 32, at 79.   [32] [1989] QB 26.

striking miners. The Home Secretary, disturbed by an apparent increase in public disorder through the 1980s, desired to give greater resources, that is to say weapons, to police chief constables. What is of interest in the present context, however, is not the politics of the dispute, nor even the way in which the court addressed (or rather failed to address) the competing political and democratic constituencies and accountability of the parties. Rather, the issue for us is the way the court dealt with questions of the prerogative.

What was the prerogative power that, in the court's judgment, gave to the Home Secretary the authority to issue the police with CS gas and plastic bullets? While there are clear precedents in support of the notion that the Crown enjoys extensive prerogative powers to defend the realm from external attack, authority is sparse (to say the least) on the existence of prerogative powers to keep the peace within the realm. Even if such a prerogative does exist (and authorities are divided on this point) it is clear that before this case there was no authority for the view that such a power extends to arming the police with CS gas and plastic bullets. Remember the statement of Diplock LJ in the *British Broadcasting Corporation* case: the courts should neither broaden nor expand the scope of prerogative authority. In the *Northumbria* case the Court of Appeal recognized that, as Nourse LJ expressed it, 'references in reported cases and authoritative texts to a prerogative of keeping the peace within the realm are admittedly scarce'[33] yet the court proceeded to hold—wholly contrary to the Diplock dictum from the *British Broadcasting Corporation* case—that notwithstanding this lack of authority, the Home Secretary could lawfully use prerogative power as justification for arming the police.

That the courts are prepared to grant to the Crown such elastic and ill-defined powers, and to subject their exercise to such modest—even superficial—review, constitutes the second way in which the executive will find the rule of law a much less onerous check on its powers than it might at first have seemed.

CONCLUSIONS: BEYOND THE CROWN?

We should take care not to exaggerate the point: it is not the case now (although in earlier times it might have been true) that the courts will automatically accept any legal argument put to them by the executive in the name of the Crown. We have seen in previous chapters how in

---

[33] Ibid., at 56.

R v Secretary of State for the Home Department, ex parte Fire Brigades Union the Home Secretary's use (or misuse) of prerogative power was held by the House of Lords to have been unlawful. So too have we seen how in *M v Home Office* the House of Lords held that the courts do have the jurisdiction in appropriate cases to find Ministers of the Crown in contempt of court. Both of these modern and important public law precedents are evidence of the fact that at least the servants and agents of the Crown no longer operate entirely beyond the rule of law, even if the same cannot be said for the monarch herself.[34] However, it should not be thought that relatively recent court decisions such as these mean that the Crown—in the sense of either Crown-as-monarch or Crown-as-executive—now operates entirely within the framework of the rule of law. As the law stands, the Crown is partly regulated by and accountable to law, and is partly—still—above and beyond the law.

Thus, despite the advances that have been made in cases such as *Fire Brigades* and *M*,[35] neither the Crown-as-monarch nor the Crown-as-executive has yet been brought entirely within the reach of public law. The *Northumbria* case is a good example of the kind of executive action which even now may escape effective judicial scrutiny on the ground that, somewhere along the line, it can be said to be connected to some historic prerogative power—even if the alleged authority for such a claim is sparse. The *Northumbria* case is not the only example of the continuing legal difficulties that are created by the problem of Crown authority. In addition to the issue illustrated by that case, there are perhaps three further areas of difficulty: first relating to the legal identity of government departments and to the status of civil servants; secondly relating to the various privileges and immunities of the Crown; and finally relating to the liability of the Crown. We are touching here on the most complex and technical areas of public law, but the point here is not to descend into detail—for that the reader is encouraged to consult the specialist literature cited in the bibliographical essay—but rather simply to outline the nature of the problem in general terms.

On the first issue, as we saw above in our consideration of the institutions of central government, departments and civil servants are regulated as much by convention as they are by law. Indeed the law has in a number

[34] As we saw in chapter 2 above, the ruling in *M v Home Office* applies only to the Crown-as-executive and, expressly, not to the Crown-as-monarch.
[35] To these two could be added a third, equally seminal, case: *Council of Civil Service Unions v Minister for the Civil Service* [1985] AC 374 (the so-called GCHQ case), discussed in chapter 6, below.

of respects struggled to keep pace with the growth of modern, professional government. The shape of government departments, and the complex relations between civil servants, Ministers, Parliament, and the public have developed without and despite the law, rather than under the authority and within the framework of the law. Yet despite the marginal role played by English law in the shaping of government, from time to time questions do arise that require legal resolution. On such occasions the courts have often struggled to translate the structures and responsibilities of contemporary government into recognizable legal terms—there seems to be some considerable distance between the way government has developed in practice and the way the law continues to conceive of government. It is frequently the case, for example, that a statute will confer on a Secretary of State a discretion to make certain decisions. In practice the overwhelming majority of such decisions will be made not by the Secretary of State himself (or, albeit rarely, herself) but will instead be made by a civil servant working in the Secretary of State's department. There is absolutely nothing unusual about this—it is an everyday feature of modern practical government. But what is the formal legal status of such a decision where it is made not by the Secretary of State, but by the civil servant? The answer, which comes from a seminal administrative law case, *Carltona*,[36] is that the law will recognize the civil servant's decision as being that of the Secretary of State. This, it has to be said, is something of a fudge—far from recognizing the practical reality that civil servants enjoy considerable decision-making powers and responsibilities in their own right, powers and responsibilities which will routinely operate at considerable remove from the Secretary of State, the court in *Carltona* simply ignored the distinction between the Minister and the civil servant and pretended that they are both the same thing—legally indistinguishable parts of a single unit, the government department, united together in the service of the Crown.

Fudge it may be, but until recently it has been a remarkably successful one. That may change, however, with the advent of next steps agencies: will the *Carltona* principle apply where the civil servant works not in the Secretary of State's department, but in a hived-off next steps agency? There is no clear answer to this problem—it is an example of the difficulty the law has in seeking to come to terms with the structure of contemporary government. Instead of having developed a modern and sophisticated understanding of the State, of government, of departments,

---

[36] *Carltona v Commissioners of Works* [1943] 2 All ER 560.

Ministers, and civil servants, the law has been unable to move beyond the increasingly unhelpful metaphor of the Crown. A century ago Maitland wrote that 'the Crown is a convenient cover for ignorance: it saves us from asking difficult questions'.[37] Perhaps Maitland was, in this instance, only half right—the metaphor of the Crown has indeed saved the law from having to ask difficult questions (developing a modern and sophisticated understanding of the State would not be straightforward), but this has not been convenient. On the contrary, it is deeply inconvenient that frankly very basic issues such as 'what is the legal status of a civil servant's decision' remain so obscure.

The *Town Investments* case can be seen as a further illustration of the same problem.[38] The issue in this case arose out of the Counter-Inflation Act 1972, which among other things limited the ability of landlords to increase rents. The Act expressly stated that it did not bind the Crown. The question in the case was whether a lease to a government department fell within the scope of the Act, or fell within the scope of the Crown's immunity from the effects of the Act: is a government department (in this instance the Department of the Environment) in law a part of the Crown, or not? That the case went all the way to the House of Lords indicates again the extent of the difficulties the law has in identifying the scope of the Crown and in answering even the most basic questions about the relationship of modern government departments to the ancient powers and privileges of the Crown.

The second area of difficulty concerns the Crown's various legal immunities and privileges. The law grants to the Crown a number of immunities and privileges. Some of these are relatively harmless, even amusing. There is, for example, a privilege relating to whales. Whales are in law 'royal fish'. When a whale is captured in the seas adjoining the coast of the kingdom, regardless of who does the capturing, the head of the whale belongs by prerogative right to the king while the tail belongs to the queen. The reason for this is that in former times it was important to keep the queen's wardrobe well-stocked with whalebone. Unfortunately however, whoever invented this particular Crown privilege knew little of the anatomy of whales, as the whalebone is located entirely in the head! Leaving whales to one side, there is a rather more serious aspect to the law of Crown privileges. It is this: if the law grants to a body a series of privileges and immunities, it is obviously going to be of the utmost

---

[37] F. Maitland, *The Constitutional History of England* (Cambridge, 1908), at 418.
[38] *Town Investments v Department of the Environment* [1978] AC 359.

importance to be as clear as possible about who that body is that is to be the beneficiary of the privileges and immunities. Unfortunately, clarity is not a feature that many would associate with the law of Crown privileges. Two examples will suffice to illustrate the point.

The first concerns taxation. As we saw in our consideration of *British Broadcasting Corporation v Johns* above, the Crown is not legally compelled to pay tax. The legal source of this (extraordinarily valuable[39]) immunity lies in the notion that the Crown is not bound by statute save where the statute states to the contrary, either expressly or by necessary implication. As taxation is a matter governed exclusively by statute (it is a requirement of the Bill of Rights 1689 that only Parliament may authorize taxation), and as tax statutes do not bind the Crown (or so it has been held), the result is that such taxation as the Crown pays is voluntary.[40] The issue here is, how far does the immunity from taxation extend? On examination we find that it has been allowed to extend far beyond the Crown itself. Numerous members of the royal family benefit from tax-free annuities, from the Prince of Wales down to a plethora of minor and lesser royals. This is exactly the danger when the law carves out privileges for people. For the monarch herself to enjoy certain immunities is one thing, but to extend those immunities throughout her family is another thing altogether.

Our second example concerns not the extension of the Crown-as-monarch into the broader royal family, but relates rather to the Crown-as-executive. Another important Crown privilege is that under certain circumstances the Crown may certify that otherwise admissible evidence should not be produced in court. This is a power that is now exercised not by the monarch herself, but by government Ministers. Where it is, in the government's view, contrary to the public interest for evidence to be produced in open court (because, for example, if made public the evidence might compromise national security), the government may seek to withhold such evidence from a court, even where the evidence would, if released, materially aid a party to a legal dispute. This Crown privilege is known as public interest immunity (PII). It is a powerful weapon in the hands of the government, enabling it to seek valuable

[39] In the early 1990s it was estimated that Elizabeth II, the richest woman in the world, saved in the region of £20,000 every day (£7.3 million *per annum*) from not paying tax on her personal wealth.

[40] The present Queen came to an agreement with the government in 1993 that from April of that year she would volunteer to pay some tax on her personal wealth: for details, see A. Tomkins, 'Crown Privileges', in M. Sunkin and S. Payne (eds.), *The Nature of the Crown: A Legal and Political Analysis* (Oxford, 1999), at 187–188.

control over the flow of information into court. Its exercise is from time
to time extremely controversial, such that governments have come close
to falling over its abuse.[41]

The point here, though, is once again the scope of the immunity: who
is able to claim PII, and under what circumstances? As with the question
of the Crown's immunity from taxation, so too here has the law been lax
in its control over the expansion of PII. The courts have held, for
example, that it is not only the Crown which may claim PII—private,
non-State organizations such as the National Society for the Prevention
of Cruelty to Children have been permitted to benefit from PII.[42] The
courts have also lacked rigour in laying down limitations on the circumstances in which the government may claim PII, with some cases having
apparently suggested that PII may be claimed in criminal as well as
in civil trials (thus preventing defendants from being able to defend
themselves properly when being prosecuted by the same State that is withholding evidence from them) and others having suggested that in some
circumstances the government is obliged to claim PII even where it does
not wish to do so, thereby restricting the flow of information into the court
in an even more oppressive manner. These suggestions (that PII may be
claimed in criminal trials, and that in some circumstances the government
is required to claim PII) have since been doubted, but, again, the story of
public interest immunity is a further reminder of the dangers that will
remain inherent in English public law for as long as it continues to grant
privileges and immunities to the Crown without more clearly defining
them.

Our final area of difficulty concerns the liability of the Crown. We have
already seen what a complex topic this is: *M v Home Office*, discussed in
the previous chapter, is one of the leading authorities on this topic. The
liability of both the Crown-as-monarch and the Crown-as-executive are
exceptionally problematic areas for the law. This has been particularly the
case with regard to the common law. At common law, the Crown can do
no wrong, and the Queen cannot be sued in her own courts. Until 1947
these rules operated significantly to limit the extent to which the
Crown—either as monarch or as executive—could be liable for breach
of contract or for negligence. In 1947, an important reforming statute

---

[41] See e.g. the controversy over the Major government's use of PII certificates in the
Matrix Churchill trial in 1992, the collapse of which led to the Scott inquiry on arms-to-
Iraq: see A. Tomkins, *The Constitution after Scott: Government Unwrapped* (Oxford, 1998),
chapter 5.
[42] See *D v NSPCC* [1978] AC 171.

was passed, the Crown Proceedings Act, which attempted to bring the contractual and tortious liability of the Crown somewhat closer to the normal legal position. But even the 1947 Act has not proved to be entirely successful in this regard, the courts on a number of occasions having interpreted the Act in ways that continue to favour and to offer special exemptions to the Crown, restricting legal liability of both monarch and executive. One of the most important examples arose in the celebrated *Factortame* litigation,[43] case law which is central to the modern law of the sovereignty of Parliament, and which is considered in detail in the next chapter.

This is a familiar pattern. If the law has struggled to bring the power and authority of the Crown within the framework of legal accountability, this has been especially the case with regard to the common law. For every breakthrough there is always a case such as *Northumbria Police*, *Town Investments*, or *Factortame* to remind us of the limitations that continue to bedevil the rule of law and to constrain the reach of the court-room. Across a wide variety of public law contexts it has been statute, rather than common law, that has done most to delimit the Crown. This is as true for questions of succession and for determining the identity of the monarch as it is for issues concerning the Crown's property holdings.[44] It is also true in the context of Crown liability.

All of this will have to change if English public law is to mature. Public lawyers tend not to like to think of their subject as being under-developed and immature, and consequently underplay the significance of the Crown, both as regards the monarch herself and in terms of the Crown as a source of broader executive authority. Yet it is a dangerous and foolish pretence to under-estimate the continuing and extraordinary powers of the Crown: as Joe Jacob has observed, in blunt and disturbing language that lingers in the mind, 'At the heart of Britain, law does not rule. The Crown is at this centre. If there are laws, they are not justiciable in any ordinary sense and not discernible by any legal technique. We may grant that the boundaries of this core are defined by law and, certainly, that its scope is diminishing; but, in this centre, the rule of law does not operate.'[45]

---

[43] See *R v Secretary of State for Transport, ex parte Factortame* [1990] 2 AC 85.

[44] On the former, see the Act of Settlement 1701 and the various Demise of the Crown Acts; on the latter, see the Crown Private Estates Acts 1800 and 1862, among other examples.

[45] J. Jacob, *The Republican Crown: Lawyers and the Making of the State in Twentieth Century Britain* (Aldershot, 1996), at 1.

4

Parliament

Parliament, after the Crown, is the second of the two sovereign authorities known to English public law. This chapter considers the public law powers of Parliament, just as the previous one considered the public law powers of the Crown. This chapter is in four sections: first we consider the three functions of Parliament and their historical development; secondly we discuss the composition of the two Houses of Parliament; thirdly we consider the so-called 'sovereignty of Parliament', more accurately the notion that in English law Acts of Parliament enjoy legislative supremacy; and finally we turn to the revealing, but often overlooked, topic of the privileges of Parliament.

THE THREE FUNCTIONS OF PARLIAMENT

As we saw in chapter 2, Parliament emerged in the fourteenth century out of the Crown's need to obtain consent for such matters as the raising of revenue. Parliament was simply a body that the king would summon for the purpose of granting to the Crown the authorization that it needed to raise revenue through various forms of what we would now call taxation. In this sense the first function of Parliament is to support the government. In the fourteenth century the business of government was conducted directly by the Crown and the Privy Council. Parliament was summoned by the Crown for the purpose of voting supply, that is to say, for the purpose of granting to the Crown such moneys as it needed in order to continue the expensive business of government. Over the course of the last 700 years both the shape of the government and the authority of Parliament have changed, of course, but the essentials of the fourteenth century model remain even now.

To this day the first function of Parliament is to maintain the government in office. The government, that is to say the Ministers of the Crown headed by the Prime Minister, must come regularly before Parliament in order to obtain parliamentary support for its policies, and in particular for its proposals concerning taxation and revenue. Without such continuing support no government can survive in office. Parliament remains in the twenty-first century, just as it was 700 years ago, the institution through which the Crown's government must govern. Another way of expressing this is that Parliament exists in order to supply the government of the day. This is true in two senses: first Parliament supplies the members of the government, in that all Ministers of the Crown are required by constitutional convention to be members of one of the two Houses of Parliament. Secondly, Parliament votes supply—that is to say, money—to the government so that it has the financial resources it needs to govern. This is why there is a budget every year. Budget day is the day on which the Minister of the Crown with responsibility for Her Majesty's Treasury (the Chancellor of the Exchequer) presents to Parliament the government's financial proposals for the coming year. If Parliament approves the government's proposals, it will pass the budget (in law the Finance Act) and the government will continue. If Parliament does not approve, the government will fall. In public law, therefore, Parliament is the institution through which the government must govern, and it is the first responsibility of the government to ensure that it continues to enjoy parliamentary support, for in English public law no government can operate without it.

The second function of Parliament is the representation of grievances. As Parliament was called by the king in order to grant to him the supply he needed, it quickly became apparent that Parliament was in an excellent position to act as a vehicle through which grievances could be brought before the Crown. If a parliamentarian could, by someone with a grievance against the Crown, be persuaded of the justice of that grievance, then Parliament as a whole might in turn be persuaded not to grant to the king his essential supply without the king first acting upon and redressing the grievance. In other words, Parliament could bargain with the Crown, and could even impose conditions on the Crown, a power of which no-one besides Parliament could boast. Successful monarchs in early modern England were those who learnt how to live with this process of regular parliamentary bartering and negotiation (just as successful governments now are those that learn how to garner and nurture strong parliamentary support). It was one of the principal causes of the Civil War in the 1640s that the Stuart monarchs had so failed in this task.

As a result of Parliament's ability to bargain with the Crown, both Houses of Parliament rapidly acquired representative functions. The House of Lords represented the interests of the landed aristocracy, and the House of Commons represented the interests of those who selected, and in later centuries elected, its members. These parliamentary powers of representing grievances to the Crown developed during a period in which the courts displayed considerable hostility to litigants who dared to bring to the judiciary complaints against the Crown. Even as late as the seventeenth century, as John Hampden and others found to their cost, the court-room was no place to bring action against the king's government.[1] Almost by default, therefore, Parliament developed in early modern England as the principal institution through which the Crown and the government could be held to account. This was particularly the case with regard to the House of Commons—those whom it represented tended to have more pressing grievances against the Crown than did the more privileged classes of the landed gentry. Thus Parliament, and especially the House of Commons, became not only the institution that supplied and maintained the government, but also the institution that stood in principal opposition to the government. There is an obvious paradox here, as the first and second functions of Parliament may pull the institution in two diametrically opposed directions. This tension, between support and opposition, remains critical to understanding the contemporary constitutional roles of Parliament, and will be a prominent theme of both this chapter and the next one.

While the first and second functions of Parliament may pull the institution in two different directions at once, this does not have to be the case. The two functions can be successfully combined. Indeed, it is when the two functions are successfully combined that Parliament will be at its most effective. The product of this combination of powers we call scrutiny. Parliament's formal powers over supply, combined with its representative functions, mean that in practice a considerable amount of Parliament's time is taken up with the task of scrutinizing the executive. Scrutiny of the finances, the policies, the administration, and the decisions of government departments is an enormous undertaking, and it is one of the most important constitutional responsibilities of modern Parliament. Such scrutiny is complex, and can take many forms, ranging from relatively high-profile but low-intensity debates in the chamber, to the more rigorous, if sometimes less well-publicized, investigations of departmental and other select committees. The practical operation of these and other forms of parliamentary scrutiny of the executive is the subject of the next chapter.

The final function of Parliament is to legislate. This may seem the

---

[1] For *Hampden's Case* and others like it, see chapter 2 above, at 43.

most obvious of Parliament's tasks, but of the functions we have identified here it is the one over which Parliament actually has the least authority. This may seem counter-intuitive, and it needs to be carefully explained. Public lawyers have become accustomed to conceiving of Parliament as being principally the national legislature. This has resulted in two unfortunate tendencies. On the one hand, public lawyers have tended to underplay the continuing constitutional significance of the first and second functions of Parliament. On the other hand they have tended to overplay Parliament's contribution to law-making. This is in large part due to the influence of Dicey. Dicey, it will be recalled, argued that British constitutional law is based on two main rules: the sovereignty of Parliament (which governs the relationship between the law and Parliament) and the rule of law (which governs the relationship between the law and the executive). The 'sovereignty of Parliament' was the term Dicey adopted to describe the rules that in the hierarchy of norms govern the legal status of statutes, that is to say, of Acts of Parliament. As we saw in outline in chapter 2 above, these rules provide first that Parliament may legally make or unmake any law whatsoever, and secondly that under English law no-one has the power to override or to set aside an Act of Parliament.

It has to be said that the phrase 'the sovereignty of Parliament' is a singularly unhappy one. What the doctrine tells us is that there is nothing in the English legal order higher than an Act of Parliament. An Act of Parliament is a measure that has been formally approved and adopted by both Houses of Parliament and to which the monarch has assented. The only exception to this is that under certain strictly limited circumstances legislation may be passed without the consent of the House of Lords. The doctrine therefore refers not to Parliament as such, but rather to one particular form of legislative instrument which Parliament, or more properly the Queen-in-Parliament, may pass into law—namely, statutes, or Acts of Parliament. Thus, the doctrine of the sovereignty of Parliament is more accurately described as the *legislative supremacy of Acts of the Queen-in-Parliament*. Much unnecessary confusion will be avoided if it is remembered that it is not *Parliament* that enjoys sovereignty under this doctrine, but *Acts of Parliament*.

Dicey gave to his doctrine of the sovereignty of Parliament a very strong content. The Diceyan conception of the sovereignty of Parliament suggests for example that no Parliament can be bound by its predecessors; that it is legally impossible for Parliament to entrench the laws that it passes such that they bind future Parliaments; and that these rules apply just as much to the manner and form of legislation as they do to the substantive content of legislation. Part of the reason that public lawyers have focused on Parliament's legislative powers at the expense of its other constitutional functions is that a number of the most important constitutional developments of the twentieth century have proved exceptionally difficult to fit into the strict model of the sovereignty of Parliament that Dicey preferred. At the time when Dicey wrote, for example, Britain possessed a global empire and its imperial Parliament in Westminster legislated for colonies on almost all of the world's continents. During the course of the twentieth century all but a handful of these colonies obtained their independence. If Parliament cannot bind its successors, what is the legal effect of Parliament in (say) 1950 declaring that a particular colony is independent if a later Parliament in (say) 1960 decides to revoke that acknowledgement of independence and to resume its former imperial task of legislating for the territory? Constitutional lawyers and commentators of the mid twentieth century, from Jennings and De Smith to Heuston and Marshall, invested a considerable amount of energy in trying to reconcile the fact (and the conclusivity) of post-colonial independence with the Diceyan doctrine of the sovereignty of Parliament. If post-colonial independence generated one set of problems for the Diceyan conception of parliamentary sovereignty, the United Kingdom's accession with effect from 1 January 1973 to the European Economic Community (as it then was—now the European Union) gave rise to another. How to reconcile the sovereignty of Parliament with the supremacy of European law has been both controversial and complicated, as we shall see.

In the light of all this, perhaps it is not surprising that public lawyers have given such greater prominence to consideration of Parliament's legislative functions than they have to its other functions of supply, representation, and scrutiny. This should not blind us to the fact, however, that conceiving of Parliament as being principally a legislature is a relatively recent development, which dates only from the end of the nineteenth century. Certainly Bagehot, writing in the 1860s, did not share this view.[2] Not only is it a relatively recent portrayal of Parliament to depict it as mainly being concerned with legislation: it is also the case that even now

---

[2] For Bagehot the House of Commons had five functions, of which legislation was the fifth. The others were: to act as the electoral college, to supply the government, to express the mind of the English people, and to teach the nation what it does not know. As for the House of Lords, Bagehot gave the upper house two functions: to delay and to revise. See W. Bagehot, *The English Constitution* [1867] (ed. P. Smith, Cambridge, 2001), chapters 5–6.

Parliament has a weaker hold over its legislative powers than it does over its other constitutional functions. Parliament's legislative powers are constrained by three factors. First, while Parliament has responsibility for law-making on the national level, this is now only one of many levels at which law is made. Law is also made locally by local authorities; regionally by bodies such as the Scottish Parliament and the Welsh and Northern Irish Assemblies; at the European level; and internationally. While Parliament has some oversight with regard to all four of these non-parliamentary levels of law-making, such oversight is an aspect of Parliament's functions as a scrutineer, rather than as a legislator.

Secondly, even at the national level, it is far from the case that Parliament is the only legislator. In addition to Parliament's legislative power, the executive also enjoys considerable law-making power at the national level. Statute is not the only legally recognized form of national legislation. Such rules may also be made by Order in Council—that is to say by the executive acting under the prerogative. Further, much legislation is delegated or secondary rather than primary. While Parliament passes statutes (primary legislation), delegated and secondary legislation is generally made within the executive. Parliament may be consulted, but its role is limited. In the context of delegated legislation Parliament looks anything but a sovereign legislature.

Finally, even in that part of the legislative matrix that is Parliament's domain—primary legislation on the national level—how much control does Parliament really have over 'its' legislation? In practice the legislative agenda of Parliament has for some time fallen under the control of the government of the day. Few Bills are now passed that are genuinely Parliament's own, rather than having been proposed by the executive. Similarly, only a tiny number of the government's Bills are rejected by Parliament. During Mrs Thatcher's eleven years as Prime Minister her government suffered only one legislative defeat on the floor of the House of Commons—the Shops Bill in 1986, which if passed would have liberalized Sunday trading laws. This is not to say that Parliament will not amend government legislation, and indeed Parliament will routinely require amendments to be made to government legislation, sometimes insisting on amendments which the government would strongly prefer not to have to make. Notwithstanding Parliament's undoubted amendatory powers, however, is it not the case that far from being a sovereign law-maker, today's Parliament is more accurately described as the institution through which the government legislates?

These then are the three public law functions of Parliament: supply, representation, and legislation. As can be readily seen, Parliament, like the Crown, is neither a simple nor a straightforward institution. It is multifaceted, complex, and subtle. Public lawyers simplify their accounts of Parliament at their peril. In particular, to see Parliament as being little more than a legislature would be a grave mistake.

Before moving on to consider the question of who it is that actually gets to exercise these various parliamentary functions we need first to add a brief word on the structure of Parliament. We have been considering Parliament as if it is a single unit, which of course it is not. The Westminster Parliament (unlike the Scottish Parliament and the European Parliament) is a bicameral Parliament. That is to say, it has two Houses. How are the various functions of Parliament shared between the two Houses, and is the present division of responsibilities in need of revision?

The answer to the first part of this question is simple. In all the functions of Parliament, it is the House of Commons that takes the lead. With regard to supply, representation, the presentation of grievances, scrutiny, and legislation, the House of Lords plays a merely supporting role. This has not always been the case, but over the course of the last three centuries the balance of power between the Lords and the Commons has gradually shifted—at the expense of the Lords, in favour of the Commons. This is perhaps a slightly over-simplistic statement. The relationship of the two Houses to one another has not always been consistent across the various parliamentary functions. Even when the Commons and the Lords had more or less equal legislative power, for example, it was already the case that in matters of supply the Commons played the superior role.

It is in the context of Parliament's legislative function that power has most recently shifted from the Lords to the Commons. This rather dramatic shift occurred in 1911.[3] It should not be thought however, that 1911 marks the moment at which the decline of the House of Lords commenced. In all of the other, non-legislative, areas of parliamentary activity, the Commons had already overtaken the Lords long before the beginning of the twentieth century. Recall that Bagehot, writing in the 1860s, saw that the House of Lords even then had but two powers—a power to revise and a power to delay.[4] The effect of the Parliament Act

---

[3] The story of the constitutional crisis of 1909–1911 was told in the previous chapter. The crisis passed with the enactment of the Parliament Act 1911, the legislation which reduced the legislative power of the Lords, and enabled the Commons and the Crown to legislate, in certain circumstances, despite the dissent of the House of Lords.

[4] See n. 2 above.

1911 was simply to bring the legislative relations between the two Houses into line with the pre-existing parliamentary norm.

QUESTIONS OF COMPOSITION: COMMONS AND LORDS

The composition of the House of Commons is a reasonably straight-forward matter. To become a Member of the House of Commons (that is to say an MP[5]) you have to win a seat at a constituency election. The United Kingdom is divided into 659 electoral districts, called constituencies. Each constituency elects one candidate to become its MP. Thus, there are 659 MPs, all of whom are directly elected, and each of whom represents one constituency. There are two sorts of constituency elections: general elections, and by-elections. A general election is when there is a simultaneous election in every one of the 659 constituencies. Statute now provides that there must be a general election at least every five years.[6] A by-election is when there is an election only in one constituency, to replace a Member who has died or who decides to leave Parliament.

Almost all constituency elections, both general and by-elections, are won by candidates put forward by major political parties. Indeed in the last three general elections (1992, 1997, and 2001) only two constituencies returned independent candidates: one in the 1997 election and one in the 2001 election. All remaining elected candidates were representatives of a political party. The major political parties (Labour, Conservative, and Liberal Democrat) will field candidates in all English constituencies.[7] Thus, the critical step in seeking to become an MP is to be selected by your party of choice as that party's candidate in a constituency which that

[5] MP stands for Member of Parliament. The designation of Members of the House of Commons as MPs is slightly unfortunate. Parliament is composed of both the House of Commons and the House of Lords, so it might be thought that an MP—a Member of Parliament—would be someone who is a Member of either House. This is not, however, the case. Only Members of the Commons are known as MPs. Members of the Lords are known as peers.

[6] Parliament Act 1911, s. 7, amending the Septennial Act 1715. The prerogative power of dissolving Parliament—the formal legal device that triggers a general election—was discussed in the previous chapter.

[7] Electoral politics is different in Scotland, Wales, and Northern Ireland. In Scotland and Wales there are four major parties: Labour, Conservative, and Liberal Democrat, plus either Scottish National or Plaid Cymru (the Welsh nationalists). Northern Ireland is different again. Of the major English parties, only the Conservatives field candidates in Northern Ireland. The major parties in Northern Ireland are the two nationalist parties (Sinn Fein and the SDLP) and the two unionist parties (the UUP and the DUP).

party is likely to win. There is a core of constituencies (mainly in the rural parts of the south of England) that the Conservative party counts as safe Conservative seats—that is to say, as constituencies that can safely be relied on to elect the Conservative party's candidate. Equally, there is a core of constituencies (mainly in the north of England, and in parts of Scotland and Wales) that the Labour party counts as safe Labour seats. Safe seats account for at least half of the 659 available. The others, known as marginal seats, may swing from one party to another—from Labour to Scottish National, from Conservative to Liberal Democrat, and so forth. Being selected by your party as the candidate in a marginal constituency clearly offers a less secure political career than being selected in a safe seat.

The electoral system used for elections to the House of Commons is known as the 'first past the post' system. This system is often contrasted with systems of proportional representation which are common elsewhere in Europe.[8] Under the first past the post system the winner takes all. The goal is not to secure more votes than *every* other candidate, but merely to secure more votes than *any* other candidate. This means that to be elected a candidate does not have to score more than 50 per cent of the votes cast—he or she[9] could be elected with as little as 20 per cent, on condition that no other candidate scored more. That would be a rather unusual result, however. A more typical result would look something like this: Labour candidate 36 per cent, Conservative candidate 30 per cent, Liberal Democrat candidate 24 per cent, remainder of votes cast (for minor parties and independent candidates) 10 per cent. It is to be noted that even though the majority of voters cast their votes against the Labour party's candidate, that candidate would nonetheless win the seat, as no other single candidate polled more votes.

When it came into office in 1997 the Labour government appointed Lord Jenkins to chair an inquiry into the question whether the electoral system used for elections to the House of Commons should be reformed. The Liberal Democrat party has long urged that the system ought to be altered so as to adopt at least aspects of proportional representation. For a time it was thought that change may be upon us—the newly created

---

[8] See chapter 3, n. 7, which briefly outlines the differences between first past the post and proportional representation.

[9] The House of Commons remains dominated by men. The 1997 election was the first in which over 100 women MPs were elected. There are currently 118 women MPs. This is a poor ratio, but it compares favourably to the number of women on the bench. There are currently twelve law lords (all of whom are men), 35 Court of Appeal judges (of whom two are women), and 105 High Court judges (of whom six are women).

Scottish Parliament and the Welsh and Northern Irish Assemblies all included aspects of proportional representation in their electoral systems, and when it reported the Jenkins commission recommended reform along similar lines for the House of Commons. However, it now appears that there is little political appetite for such change within the government, or indeed within the broader Labour party, and the issue has for the time being dropped considerably down the political agenda once more.[10]

Whereas the Commons is entirely elected, the House of Lords is entirely unelected. There are four types of peer: hereditary peers, life peers, law lords, and bishops. Until 1999 the majority of peers were hereditary peers. That is to say, they were members of the House of Lords because they had inherited the right to sit and vote in Parliament from their fathers. Hereditary peerage was conferred by prerogative right by the Crown (exercised in practice on the advice of the Prime Minister). The effects of the 1999 reforms are considered below. Life peerage was made possible by virtue of the Life Peerages Act 1958 (before 1958 all peers apart from the law lords and the bishops were hereditary). A life peer sits in the Lords until death, but upon death the right is not inherited—a peerage of this form lapses upon the death of the person on whom it was conferred. As with hereditary peerages, life peerages are created by the Crown on the advice of the Prime Minister. Law lords are life peers, but their peerages are created not under the 1958 Act but under the Appellate Jurisdiction Act 1876. Judges serving on the judicial committee of the House of Lords retire from judicial office at the age of 70, but they continue to hold their peerages for life. There are currently twelve judges serving on the judicial committee, but a total of twenty-seven law lords in the House, fifteen of whom are retired. These three groups (hereditary peers, life peers, and law lords) are all temporal peers. In addition to the temporal peers, there is one last group of peers—the spiritual peers. This group is composed of the two Archbishops (Canterbury and York) together with the twenty-four most senior bishops of the Church of England, all of whom are automatically made members of the House of Lords.

The Labour government that was elected in 1997 came into office promising considerable constitutional change. One aspect of its reform programme was to revisit the question of the membership of the House of Lords. The government proposed a two-stage reform. The first stage

---

[10] This is not to say that it may not be resurrected, of course. For the report of the Jenkins commission, see *Commission on the Voting System*, Cm. 4090 (London, October 1998).

would be to remove the hereditary peers from the House of Lords, and the second stage would constitute a more thorough-going reform. The first stage was put into effect by the House of Lords Act 1999. This Act abolished the right of the hereditary peerage to sit in the House of Lords, with the result that several hundred peers were required to leave the House. Not all hereditary peers were required to do so, however. The government was forced to accept an amendment to its Bill which allowed ninety-two hereditary peers to continue to serve in the House of Lords, albeit that when these ninety-two die, their peerages will die with them and will not be inherited.

The second stage of reform is more ambitious. It seeks a more fundamental reform the aim of which is a 'more representative and democratic' House.[11] To this end the government in 1999 appointed a Royal Commission to make recommendations on what a reformed House of Lords should consist of. The all-party commission, chaired by the former Conservative Minister Lord Wakeham, reported in early 2000. It recommended that in a House of no more than 550 members, the majority should be appointed (by a statutory and independent Appointments Commission), and that the minority should be elected. Three different models of election were proposed, with the choice of which model to adopt being left open. Under the commission's recommendations there would be two sorts of appointed members: independent and political. Both sorts would be appointed by the Appointments Commission. The bishops and the law lords would remain in the House, although the bishops would be reduced in number. The Wakeham commission further recommended that the length of term for both elected and appointed members should be in the region of twelve to fifteen years, a period considerably longer than that for elected office, and recommended in order to ensure greater independence. The view of the Wakeham commission was that the powers and functions of the House of Lords should remain essentially unchanged.[12]

During the 2001 election campaign the Labour party pledged that it would implement the recommendations of the Wakeham commission, and that it would consult on the way in which this would be done. Accordingly, in November 2001 the government published a White Paper containing its proposals on how to proceed. While the White Paper was

---

[11] Labour party manifesto for the 2001 general election, *Ambitions for Britain* (London, 2001), at 35.

[12] Report of the Royal Commission on the Reform of the House of Lords, *A House for the Future*, Cm. 4534 (London, January 2000).

based on the Wakeham report, there were a number of important points of divergence. The government proposed that in a House of 600 members, 120 (20 per cent) should be elected, 120 should be independent members appointed by a statutory Appointments Commission, and up to 332 should be political nominees appointed by the political parties. In addition there would remain sixteen bishops and twelve law lords. Unlike the Wakeham commission, the government stated that it favoured a shorter term of ten or even five years, although it did not express a final view on this point.[13]

The government's proposals were not well received. Two issues in particular caused considerable discontent: the size of the elected element and the extent of the Prime Minister's patronage. Wakeham himself was deeply critical of the government's White Paper, arguing strenuously that the reduced role of the independent Appointments Commission (which under the government's proposals would be able to nominate only 20 per cent of the members, leaving the political appointees in the hands of the political parties) and the shortened terms of office would significantly impair the effectiveness of the second chamber. The all-party (but Labour-dominated) House of Commons Select Committee on Public Administration published in February 2002 a report in response to the government's White Paper that was deeply critical of it. The Select Committee argued strongly that the second chamber should be predominantly elected (it proposed that 60 per cent of its members should be directly elected), and that all of the nominated members should be appointed by the Appointments Commission, and none by the political parties themselves. It also recommended that the size of the chamber should be reduced to 350, and that both the bishops and the law lords should cease to serve as members.[14]

In February 2003 both Houses of Parliament voted on a series of reform proposals. The options available ranged from an entirely appointed House of Lords to an entirely elected one, with various proportions of elected to appointed members in between. In the event the two Houses could not agree on a preferred option—indeed, there was no majority in the House of Commons for any of the options. Such an impasse suggests that further reform of the House of Lords is now about as distant a prospect as is electoral reform for the Commons. Some

---

[13] *The House of Lords: Completing the Reform*, Cm. 5291 (London, November 2001).
[14] Select Committee on Public Administration, *The Second Chamber: Continuing the Reform*, 2001–02 H.C. 494, February 2002. The powers and functions of select committees are considered in the next chapter.

commentators have speculated that the government does not really wish to proceed with the second stage of House of Lords reform, and that it will be quite happy to say that it tried, but could not attain a consensus, and so continue with the 'transitional' House that we currently have. After all, a cynic would point out, it is in the government's interests for there to be no further reform, as the current arrangement of an entirely appointed House where the Queen creates peers uniquely on the advice of the Prime Minister (albeit that the Prime Minister consults other party leaders) suits the government quite nicely.

Thus, for the time being, the House of Lords is only partially reformed. Its current composition is as follows: there are 557 life peers appointed under the Life Peerages Act 1958, ninety-one former hereditary peers, twenty-seven law lords, and twenty-six bishops. This makes a total of 701 peers, of whom 116 are women. Of these 701 peers, 219 are Conservative, 191 Labour, sixty-five Liberal Democrat, and 178 cross-bench. Cross-bench peers take no party whip, and act as independents, their existence and indeed prominence in the chamber being one of the principal ways in which the Lords is different from the Commons, the Commons, being as we saw above, entirely dominated by party. While no party has an overall majority in the House of Lords, the Conservative party has the largest single number of peers (although, it should be noted, it was a very considerably larger number before the hereditary peerage's right to sit was abolished by the 1999 Act). The average age of the current membership of the House of Lords is 67 years. That for the House of Commons is 52.

LEGISLATIVE SUPREMACY: THE 'SOVEREIGNTY OF PARLIAMENT'

The doctrine of legislative supremacy provides that as a matter of English law there is no source of law higher than a statute. This means that the Queen in Parliament may make or unmake any law whatsoever, and that no court or other body may override or set aside any Act of Parliament. These rules are relatively simple to state, but they have caused more controversy and legal confusion than perhaps any other single area of public law. It is the purpose of this section to try to cut through the confusion, to explain what the rules of supremacy mean, and to examine the knotty question of how these rules may be reconciled with European legal norms that push—or at least appear to push—in a different direction. The argument here will suggest that for public lawyers, while the issues do present some difficulties, they are neither quite so convoluted nor as problematic as some commentators have made out.

There are five main areas of controversy. The first concerns the source of the rules of supremacy; the second the scope of the rules as English law stood before 1973; and the third the scope of the rules as English law has stood since 1973. 1973 is the critical date because it was on 1 January of that year that the United Kingdom became a member of the European Communities. Once we have considered these issues there are two further, more recent, areas of concern that will have to be addressed briefly. These are the impact of human rights law and the concept of 'constitutional statutes'.

(A) THE SOURCE OF THE DOCTRINE

The doctrine of legislative supremacy is a rule of law, not a constitutional convention. What then is the legal authority for the rule? What is its source? There are two alternatives: authority might be found either in statute or in common law. The first of these options may relatively quickly be dismissed. Parliament has never legislated so as to confer legislative supremacy on itself. It may well be that Parliament now legislates in the general expectation that its statutes will enjoy legislative supremacy, but general parliamentary expectations are not, of course, sources of law. It is sometimes suggested that the Bill of Rights 1689 is an Act that can be read as providing statutory authority for the doctrine of legislative supremacy, but such a reading of the Bill of Rights is mistaken. As we saw in chapter 2, the Bill of Rights is concerned with the relationship of the Houses of Parliament to the Crown. Legislative supremacy, by contrast, is concerned with the relationship of Acts of Parliament to the law. For sure the Bill of Rights can be read as enshrining the notion that Parliament (as an institution) enjoys certain powers *vis-à-vis* the Crown, but none of its provisions is concerned with legislative supremacy. For a Bill to be passed as an Act of Parliament that has the force of law requires, of course, the assent of both the Houses of Parliament and of the Crown. Acts of Parliament are in this sense instances of Parliament and the Crown acting together. The Bill of Rights 1689, by contrast, is concerned with the constitutional regulation of the relationship between Parliament and the Crown when they are in disagreement with one another, not when they are acting together.

The doctrine of legislative supremacy is a doctrine of the common law. Like any other rule of the common law it may be developed, refined, re-interpreted, or even changed by the judges. Thus, the doctrine of legislative supremacy may be fundamental in the sense that it is basic to the constitution, but it is no more entrenched or unchangeable than any other rule of English law. Much unnecessary confusion about the nature of legislative supremacy can be avoided if this is borne in mind. Not only may the doctrine be changed: it has been changed. It was far less clear before the English Civil War, for example, that the common law unquestioningly accepted the binding authority of statute. Lord Coke CJ famously remarked in 1610 in *Dr Bonham's Case* that 'when an Act of Parliament is against common right and reason, or repugnant, or impossible to be performed, the common law will control it, and adjudge such Act to be void'.[15] Since the resolution of the long seventeenth century conflict between Parliament and the Crown, however, the common law has much more clearly identified statutes as having supremacy in the hierarchy of legal norms. Parliament won the conflict with the Crown, and the courts have formally recognized this fact by according to Acts of Parliament a legal status higher than that of judge-made law. Acts of the Crown-in-Parliament are more powerful than the decisions of Her Majesty's judiciary.

There is something important to be observed here: underpinning the strictly legal doctrine of legislative supremacy is the courts' recognition of a political reality. Before the Civil War, Parliament was just one among a number of competing authorities, and the courts recognized it as such. Parliament's victory in the Civil War, reaffirmed forty years later in the Bill of Rights, however, meant that it had conclusively asserted itself, and had thereby acquired for itself greater power and authority than it had been able to enjoy beforehand, and, again, the courts recognized the new political reality by making it clear that in the common law statute reigned supreme. The lesson to be learnt from this experience is that if the political reality changes once again, there is nothing to stop the common law from changing with it. We shall return to this point when we consider the impact of the European Community, below.

(B) THE SCOPE OF THE DOCTRINE

Before we come to that, however, we need first to consider a number of issues relating to the scope of legislative supremacy as the law stood

---

[15] (1610) 8 Co Rep 114a, at 118. It should not be thought from this quotation that there was no judicial recognition of legislative supremacy before the Civil War. Goldsworthy has shown in his masterly study that there was considerable recognition of legislative supremacy in the fourteenth to seventeenth centuries. It is just that such judicial recognition was neither as clear nor as consistent before 1700 as it has been since. See J. Goldsworthy, *The Sovereignty of Parliament: History and Philosophy* (Oxford, 1999).

before 1973. We have seen that the courts may change the doctrine of legislative supremacy. Does Parliament also have this power? It might be thought that the answer to this question is obvious: if Parliament may make or unmake any law whatsoever, surely this must include the ability to make (or unmake) a law that altered the doctrine of legislative supremacy. Such simplicity is in this instance deceptive, however. A law that altered the doctrine of legislative supremacy would be a law that reduced it: after all, the doctrine could hardly be further expanded! Herein lies the problem. If Parliament passes an Act that reduces the legislative competence of a future Parliament, then the future Parliament will no longer be legislatively supreme. Some commentators—most notably Dicey and Wade—have strongly argued that Parliament does not possess this power. That is to say that the only law that Parliament may not make is one that reduces the legislative supremacy of future Parliaments: Parliament 'may not bind its successors'. According to this interpretation it is not only the present Parliament that enjoys legislative supremacy, it is all Parliaments, present and future.

Not all commentators agree with this reading of the rules of supremacy. Jennings, Heuston, and Marshall, among others, have argued that there are circumstances in which Parliament may bind its successors. The most important aspect of their argument is that even if Parliament may not bind its successors as to the substance of legislation, Parliament may bind its successors as to the 'manner and form' of legislation. Suppose that Parliament in 1955 passes an Act that provides that 'no repeal of this Act shall be valid unless passed by a two-thirds majority in both Houses of Parliament'. Suppose further that in 1965 Parliament passes an Act that repeals the 1955 legislation, but that the requisite two-thirds majorities are attained in neither House. Is the repeal effective, or does the 1955 Act remain good law because the procedural stipulation that it laid down has not been satisfied? There is no clear authoritative answer to this question in English law. Different cases point in different directions.

The best authority in favour of the view that the 1965 repeal would be effective notwithstanding the failure to meet the procedural stipulations of the 1955 Act is *Ellen Street Estates v Minister of Health*.[16] This case suggests that Parliament may not bind its successors even as to the manner and form of future legislation. The case concerned compensation for landowners whose properties were compulsorily acquired as part of the government's programme of slum clearance in the east end of London in

---

[16] [1934] 1 KB 590.

the inter-war years. Arrangements for such compensation were laid down in the Acquisition of Land (Assessment of Compensation) Act 1919, section 7(1) of which provided that orders of compulsory purchase and related matters dealt with under the Act 'shall . . . have effect subject to this Act, and so far as inconsistent with this Act those provisions shall cease to have or shall not have effect'. The Housing Act 1925 subsequently enacted further provisions on compensation, the effect of the new provisions being in some respects inconsistent with those provided for in the 1919 Act. Before the court it was argued that the provisions of the 1925 Act should not be enforced, as they were in conflict with the terms of the 1919 Act. Both the Divisional Court and the Court of Appeal dismissed this argument, Maugham LJ in the Court of Appeal ruling that 'The Legislature cannot, according to our constitution, bind itself as to the form of subsequent legislation'.[17]

To return to our hypothetical, the best authority in favour of the view that the 1965 repeal would not be effective, and that as a result Parliament may bind its successors at least as to the manner and form of subsequent legislation, is a Privy Council decision, *Attorney-General for New South Wales v Trethowan*.[18] In this case the Privy Council struck down two measures which had been passed by the legislature of New South Wales in Australia on the ground that they did not comply with procedural requirements laid down by an earlier measure of the New South Wales legislature. However, it is difficult to see what weight this decision would have in English law, as the legal character of the New South Wales legislature was at the material time different from that of the Westminster Parliament. The New South Wales legislature was subject to the Colonial Laws Validity Act 1865, section 5 of which provided that:

Every colonial legislature shall . . . in respect to the colony under its jurisdiction, have, and be deemed at all times to have had, full power to make laws respecting the constitution, power, and procedure of such legislature; provided that such laws shall have been passed in such manner and form as may from time to time be required by any Act of Parliament, letters patent, Order in Council, or colonial law . . .

The Privy Council made it clear that its judgment depended entirely on

[17] Ibid., at 597. The decision in the *Ellen Street Estates* case affirmed an earlier decision of the Divisional Court that had been concerned with the same statutory provisions: see *Vauxhall Estates v. Liverpool Corporation* [1932] 1 KB 733, in which Avory J had held (at 743) that 'no Act of Parliament can effectively provide that no future Act shall interfere with its provisions'.
[18] [1932] AC 526.

this provision. This significantly reduces the importance of the case as a matter of English law, as neither this provision nor any other like it applies to the Westminster Parliament, as we have seen. To conclude on the question whether Parliament may bind its successors, while there is no clear answer, the weight of authority appears to lean in the direction of the Diceyan view that, as a matter of English law, Parliament may bind its successors neither as to the substance nor as to the manner and form of subsequent legislation.

A second issue concerning the scope of legislative supremacy is the doctrine of implied repeal. Most of the time, when a later Parliament wishes to repeal statutory provisions passed by an earlier Parliament, the later Parliament will state its intention expressly. Almost all Acts contain a schedule listing the provisions of earlier Acts that are expressly repealed by the new Act. This is a simple and unremarkable matter of routine legislative drafting and is of course fully in accordance with the doctrine of legislative supremacy: Parliament may make *or unmake* any law whatsoever. What of the situation, however, where there are two Acts of Parliament that conflict, but where the later Act has not expressly repealed the earlier one? In order to deal with this scenario the courts have developed the doctrine of implied repeal. This doctrine holds that the provisions of the later Act prevail over those of the earlier one even where the later one has not expressly repealed the earlier one.

The leading authority on this important aspect of legislative supremacy is *Ellen Street Estates v Minister of Health*.[19] In this case, which was considered above in relation to the 'manner and form' argument, Scrutton LJ held that 'Parliament can alter an Act previously passed . . . by enacting a provision which is clearly inconsistent with the previous Act'.[20] Maugham LJ agreed, and explained that 'it is impossible for Parliament to enact that in a subsequent statute dealing with the same subject-matter there can be no implied repeal'.[21] We shall have cause to return to the question of implied repeal when we consider the impact of the United Kingdom's membership of the European Community on the doctrine of legislative supremacy. The point to note here is the narrow application of the notion of implied repeal. For the court to hold that one statute impliedly repeals another, the two statutes must be 'clearly inconsistent' and must each deal with the 'same subject-matter'.

---

[19] See n. 16 above.   [20] Ibid., at 595–596.   [21] Ibid., at 597.

(C) THE IMPACT OF THE EUROPEAN COMMUNITY

The biggest challenge to the doctrine of legislative supremacy in recent years has been posed by the United Kingdom's accession to the European Community. This is because, as a matter of EC law, it is Community law that prevails in any conflict with national law—even with national constitutional law. At the very heart of the Community's legal system lies the doctrine of the supremacy of Community law. If Parliament passes an Act that violates a provision of Community law, under the English legal doctrine of legislative supremacy it will be the Act of Parliament that prevails, notwithstanding the incompatibility with Community law. Under EC law, however, it will be the provision of Community law that prevails, under the doctrine of the supremacy of EC law.[22] The story of how this apparent conflict (between the legislative supremacy of statute on the one hand and the supremacy of EC law on the other) has been resolved is the one that is analysed in this section of this chapter.

The starting point is the legal instrument which in English law effected the accession of the United Kingdom into the European Community. That instrument is the European Communities Act 1972 (ECA). No discussion of the cases that have considered the issue of how to reconcile legislative supremacy with EC law can be successful without first considering the detailed terms of this all-important statute. There are three provisions that need to be set out: section 2(1), section 2(4), and section 3(1). Section 2(1) is in the following terms:

All such rights, powers, liabilities, obligations and restrictions from time to time created by or arising by or under the Treaties ... as in accordance with the Treaties are without further enactment to be given legal effect or used in the United Kingdom shall be recognised and available in law, and be enforced, allowed and followed accordingly ...

The effect of this rather awkwardly worded provision is to bring into domestic legal force all provisions of Community law that are to be given

---

[22] The doctrine of the supremacy of EC law was laid down by the European Court of Justice in its ground-breaking decision in Case 6/64, *Costa v ENEL* [1964] ECR 585 in which the Court held that by the creation of the European Community 'the Member States have limited their sovereign rights, albeit within limited fields, and have thus created a body of law which binds both their nationals and themselves'. This principle was subsequently amplified in Case 11/70, *Internationale Handelsgesellschaft* [1970] ECR 1125 in which the ECJ held that Community law 'cannot be overridden by rules of national law, however framed'. It is to be noted that both of these cases were decided before the United Kingdom acceded to the European Community, and were well settled and widely known principles of EC law before 1972.

legal effect 'without further enactment'. Under Community law there are two sorts of provisions that are to be given domestic legal effect without further enactment: those which are 'directly applicable' and those which are 'directly effective'. Before proceeding any further with our analysis of the ECA and of the impact of EC law on the doctrine of legislative supremacy, it is necessary to take a short detour into the world of EC law in order that we may discover what the terms 'direct applicability' and 'direct effect' mean.

Community law is a complex legal system, composed of multiple legal sources. There are five principal sources of Community law: the Treaties themselves, Regulations, Directives, Decisions, and Recommendations.[23] Article 249 EC provides that, of these, two are directly applicable. These two are Treaty provisions and Regulations. Under Community law, Treaty provisions and Regulations come into effect in the domestic legal orders of the Member States automatically and without the need for any intervening national legislative or executive action. This is the meaning of the term 'direct applicability'. The term 'direct effect' is more difficult. A provision of Community law is said to be directly effective if it is sufficiently clear and unconditional to be invoked in litigation before a national court. Whereas the notion of direct applicability is found in the text of the Treaty, the notion of direct effect is not mentioned in the Treaty itself, but is an invention of the European Court of Justice, developed in its seminal decision in the *Van Gend en Loos* case in 1962.[24] It is not only Treaty provisions and Regulations that may have direct effect: so too may Directives and other sources of Community law. The direct effectiveness of a provision depends not on its source (Regulation or Directive) but on its substantive content (is it sufficiently clear and unconditional). Thus, not all Treaty provisions, Regulations, or Directives possess direct effect: only those which are in the opinion of the Court of Justice sufficiently clear and unconditional are directly effective.

If we take this back to the terms of section 2(1) of the ECA, we can see that the purpose of this subsection is to bring into domestic legal force all directly applicable and directly effective provisions of Community law.[25]

---

[23] This is laid down in Art. 249 EC (formerly Art. 189 of the EC Treaty).

[24] Case 26/62, *Van Gend en Loos* [1963] ECR 1.

[25] Provisions of Community law that are neither directly applicable nor directly effective but which are nonetheless required by EC law to be brought into force in the national legal orders of the Member States are dealt with for the United Kingdom by s. 2(2) of the ECA. This subs. empowers the relevant government Minister to make the necessary provision by means of delegated legislation.

Note the word 'all' in the previous sentence. The terms of section 2(1) apply not only to directly applicable and directly effective provisions of Community law as Community law stood at the date of the coming into force of the statute (1 January 1973) but apply also to all future directly applicable and directly effective provisions of Community law.

Section 2(4) includes the following provision: 'any enactment passed or to be passed . . . shall be construed and have effect subject to the foregoing provisions of this section'. 'Enactment' here means any legislative measure, including Acts of Parliament. 'Construed' means construed by a domestic court. The effect of section 2(4) is that all courts in the United Kingdom are required to construe and to give effect to all legislation (primary and secondary) of whatever date—whether passed before 1973 or after—subject to 'the foregoing provisions of this section'. As we just saw, the effect of the foregoing provisions of section 2 is to bring directly applicable and directly effective Community law of whatever date into domestic legal force. Thus, the meaning of section 2(4) is that domestic courts are required to construe and to give effect to parliamentary legislation 'subject to' the terms of directly applicable and directly effective Community law, regardless of the date of either.[26] Given that section 2(4) applies not only to legislation made before 1973, but also apparently to legislation to be made after that date, this appears on one reading to constitute an attempt by the Parliament of 1972 to bind its successors— something that, as we saw in the previous section, Parliament is not generally free to do. Whether section 2(4) has been so regarded in subsequent cases is a question we shall discuss shortly.

First, however, we must consider one further provision of the ECA: section 3(1). This provides that 'For the purpose of all legal proceedings any question as to the meaning or effect of any of the Treaties, or as to the validity, meaning or effect of any Community instruments, shall be treated as a question of law . . .'. When something is 'treated as a question of law' this means that the domestic courts have the competence authoritatively to determine it and to adjudicate on disputes arising under it. Thus, section 3(1) confers on domestic courts in the United Kingdom the power to determine and to adjudicate on disputes arising under Community law. This is a feature of Community law that distinguishes it from regular public international law: unlike international law, Community law

---

[26] Combining subs. 2(2) and (4) leads to the result that domestic courts must also construe and give effect to parliamentary legislation subject to any delegated measure made by a Minister under s. 2(2).

can be (indeed must be) enforced by local domestic courts and tribunals throughout the Member States of the Community. The European Court of Justice in Luxembourg may be the supreme court in the European judicial architecture, but it sits at the top of an exceptionally large pyramid. The point to note about the conferment on domestic courts in the United Kingdom of a jurisdiction to hear and to decide cases concerning Community law is that this is not a jurisdiction that the courts have conferred on themselves. Rather, courts in the United Kingdom possess this power for one reason and for one reason only: namely, because Parliament legislated it, in section 3(1) of the ECA 1972.

For a considerable period after their enactment these provisions caused relatively little controversy. When domestic courts were called on to interpret aspects of English law that pre-dated the ECA, no question of legislative supremacy was raised when the courts found themselves compelled to construe or to give effect to the old law subject to new European requirements. It has always been open to Parliament to issue instructions to the judges to the effect that they should interpret old statutes in new ways. Even when courts were called on to interpret aspects of English law that post-dated the ECA, the judges managed to perform this task without upsetting the conventional understandings of legislative supremacy. As Lord Diplock pointed out in *Garland v British Rail* in 1983:

it is a principle of construction of United Kingdom statutes, now too well established to call for citation of authority, that the words of a statute passed after [a] Treaty has been signed and dealing with the subject matter of [an] international obligation of the United Kingdom, are to be construed, if they are reasonably capable of bearing such a meaning, as intended to carry out the obligation, and not to be inconsistent with it.[27]

On this reading, section 2(4) of the ECA requires the courts to do nothing that they would not in any event have done by virtue of the common law rule that all statutes passed after the Crown has ratified an international treaty are, if at all possible, to be interpreted by the courts so as to be in conformity and not in conflict with the Crown's international treaty obligations. The doctrine of legislative supremacy provides that the courts may not overturn or set aside a statute, but they may of course interpret statutes, and there is nothing in the doctrine to prevent them from interpreting statutes, in appropriate cases, in the light of the

---

[27] *Garland v British Rail Engineering* [1983] 2 AC 751, at 771.

Crown's international treaty obligations, including its obligations under the treaties that constitute the European Community.

Lord Diplock's dictum in *Garland* applies when a statute is being interpreted in the light of the EC Treaty. What of the situation in which the courts are required to interpret a statute in the light of a subordinate EC measure, such as a Directive? The European Court of Justice ruled in 1984 that, as a matter of Community law, 'in applying . . . the provisions of a national law specifically introduced in order to implement [a] Directive . . . national courts are required to interpret their national law in the light of the wording and the purpose of the Directive'.[28] Consequently, in cases such as *Pickstone v Freemans*,[29] which was concerned with equal pay, and *Litster v Forth Dry Dock and Engineering*,[30] which was concerned with employee protection, English courts gave generous and purposive readings to, respectively, the Equal Pay Act and the Transfer of Undertakings Regulations in order to ensure that English law complied with Community law even where narrower or more literal interpretations of domestic law might have led to a different result. Here again, these cases pose no threat to the doctrine of legislative supremacy. These cases are concerned with statutory interpretation, not statutory invalidation. What they disclose is considerable (but not unlimited[31]) judicial enthusiasm for and engagement in the enterprise of embedding EC law as effectively as possible in the United Kingdom.

The period of relatively uncontroversial application of the ECA ended with *Factortame*. *Factortame* is a series of cases spanning more than ten years. The cases include decisions of enormous constitutional significance, both for English law and for Community law. In the present context we are not concerned with the whole series of cases, but only with two of the earlier decisions, both decisions of the House of Lords. For

---

[28] Case 14/83, *Von Colson and Kamann v Land Nordrhein-Westfalen* [1984] ECR 1891. This rule of construction, known in EC law as the doctrine of indirect effect, was controversially extended by the ECJ in Case C-106/89, *Marleasing v La Comercial* [1990] ECR I-4135, in which the Court stated that whenever there is an apparent conflict between the terms of a Directive and those of national law, the national court is, as far as possible, required to interpret the national law in the light of the Directive, regardless of whether the national law was designed to implement the Directive or not, and regardless of whether the national law was adopted before or after the Directive.

[29] [1989] AC 66.

[30] [1990] 1 AC 546.

[31] That there were limits to the extent to which the courts would depart from literal interpretation in favour of purposive construction is illustrated by *Duke v GEC Reliance* [1988] AC 618.

ease of reference we shall call these cases *Factortame I* and *Factortame II*.[32] Before coming to the various decisions, we must first outline the facts. The cases were brought by a large number of companies which between them owned some ninety-five fishing boats that had been registered under the Merchant Shipping Act 1894 as British and had accordingly been permitted to fish in British waters. The majority of the directors and shareholders of the companies were Spanish nationals. The Thatcher government wished to change the scheme for registration of fishing boats, and to this effect Parliament passed the Merchant Shipping Act 1988, which replaced the 1894 Act. Under the 1988 Act, boats formerly registered as British were required to re-register. The ninety-five boats in question failed to qualify for re-registration under the terms of the 1988 Act. Factortame and the other applicants brought proceedings in the Divisional Court arguing that the relevant provisions of the Merchant Shipping Act 1988 were contrary to European Community law and should accordingly be set aside.

The Merchant Shipping Act 1988, section 14(1) provided that 'a fishing vessel shall only be eligible to be registered as a British shipping vessel if—(a) the vessel is British-owned'. Section 14(7) provided that for the purposes of section 14(1) the term 'British-owned' meant either that the legal title to the vessel had to be vested in a person who is a British citizen resident and domiciled in the United Kingdom, or, for vessels that were owned by a corporation, that at least 75 per cent of its shareholders and 75 per cent of its directors had to be British for the vessel to be registrable as British. Factortame argued that these provisions were contrary to a number of principles of Community law, including the right not to be discriminated against on the basis of nationality and the rights to free movement of services and to freedom of establishment. The government defended the action by arguing that while the rights asserted by Factortame were generally applicable in Community law, they did not apply here, as the fisheries industry was one area of Community policy where special considerations applied, in the interests of protecting national fishing fleets, fishing communities, and indeed the fishing stocks themselves. There was considerable argument on this point—which as a matter of Community law is far from straightforward. We shall refer to this point as the substantive question, that question being: are the relevant provisions of the Merchant Shipping Act 1988 contrary to Community law?

---

[32] Reported as *R v Secretary of State for Transport, ex parte Factortame* [1990] 2 AC 85, and *R v Secretary of State for Transport, ex parte Factortame (No. 2)* [1991] 1 AC 603.

Having heard argument on the substantive question, the Divisional Court came to the conclusion that it did not know the answer to the question, and so it utilized its power to refer the matter to the European Court of Justice (ECJ).[33] This convenient device, whereby national courts may refer questions of the interpretation of Community law to the ECJ, is a central pillar of the European judicial architecture and has proved to be of critical importance to the smooth operation of Community law. The substantive question is of no further concern to us: it raises no point of English public law. Knowing the answer to the substantive question is important if you are a student of European fisheries law, but if that is what you are interested in you are probably reading the wrong book.[34] What matters for public law is what happened next.

It would take the ECJ some two years to answer the substantive question. If during this time the applicants continued to be unable to secure British registration for their vessels, they would suffer irreparable damage, such that many would lose their livelihood. The applicants therefore applied to the Divisional Court for interim relief, the effect of which would be that the relevant provisions of the Merchant Shipping Act 1988 would be disapplied pending the outcome of the substantive point. The Divisional Court granted the relief. The government successfully appealed to the Court of Appeal, and the applicants further appealed to the House of Lords. It is this appeal which we will refer to as *Factortame I*. The question in *Factortame I* is not the substantive question about the compatibility of English fishing law with Community law. Rather, the question in *Factortame I* is a jurisdictional question, and this jurisdictional question is of profound importance for public law. The question is whether the courts have the power to grant interim relief the effect of which would be to suspend the operation of an Act of Parliament.[35]

The House of Lords ruled that in English law the courts have no jurisdiction to grant the remedy that the applicants were seeking. The key to this decision is the Crown Proceedings Act 1947, section 21(2). This provides that 'The court shall not in any civil proceedings grant any injunction or make any order against an officer of the Crown'. Now, the

---

[33] See Art. 234 EC (formerly Art. 177 of the EC Treaty).

[34] For the curious, the ECJ decided that the Merchant Shipping Act was in violation of Community law. Further cases have been concerned with such questions as whether the breach of EC law was sufficiently serious to merit an application for damages (it was held that it was), and what the quantum of damages should be.

[35] Interim relief, or an interim remedy, is a remedy that is granted by a court during the course of litigation rather than at the end of litigation. The term interlocutory relief is also used to describe such a remedy.

respondent in *Factortame I* (and indeed in *Factortame II*) was the Secretary of State for Transport, who is of course a Minister of the Crown. The interim remedy sought by the applicants would constitute an order of the court made against the respondent, which is to say in this case an order of the court made against an officer of the Crown. In the House of Lords Lord Bridge interpreted section 21(2) of the Crown Proceedings Act as forbidding the court, under English law, from making such an order. This was a controversial interpretation. Earlier lower court decisions had ruled that the term 'civil proceedings' in section 21(2) included actions commenced by writ, but excluded applications for judicial review (such as the present case). If this interpretation had been followed by the House of Lords in *Factortame I*, then the bar contained in section 21(2) would not have applied, and the court would have been free to grant the remedy. As it was, however, Lord Bridge overruled the earlier case law. This decision thus provides a further example of a theme explored in the previous chapter: namely, that the courts will grant to the Crown extraordinary latitude throughout public law, and in particular in the law of remedies.[36]

It is a noteworthy feature of *Factortame I* that its reasoning is not dressed up in the garb of grand constitutional theory and the doctrine of legislative supremacy. Indeed, Lord Bridge barely even mentions legislative supremacy. The judgment is based not on constitutional principle, but on a narrow reading of a somewhat technical point of the law of remedies against the Crown. The broader constitutional picture was not to come to the fore until the next stage of the case.

Having concluded that there was no jurisdiction in English law to enable the court to grant the remedy which the applicants sought, Lord Bridge then proceeded to consider whether the applicants were entitled to a remedy under European Community law. After all, it was their rights under Community law that the applicants argued were being compromised by the Merchant Shipping Act: could Community law not protect those rights at this interim stage? Thus the jurisdictional question was split into two. The first part of the question asked whether *in English law* the courts have the power to grant interim relief the effect of which would be to suspend the operation of an Act of Parliament. As we have seen, the House of Lords answered this question in the negative— not because of the doctrine of legislative supremacy, but because of a

---

[36] See chapter 3, at 88–9. This aspect of the House of Lords' decision in *Factortame I* was subsequently reconsidered in *M v Home Office* [1994] 1 AC 377.

technicality (albeit a very important technicality) in the law of remedies against the Crown. The second part of the question asked whether *in Community law* the courts have the power to grant interim relief the effect of which would be to suspend the operation of an Act of Parliament. The House of Lords concluded that it did not know the answer to this second part of the jurisdictional question, and so referred it to the European Court of Justice.

The Court of Justice held that the applicants were entitled under Community law to interim protection. In the light of this ruling the House of Lords then granted the relief that the applicants had sought: this is *Factortame II*. The remedy granted by the House of Lords was an injunction preventing the Secretary of State from exercising his powers under section 14 of the Merchant Shipping Act 1988 to withhold or to withdraw registration of shipping vessels that failed to meet the requirements of nationality, residence, and domicile set out in that section. Thus, the effect of the order was to suspend the operation of an Act of Parliament. The question for public lawyers is: can the granting of this remedy be reconciled with the doctrine of legislative supremacy and, if so, how?

A wide variety of answers to this question have been offered by commentators. Wade has famously suggested that no reconciliation is possible, and that *Factortame II* demonstrates that Parliament in the European Communities Act 1972 effected what he has described as a 'revolution' in the law.[37] Others have robustly criticized this view.[38] Let us now examine a little more closely what the House of Lords decided in *Factortame II*, and how it fits in to the doctrine of legislative supremacy. The starting point must be the terms of the European Communities Act 1972: no analysis of *Factortame II* can succeed without considering the central provisions of this Act. The key provision is section 3(1), which was discussed above. The House of Lords decided in *Factortame II* that, in the light of the ruling from the ECJ, the applicants were *as a matter of Community law* entitled to the protection of interim relief. In other words, the House of Lords granted the remedy not in its capacity as a court of English law, but in its capacity as a court empowered to determine questions of Community law. Now, from where did the House of Lords get its power to determine questions of Community law? The answer of course is section 3(1) of the ECA. As we saw above, courts in the United

[37] See H. W. R. Wade, 'Sovereignty—Revolution or Evolution?' (1996) 112 *Law Quarterly Review* 568.
[38] See e.g. T. R. S. Allan, 'Parliamentary Sovereignty: Law, Politics, and Revolution' (1997) 113 *Law Quarterly Review* 443.

Kingdom possess the power to determine questions of Community law for one reason and for one reason only: namely, because Parliament legislated so as to confer that power on them, in section 3(1) of the ECA.

On this reading, all the House of Lords did in *Factortame II* was to enforce the will of Parliament as laid down in statute. Parliament legislated in 1972 that courts in the United Kingdom were to enforce Community law, and that is all that the House of Lords was doing in *Factortame II*. *Factortame II* was a case in which, acting under instructions contained in the 1972 Act, the House of Lords was enforcing Community law, and the legislative supremacy of Acts of the United Kingdom Parliament has never been a doctrine of Community law, only of English law. The House of Lords did not take on a jurisdiction to enforce Community law because the European Court of Justice required that it do so, or because the House of Lords volunteered for it, but because Parliament legislated for it, in section 3(1). There was no revolution here. *Factortame II* could be read as revolutionary only if it were read as a case decided under the rules of English public law, and such a reading would be in grave error, as the opening paragraph of Lord Bridge's speech in the case shows. Lord Bridge explained perfectly clearly that, whereas *Factortame I* had been decided by the House of Lords in its capacity as a court of English law, the question in *Factortame II* was 'whether Community law [has] invested us with . . . jurisdiction' to grant interim relief in certain circumstances.[39]

What then are the implications of the decision for the doctrine of legislative supremacy? Recall that there are two limbs to the doctrine. The first is that Parliament may make or unmake any law whatsoever. Is this still the case? Does Parliament, post-*Factortame*, retain the power to make or unmake any law? The answer is absolutely, yes. There is nothing in *Factortame* to suggest that Parliament cannot make a law that is contrary to Community law. Parliament might have difficulties in having its law effectively enforced, but that is a separate issue (to which we shall shortly turn) and does not speak to Parliament's capacity to make law. The first limb of the doctrine of legislative supremacy is thus entirely untouched by *Factortame*.

The second limb provides that nobody may override or set aside an Act of Parliament. Now, as a matter of English law this remains the case, but as a matter of European Community law it never was the case: from as

---

[39] [1991] 1 AC 603, at 658. The same all-important distinction is made by Lord Goff at 661–662.

long ago as 1964—eight years before the United Kingdom joined the Community—it was clear from the case law of the Court of Justice that in a conflict between national law and directly applicable or directly effective Community law, the latter would as a matter of Community law prevail over the former.[40] As soon as the House of Lords (and all other courts in the United Kingdom) became empowered by section 3(1) of the ECA to determine questions of Community law, it was clear from reading the text of the 1972 Act alongside the pre-existing jurisprudence of the Court of Justice that it was no longer true that nobody in England could set aside an Act of Parliament.

To clarify: it remains the case that under English law nobody has the power to override or to set aside a statute, but it is no longer the case that English law is the only law that is applicable in England. Since 1 January 1973 there have been two legal systems operating in this country, not one, and the doctrine of the legislative supremacy of statute is a doctrine known to only one of those two systems. This is not a revolution: it is rather the incorporation of a new legal order into a very old country. European Community law is, moreover, a new legal order that is to be enforced by the same courts as enforce domestic law. They may be the same courts, but they are not enforcing the same law. The House of Lords is one court with two jurisdictions, one in domestic law (which does not allow the court to set aside a statute) and one in Community law (which in certain circumstances does). Thus, as these legal systems currently stand, the doctrine of legislative supremacy may be stated as follows: Parliament may make or unmake any law whatsoever, and under English law nobody may override or set aside a statute. Even Dicey could surely have lived with that!

It is sometimes suggested that while the essentials of legislative supremacy are left intact by *Factortame*, the doctrine of implied repeal has been affected. That the House of Lords did not hold that the Merchant Shipping Act 1988 impliedly repealed the European Communities Act 1972 is taken by some commentators as evidence of the fact that the doctrine of implied repeal has been changed, or even abandoned. This view, while often repeated, is misconceived. There are two reasons for this. The first is that the provisions of the Merchant Shipping Act were not in conflict with those of the European Communities Act: rather, they were in conflict with certain Articles of the Treaty of Rome. The doctrine of implied repeal simply did not apply: it is concerned with conflicts

[40] See n. 22 above.

between one statute and another, not with conflicts between statutes and other sources of law such as Treaty Articles.

The second reason is that even if there had been an allegation that the Merchant Shipping Act was in conflict with the European Communities Act (which there was not), the doctrine of implied repeal would still have been irrelevant to the case. This is because, as we saw above, implied repeal concerns incompatibilities between two statutes that both deal with the same subject-matter, as Maugham LJ made clear in his judgment in the leading case of *Ellen Street Estates v Minister of Health*.[41] The Merchant Shipping Act and the European Communities Act did not deal with the same subject-matter. The one concerned fishing and the other concerned the legal relationship between the United Kingdom and the European Community. It is frankly preposterous to suggest that there could have been an issue of implied repeal here: what provision of the Merchant Shipping Act could be said to have impliedly repealed what provision of the European Communities Act? The key provisions of each have been set out above: sections 2 and 3 of the ECA, and section 14 of the Merchant Shipping Act. Take another look at them and ask yourself which words of section 14 of the 1988 Act could meaningfully be said to have impliedly repealed which words of sections 2 or 3 of the ECA?

The final question to consider in the light of *Factortame* is this. Suppose that Parliament now wishes to re-enact the terms of the 1988 Merchant Shipping Act, or something very similar. Suppose that Parliament is so concerned about the over-fishing of depleted fish stocks in the waters surrounding the United Kingdom that it deems it necessary strictly to limit access to those waters, and decides that only small numbers of local fishermen will be granted fishing permits. The Spanish, and for that matter all non-British nationals, are excluded. Parliament knows that enacting such a policy into law will fall foul of European law, but Parliament wishes nonetheless to proceed with its policy. For Parliament, protecting national fish stocks is simply more important than observing European law. What would Parliament now have to do, in the light of *Factortame*, to ensure that its statute is upheld and enforced by the domestic courts? There are, it seems, two options. The first is that Parliament could withdraw the United Kingdom from the European Community and repeal the European Communities Act. This would be a rather dramatic step to take for the sake of a few cod, it might be thought, but it is nonetheless an option that Parliament does have. It is always to be

---

[41] See n. 16 above.

remembered that such national sovereignty as is for the time being shared with the European Community is not beyond the recall of Parliament: Parliament may at any time and for any reason or for none withdraw the United Kingdom from the Community.

A second option is perhaps less unlikely. Suppose that Parliament passes an Act that provides in section 1 that 'the terms of the Merchant Shipping Act 1988 are hereby re-enacted'; and further provides in section 2 that 'this Act shall be construed and have effect notwithstanding any provision to the contrary in either (a) the European Communities Act 1972 or (b) Community law'. Would the effect of such a 'notwithstanding' clause not be to oust the jurisdiction of the domestic courts to enforce Community law over this particular Act? The legal robustness of such a clause has never been tested, as Parliament has not yet desired knowingly to legislate in such a way as would violate Community law, but there is a strong argument that, if faced with such a clause, domestic courts would regard themselves as bound to uphold the statute and to disregard Community law. After all, domestic courts have the power to enforce Community law only because Parliament has conferred such a power on them, and what Parliament can confer on the courts Parliament can take away. A 'notwithstanding' clause such as this would not entirely remove the power of domestic courts to enforce Community law: rather, it would simply exclude this one statute from that jurisdiction.

Even if such a 'notwithstanding' clause were to prove successful in protecting the statute in domestic courts, such a move would clearly be contrary to Community law, and the European Commission would have no hesitation in bringing the United Kingdom before the Court of Justice on an infringement action.[42] The Court of Justice might even go so far as to levy a penalty payment (that is to say, a fine) on the United Kingdom. But these are problems of Community law, not of English public law. As far as English public law is concerned, even after *Factortame* Parliament may relatively easily legislate in violation of Community law and more-over may do so in such a way that the domestic courts have no option but to uphold and enforce the legislation. If the courts overrode or set aside a 'notwithstanding' clause of the nature suggested here, perhaps that *would* be a revolution. As the law stands, however, the doctrine of legislative supremacy remains intact: any rumours pertaining to its death are, as the saying goes, premature.

---

[42] See Art. 226 EC (formerly Art. 169 of the EC treaty).

(D) THE HUMAN RIGHTS ACT 1998

A second challenge to the doctrine of legislative supremacy is posed by the Human Rights Act 1998 (HRA). This is nothing like as big or as complex a challenge as that considered in the previous section, and it can be dealt with relatively swiftly. Confusingly, there are in law two Europes, not one. The second legal Europe is the Council of Europe. This is an international body that is entirely separate from the European Community, although all fifteen Member States of the EC are (now) members also of the Council of Europe. The Council of Europe has forty-one Member States, so it is presently considerably bigger than the EC, and will indeed remain so even after the next round of EC expansion. By far the most important legal initiative of the Council of Europe is the European Convention on Human Rights (ECHR). This treaty is an international Bill of Rights. It dates from 1950, and the United Kingdom has been bound by it as a matter of international law since it came into force in the early 1960s. The ECHR is enforced by the European Court of Human Rights (ECtHR) in Strasbourg. The EC and the ECHR, and the ECJ and the ECtHR are very frequently muddled up and confused in the media, but it is essential that they be kept separate.

While the United Kingdom has been bound by the ECHR as a matter of international law since the early 1960s, the terms of the ECHR were incorporated into domestic law only in 2000, when the HRA came into force. Between the 1960s and 2000, domestic courts could not enforce the terms of the ECHR. There were limited circumstances in which domestic courts could have regard to the terms of the ECHR while enforcing domestic law, but the ECHR itself could until 2000 be enforced in respect of the United Kingdom only by the ECtHR in Strasbourg, and not by domestic courts.[43] This changed when the Human Rights Act 1998 came into force in October 2000. The HRA incorporates ECHR rights, known in English law as Convention rights, into domestic law. The HRA therefore plays a similar role in respect of the ECHR to that played by the ECA in respect of the European Community. However, the comparison ends there—and this is the important point—as the terms of the domestic incorporation of the ECHR are significantly different from those contained in the ECA.

The ECHR is a Bill of Rights. As such, it sets out a number of fundamental rights that the State may interfere with only in strictly limited

---

[43] The role of the ECHR in English public law before 2000 is considered below in chapter 6.

circumstances. These rights include the right to life; the right to freedom from torture; the right to freedom from slavery and servitude; the right to liberty; the right to a fair trial; the right to privacy; the right to freedom of thought, conscience, and religion; the right to freedom of expression; and the right to freedom of peaceful assembly and association; as well as others. Does the domestic incorporation of the ECHR mean that Parliament is no longer free to legislate in violation of these Convention rights? If so, does this amount to a restriction on the legislative supremacy of Acts of Parliament?

The legal relationship between Convention rights and the doctrine of legislative supremacy is governed by sections 3 and 4 of the HRA. Section 3 provides that 'So far as it is possible to do so, primary legislation . . . must be read and given effect in a way which is compatible with the Convention rights'. This means that whenever possible courts must endeavour to interpret statute (whenever enacted) so as to be in conformity with, and not in conflict with, Convention rights. Section 4 provides that if such an interpretation is impossible, the court may grant a new remedy, specially created by the Act, called a 'declaration of incompatibility'. A declaration of incompatibility is exactly what its name suggests it is: it is a remedy which is merely declaratory of the fact that in the court's view a statute, or a certain provision in a statute, is incompatible with a Convention right. Section 4(6) provides that a declaration of incompatibility 'does not affect the validity, continuing operation or enforcement of the provision in respect of which it is given'.[44]

The effect of a declaration of incompatibility is political rather than legal, in that Parliament will be invited to revisit its statute book, and to decide whether in the light of a declaration having been granted by a court, it wishes to continue with the provision, to amend it, or to repeal it. The final decision rests with Parliament, and if Parliament decides not to amend or to repeal a provision that has been declared by a court to be incompatible with a Convention right, so be it. Parliament continues to have the supreme legislative authority to legislate in contravention of Convention rights if it so wishes, and no domestic court or tribunal may overturn or set aside such legislation, notwithstanding the incompatibility. Thus, the Human Rights Act has been ingeniously and carefully designed so as to introduce into English public law ideas of basic or fundamental rights without disturbing the doctrine of legislative supremacy.

---

[44] On the relationship between ss. 3 and 4, see *R v A (No. 2)* [2002] 1 AC 45.

(E) 'CONSTITUTIONAL' STATUTES?

Before we leave the topic of legislative supremacy there is one final point that calls to be addressed. In a recent judgment, an experienced and influential public law judge has suggested that the common law may recognize a category he described as 'constitutional statutes'.[45] The case, popularly known as the Metric Martyrs' case, concerned the prosecution of a number of traders for using imperial measures (pounds and ounces) rather than metric measures (kilograms). For a long period traders were able to use either but, by virtue of EC Directives, after a certain point only metric measures could be used. Legal proceedings were taken against the traders concerned for continuing to use imperial measures after this cut-off point. As part of their legal argument, the traders argued that the power under which the government had transposed the Directive into English law (this power being contained in the European Communities Act 1972, section 2(2)) had been impliedly repealed by the Weights and Measures Act 1985, a statute that had in its original form permitted both metric and imperial measures to be used. The 1985 Act was amended by secondary legislation in 1994 to the effect that after a certain date only metric measures would be permitted. The traders argued that such amendment was invalid and unlawful on the ground that the statutory power that authorized the government to make the amendment (ECA 1972, section 2(2)) had been impliedly repealed by the Weights and Measures Act 1985. In the Divisional Court judgment was given by Laws LJ, who rejected the implied repeal argument and held against the traders.

What is of interest in the case is not so much the outcome as the reasoning employed by Laws LJ. He offered a number of reasons why the implied repeal argument failed. His main reason was (correctly) that there was no inconsistency between the provisions of the 1972 Act and those of the 1985 Act. If he had stopped there, all would be well, but he continued to opine that even if there had been an irreducible inconsistency between the provisions of the ECA and those of a later Act there could in any event be no implied repeal of the ECA because it was 'by force of the common law, a constitutional statute'.[46] While 'ordinary' statutes may be impliedly repealed, 'constitutional' statutes may not, according to Laws LJ. This previously unheard of category of constitutional statutes would include, in his opinion, Magna Carta, the Bill of

---

[45] *Thoburn v Sunderland City Council* [2002] 3 WLR 247.
[46] Ibid., para. 62.

Rights 1689, the Acts of Union,[47] the Reform Acts (concerning the franchise), the Human Rights Act, and the devolution legislation of 1998, as well as the ECA.

The only authority Laws LJ cited in support of these—wholly novel—propositions was *Factortame I*, of which he stated that 'in *Factortame I* the House of Lords effectively accepted that section 2(4) [of the ECA] could not be impliedly repealed, albeit that the point was not argued'.[48] Not only is it extremely unlikely that the House of Lords would ever accept a novel and controversial point that had not even been argued before it, but, as we have seen, this is emphatically not what the House of Lords held in *Factortame*. There was no issue of implied repeal in *Factortame*, as the two statutes (the ECA and the Merchant Shipping Act) each dealt with an entirely different subject-matter, such that there was no way the one could be held impliedly to have repealed the other. Only a statute that dealt with the same subject-matter as the ECA could impliedly repeal it. If Parliament were to re-legislate on the subject of the relationship between domestic and European Community law, and were to do so in a way that was inconsistent with the terms of the ECA 1972 without expressly repealing the 1972 provisions, then there is no reason why the courts would not hold that the later Act must be construed as having impliedly repealed the 1972 Act. All of this is very unlikely, of course. If Parliament were to re-legislate on the subject-matter of the ECA it would be absurd for it to do so without making express reference to the 1972 Act. Such a move would be exceptionally foolish, and extremely unlikely.

Acts can be impliedly repealed only by subsequent Acts that deal with the same subject-matter. Thus, Acts that deal with constitutional subjects can be impliedly repealed only by subsequent Acts that deal with the same, constitutional, subjects. An Act that concerns fishing, or weights and measures, cannot impliedly repeal statutes that concern constitutional law. But this is not to create a new and special category of constitutional statute that is different from ordinary statute. This is merely to restate the law of implied repeal, which has clearly been much misunderstood in recent years. Maugham LJ did not misunderstand it, and his statement of the doctrine of implied repeal in the *Ellen Street Estates* case remains good law. On a careful and thorough reading, neither the ECA,

---

[47] Contrary to the assumption made by Laws LJ, the Acts of Union have in fact been substantially amended: see C. Munro, 'Was Parliament Born Free?' in his *Studies in Constitutional Law* (London, 1987), at 66–71.

[48] N. 45, para. 61.

nor *Factortame*, nor the HRA has effected any change to the law of implied repeal as Maugham LJ stated it some seventy years ago.

PARLIAMENTARY PRIVILEGE

It will be recalled from the previous chapter that the law grants to the Crown a number of privileges and immunities. Parliament also enjoys a number of legal privileges, but these are of a wholly different nature from those enjoyed by the Crown. Parliament's privileges are enjoyed by the *Houses* of Parliament—thus in this section of this chapter Parliament refers to the House of Commons and the House of Lords only, and not to the Crown-in-Parliament whose legislative power was discussed in the previous section.

The history, development, and purpose of parliamentary privilege are entirely different from those of Crown privilege. As we saw in the previous chapter, Crown privileges are immunities and powers that the common law has voluntarily granted to the Crown, excluding the Crown from certain legal liabilities and in this sense limiting the effectiveness and the reach of the rule of law. Parliamentary privilege, by contrast, does not consist of an area of immunity that has been freely granted by the courts. Rather, parliamentary privilege has arisen as a result of Parliament's frequent struggles with the courts: Parliament has had vigorously to assert its privileges *for itself* in the face of considerable judicial hostility, in order to avoid judicial interference with parliamentary business. Unlike the Crown, Parliament has had to fight hard for its privileges—usually indeed fighting against the courts.

Parliamentary privileges enable the Houses of Parliament to undertake their constitutional functions without interference from the Crown or from the courts. They include the following: freedom of speech; freedom from arrest;[49] the right of the Houses to regulate their own composition and procedures; and the right of the Houses to enforce their privileges and where necessary to take punitive action when they are breached. We saw in an earlier chapter how in the 1620s Charles I had entered the House of Commons and arrested a number of Members who had spoken in debate against him. The House claimed that this was a breach of privilege, but the court held for the King and refused to free the Members, who were imprisoned in the Tower of London.[50] Such royal behaviour, supported

[49] That is to say, freedom from civil arrest. Parliamentary privilege does not protect Members from the ordinary operation of the criminal justice system.

[50] *Eliot's Case*: see chapter 2, n. 19.

by the courts, constituted one of the many areas of tension between the Crown and Parliament that dogged the seventeenth century. This explains the inclusion in Article 9 of the Bill of Rights 1689 the statement that 'the freedom of speech and debates or proceedings in Parliament ought not to be impeached or questioned in any Court or place out of Parliament'.

Parliamentary privilege does not need to be incorporated into statute in order to acquire legal authority. Rather like the royal prerogative, which was considered in the previous chapter, parliamentary privilege is a source of constitutional law in its own right. As such, however, it is enforced not by the courts but by Parliament itself. Thus, if parliamentary privilege is breached, the sanction and punishment will be imposed by Parliament, not by the courts. This is not to say that questions concerning parliamentary privilege will never come before the ordinary courts. From time to time they do. In such cases the courts have not always been as robust in recognizing the importance of parliamentary privilege as perhaps they ought to have been. It is as the result of such lack of judicial vigour that Parliament has on occasion felt bound to incorporate aspects of its privileges into statute: Article 9 of the Bill of Rights is a good example. Another example is offered by comparing *Stockdale v Hansard*[51] with the Parliamentary Papers Act 1840. Hansard was a printer who had published an official report by order of the House of Commons. Stockdale sued Hansard in libel in respect of allegations that had been made in the report. The House of Commons regarded the report as being covered by the parliamentary privilege of freedom of speech, but the court disagreed, and held that Hansard could be sued in libel. In the court's judgment an order of the House of Commons to publish a report did not render the publisher immune from suit. This judgment was overturned by the Parliamentary Papers Act 1840.

It is to be noted that the 1840 Act settled the dispute between the House of Commons and the court as to the scope of the privilege of freedom of speech, resolving the disagreement in favour of the view of the Commons. It does not, however, resolve the broader issue of who has the authority to determine disputes arising out of parliamentary privilege. Is the view of the House to be determinative, or is it the courts that have the power to lay down the law here? This question remains unresolved even now, such that if a new dispute were to arise between

---

[51] (1839) 9 Ad & El 1.

Parliament and the courts as to the scope of parliamentary privilege, there is no mechanism short of an Act of Parliament that can authoritatively resolve the dispute.

Part II

Accountability

'That the great affairs of the kingdom may not be concluded or transacted by the advice of private men, or by any unknown or unsworn councillors, but that such matters as concern the public, and are proper for the High Court of Parliament, which is your Majesty's great and supreme council, may be debated, resolved, and transacted only in Parliament, and not elsewhere: and such as shall presume to do anything to the contrary shall be reserved to the censure and judgment of Parliament . . .'.

PARLIAMENT, *The Nineteen Propositions*, 1642

5

Political Accountability

The preceding chapters have set out the basic structure of constitutional power in English public law. In this chapter and in the next we consider the ways in which the exercise of such power is held to account. Adopting a distinction introduced and discussed in chapter 1, in this chapter we focus on questions of political accountability, and in the next on matters of legal accountability.

ACCOUNTABLE GOVERNMENT

In both the political and the legal contexts, it is with the accountability of the Crown's government that we are primarily concerned. This is not to say that public law is not also concerned with questions of the accountability of other constitutional actors. The accountability of Parliament, of the armed forces, of the police, and of the security and secret intelligence services, among others, are all weighty topics within public law, and our focus on governmental accountability is not meant to deny the importance of these issues.[1] To concentrate on the accountability of the executive may be justified in three ways. First, the sheer centrality to public law of executive accountability makes it an essential component of any account of the subject. Secondly, it is with regard to the government that issues of accountability are perhaps most vexed. This is because they are apt to change and because at any one time the rules and practices regulating government accountability are subtle and complicated. Finally, issues of executive accountability are now among the most pressing that public law faces, and not only in England.

Relative to questions of governmental accountability, the accountability

---

[1] References to works on these issues may be found in the bibliographical essay. Even within the topic of executive accountability, not everything can be covered here. The particular aspect of executive accountability that we concentrate on in this chapter is that which relates to central, ministerial, government. Space precludes detailed consideration of the political accountability of local government, although aspects of its legal accountability are discussed in chapter 6.

of Parliament is, in the present climate, simply less problematic. This may be a somewhat surprising or even controversial observation. There are many constitutional commentators who consider that the doctrine of the sovereignty of Parliament means in effect that Parliament can do whatever it likes, is consequently unaccountable, and that this represents one of the gravest problems confronting contemporary public law. It has to be admitted that such an approach to the problem of constitutional accountability enjoys a rich heritage. Those who drafted the U.S., the Canadian, and the Australian constitutions (to cite but three of many examples) focused in their texts much more closely on limiting legislative power than they did on questions of executive accountability. This may well have been appropriate for the eighteenth and nineteenth centuries. Today, however, it is not so much the extent of Parliament's legislative competence as it is the executive's apparent control of Parliament's lawmaking powers that seems to be the practice that most urgently requires to be held to account. After all, when was the last time that a Private Member's Bill (that is, a Bill not sponsored by the government) was enacted that gave rise to serious constitutional concern? Indeed, the focus in constitutions such as that of the United States on delimiting legislative rather than executive power has created something of a vacuum. Under such constitutions, it has proven far easier to subject Congressional or legislative power to scrutiny than it has been to find effective ways of holding the executive to account. Those attempting to hold the current U.S. President to some form of constitutional account with regard to the extensive executive measures he has taken in response to the terrorist outrages of 11 September 2001, for example, are faced with an enormous problem.[2]

Perhaps the most obvious way in which the government is held to account is through the machinery and routine of democracy. The law provides that there must be a general election at least every five years. Technically of course, it is not the government as such that is elected through this process, but rather the individual members of the House of Commons.[3] However, both the political establishment and the media focus sharply during election time on the performance and policies of the government as a whole, rather than on the legislative and constituency record of particular Members of Parliament. Of course, there may be

---

[2] See e.g. N. Katyal and L. Tribe, 'Waging War, Deciding Guilt: Trying the Military Tribunals' (2001–02) 111 *Yale Law Journal* 1259.

[3] Parliamentary elections and Parliament's function of supplying the government of the day were considered in the previous chapter.

constituencies with strong local newspapers that do pay attention to the detailed records of individual MPs, but this is nowadays the exception rather than the norm. Only very rarely, such as where there are allegations of corruption, do individual constituency elections of backbench MPs gain extensive prime-time or front-page national media exposure.[4] It is not only at election time that the political establishment and the media concentrate their attention on the performance and policies of the national government. Such is now the routine of daily and weekly political comment. Neither local nor (more importantly, perhaps) European politics receives anything like the same degree of coverage in the London-based media as that devoted even to relatively trivial matters of national government.

Constant media coverage of government may be the most prominent form of scrutiny, and it may even be the form that modern governments are most concerned about, with their rapid rebuttal units and teams of spin doctors, but it is not a form of scrutiny that is required by any rule of public law. Instead, as we have seen in previous chapters, English public law provides for a system of political accountability in which Parliament, rather than the media, is the essential vehicle through which the ideas of accountability are put into practice. It is fundamental to English public law that the Crown's government may continue in office for only as long as it continues to enjoy majority support in the House of Commons. As soon as such support is withdrawn the government must either resign or seek an immediate dissolution of Parliament (that is, in effect, call a general election). The formal parliamentary mechanism by which the House of Commons indicates that it has withdrawn its support for the government is a motion of no confidence, also known as a motion of censure. The last government to lose a vote of no confidence was the Callaghan government in 1979. The very minute the vote was recorded the Prime Minister informed the House that he would seek from the Queen an immediate dissolution.

It is out of this elemental rule of public law (that the Crown's government may continue in office for only as long as it continues to enjoy majority support in the House of Commons) that the modern system of political accountability has developed. The main doctrines governing this area are the constitutional conventions of ministerial responsibility. The basic ideas underpinning the conventions of ministerial responsibility

---

[4] Martin Bell's successful campaign against Neil Hamilton in the Tatton constituency in the 1997 general election is a notable example.

were introduced in chapters 1 and 2, above. We also saw in chapter 1 how the preference that English public law has traditionally given to political over legal forms of accountability has in recent years come to be challenged. We used the *Fire Brigades Union* litigation as a case-study of the pressure to transform the constitutional order from a primarily political one into a predominantly legal one. There are numerous sources of this pressure, ranging from the influence of European law to the waning of Dicey as a constitutional authority. But a central cause of the shift from a political to a more legal model of constitutionalism is the widespread belief that the core rules of political accountability (that is to say, the conventions of ministerial responsibility) are no longer effective.

There are many commentators who take this view. Eric Barendt, for example, has written that it is now 'rare for the House of Commons to hold an individual Minister to account'.[5] In a similar vein, as editors of the widely read and influential book *The Changing Constitution*, Jeffrey Jowell and Dawn Oliver have removed from their most recent edition an essay on ministerial responsibility that was contained in the first three editions, on the ground, so they tell us, that 'the doctrine of individual ministerial responsibility has been significantly weakened over the last ten years or so, so that it can no longer be said, in our view, that it is a fundamental doctrine of the constitution'.[6] The argument here takes issue with this verdict, and suggests that it is premature to have written the obituary of ministerial responsibility. For sure, it cannot be denied that the convention of individual ministerial responsibility suffered a severe battering in the mid 1990s, the details of which are discussed later in this chapter. But the point missed by those who seek to consign the conventions of ministerial responsibility to the scrap-heap is that Parliament made a forceful and, this chapter will argue, largely successful response to the challenges that were posed for ministerial responsibility during the 1990s, the result of which is that the system of political accountability is actually *stronger* now than it has been for some years.

The argument in this chapter proceeds as follows. First, we consider the conventions of collective and individual ministerial responsibility that constitute the substantive rules of the system of political accountability. In doing so we discuss at length the critical events of the 1990s and Parliament's response to them. Once we have dealt with the substance of

---

[5] E. Barendt, *An Introduction to Constitutional Law* (Oxford, 1998), at 116.
[6] See J. Jowell and D. Oliver (eds.), *The Changing Constitution* (4th edn., Oxford, 2000), at p. viii.

the conventions, we move on to consider the various institutional processes and mechanisms Parliament has at its disposal to apply the conventions in practice. As the discussion proceeds we shall encounter three problems with political accountability, which will be described here as the three 'fault-lines' of political accountability. These are the fault-lines of openness, of ownership, and of party. While the argument here does not support the view that ministerial responsibility is a dead letter, it does concede that the system of political accountability is flawed. The fault-lines we shall identify are potentially serious. But, as we shall see, it is not as if Parliament is unaware of them or has proved unable to tackle them. There are flaws in the system, but they are not fatal.

COLLECTIVE RESPONSIBILITY

The constitutional conventions of collective and individual ministerial responsibility provide that all Ministers are responsible to Parliament for the policies, decisions, and actions of the government. The convention of collective responsibility means that all Ministers in the government must accept responsibility for the policies, decisions, and actions of the government, even if they did not personally develop or take them, and even if they personally disagree with them. Despite the fact that the convention is sometimes (and wrongly) referred to as collective Cabinet responsibility, it applies equally to Cabinet and to junior Ministers. 'Responsibility', in the context of collective responsibility, has a relatively weak meaning. Responsibility in the context of individual ministerial responsibility has a far stronger meaning, as we shall see.

Collective responsibility simply means that all Ministers must be prepared to defend government policy in Parliament. If the government takes a decision or adopts a policy with which a Minister personally disagrees, and that Minister is not prepared to support the government's position in Parliament (in terms both of his voting and of his speaking), then the Minister must resign from the government. Resignations due to breakdowns of collective responsibility are infrequent but, when they do occur, are often dramatic. Among notable examples are the resignations of Nigel Lawson (as Chancellor of the Exchequer) and Geoffrey Howe (as Deputy Prime Minister), in 1989 and 1990 respectively, over European and economic policy. It was these resignations that effectively triggered the end of Mrs Thatcher's Prime Ministership and, indeed, of her political career.

Notions of collective responsibility emerged in British government in the early eighteenth century. The first use of collective responsibility was to protect Cabinet Ministers from the monarch. Until as late as the reign of Queen Anne (1702–1714) the monarch him- or herself generally attended meetings of the Cabinet. This practice ceased with the accession in 1714 of George I (who spoke no English). After this point, because of the absence of the monarch from Cabinet meetings, the Cabinet became more likely to arrive at decisions at odds with the monarch's personal view. Angry or disappointed monarchs might consequently seek to dismiss the individual Ministers that were responsible for promoting in Cabinet policies with which the monarch subsequently disagreed. To prevent the monarch from acting in this way, the Prime Minister and Cabinet would present the monarch with a united front, making it impossible for him to take action against particular Ministers: if the king disliked government policy, he would have to dismiss the government as a whole, rather than pick off individual Ministers.

This early use of collective responsibility, however, has little to do with its modern function. Ministerial responsibility (both collective and individual) is now understood as being an obligation that Ministers owe *to Parliament*: it is not concerned with the relationship between Ministers and the monarch. The modern sense of collective responsibility did not emerge until rather later in the eighteenth century: 1780–1832 is usually given as the period in which collective ministerial responsibility to Parliament developed as a constitutional convention.

The purpose behind the modern convention of collective responsibility is that it enables Parliament easily to identify exactly what the government's position is on any given issue. Rather obviously, Parliament would not be able to hold the government to account if it did not first know what the government's policy or decision-making on a given matter was. If one Minister tells Parliament that the government's policy is one thing, and a second Minister tells Parliament that it is another, it would be impossible for Parliament effectively to pin the government down. Further, the doctrine of collective responsibility also disables Ministers from evading responsibility by stating that a certain policy or decision was not their domain, but was that of some other Minister. Suppose, for example, that there is a controversy about funding NHS hospitals. The Secretary of State for Health denies responsibility for the controversial policy, arguing in Parliament that it is all the fault of the Chancellor of the Exchequer. When the Chancellor is questioned, he too denies responsibility and blames some other Minister—the Chief Secretary to the Treasury perhaps, or another Secretary of State. The doctrine of collective ministerial responsibility prevents any unscrupulous government from getting away with nonsense such as this: even if the policy had been insisted upon by one group of Ministers over the dissent of others, the latter would remain collectively responsible to Parliament for the policy once it had been formally adopted by the government, notwithstanding any dissent they may previously have voiced within the government.

Enabling ready parliamentary identification of government policy, and preventing Ministers from evading responsibility for policy by pointing the finger at each other, can be seen as the positive aspects of collective responsibility: that is to say, as the aspects of the doctrine that facilitate political accountability of the executive. There are some more troubling aspects of the convention, however, that arguably detract from its value. Two such aspects stand out: the practice of unanimity and that of confidentiality. Let us briefly consider each of these in turn.

Government decisions are presented to Parliament and to the public as if they are all unanimous. The only formal exception is the 'agreement to differ'. This is a rare device that the Prime Minister may deploy, which effectively suspends the rules of collective responsibility for a certain prescribed time over a certain discrete matter. It was employed only three times in the twentieth century, most famously in 1975 when Labour Ministers were split over the result they desired of the referendum that was held in order to determine whether the United Kingdom would remain a Member State of the European Economic Community, as it then was. While the agreement to differ is the only formal exception to the practice of unanimity, there are many informal exceptions. Keen observers of British politics are able quickly to learn of disagreements between Ministers over a range of policy issues. It was no secret, for example, that in John Major's last Cabinet the pro-European Kenneth Clarke and the rather more sceptical Michael Portillo took diametrically opposed views with regard to Britain's relations with the European Community. Similarly, in Tony Blair's first Cabinet there were widespread reports of disagreements on a range of constitutional and Home Office policy issues between the Lord Chancellor, Lord Irvine, and the incumbent Home Secretary, Jack Straw, and on economic matters between Gordon Brown and Peter Mandelson. Stories emerge in the newspapers and elsewhere of such disagreements because the political system accommodates a number of 'safety valves'[7] that allow disgruntled or impassioned Ministers to blow off steam where they disagree with one another but are not prepared to

---

[7] This is the phrase that Rodney Brazier has used in this context: see his *Constitutional Practice* (3rd edn., Oxford, 1999), at 145.

resign over their disagreements. Leaks, unattributed briefings, semi-on-the-record conversations with lobby correspondents, and so forth are the means by which such steam is released.

How far Ministers will be allowed to go in such matters will be a matter for the judgement of the Prime Minister, a judgement which will be considerably shaped by the political climate in Westminster. In the most extreme case the Prime Minister may even feel that he himself has to resign, rather than dismiss those of his Ministers who are briefing against him. This was the course that John Major opted for in the summer of 1995 when he resigned as leader of the Conservative Party (but not as Prime Minister) and immediately put himself up for re-election as leader, with his notorious 'back me or sack me' campaign.[8] Such a display of Prime Ministerial vulnerability, however, is rare, and the more usual consequence of the practice of unanimity is to strengthen, rather than to undermine, the position of the Prime Minister. This is because it is the Prime Minister that will have the last word in determining what the policy is which his (or, once, her) Ministers must then unanimously support. It is also the Prime Minister who decides whether to employ the agreement to differ, just as it is the Prime Minister who decides exactly how much leaking and unattributable briefing he will tolerate. The practice of unanimity therefore contributes significantly to the power of the Prime Minister in being able to secure obedience from his Ministers.

Now, for those who want to argue that British government is better when it is genuine collective government, rather than government by Prime Ministerial *diktat*, this is clearly an important point, and it troubles many contemporary commentators that the Prime Minister has grown overly powerful while the Cabinet, by contrast, has atrophied. It is not clear, however, that the practice of unanimity is troubling from the point of view of political accountability. The fact that government decisions are presented as if they were unanimous does not make it more difficult for Parliament to hold the government to account. Even if there are disadvantages (in terms of the balance between Prime Ministerial and Cabinet power) of the practice of unanimity, it is not a practice which jeopardizes effective parliamentary scrutiny.[9]

---

[8] See R. Brazier, 'The Resignation of John Major' [1995] *Public Law* 513.

[9] In any event, it might be pointed out, the extent of Prime Ministerial power over his or her Cabinet colleagues should not be exaggerated, as the experience of both Margaret Thatcher (1990) and John Major (1995) testifies. Even if Cabinet is enfeebled while the government is successful, it retains the power—and, just as importantly, the willingness to use it—to topple even the most powerful of Prime Ministers.

So much for unanimity. The second aspect of collective responsibility which may give rise to cause for concern is the practice of confidentiality. All discussion among Ministers, or between Ministers and civil servants, contributing to the development of government policy is confidential. This practice is strictly complied with—or at least it is while Ministers remain in office. Once they leave office, however, it has now become commonplace for former Ministers to publish diaries or memoirs of their time in government. Thirty years ago this caused considerable excitement, not to mention High Court litigation,[10] but there have, since the mid 1970s, been detailed guidelines in place that regulate what former Ministers may, and what they may not, write about, and as long as these guidelines are followed Ministers are now regarded as being generally free to publish. That said, were a Minister to seek to publish information that was contrary to the guidelines and was consequently in breach of confidence, the Attorney-General would clearly be able to seek an injunction restraining publication.

The difficulty with confidentiality is that it severely limits openness. How can government be held effectively to account if it is closed, private, and protected by both the convention and the law of confidence? Does Parliament not first need to know what government is doing before it can successfully hold the government to account? Well, perhaps not: it could be argued that as long as Parliament knows what it is that government has decided, it does not additionally need to know a great deal about the internal processes by which government arrived at its decision. There is a strong counter-argument, however. Suppose that there is parliamentary concern over the award by the government of a contract to a particular company to manage a recently privatized rail network. Parliament wants to know what the company's role was in the earlier decision-making process within government when the government was determining the terms of the privatization. There is an allegation that the company was subsequently awarded the contract not because it submitted the most favourable bid, but because of that company's close links with government Ministers—perhaps a number of its directors have donated money to the governing political party, or some such. From this example it can be seen that it will sometimes be important, for political accountability to be effective, for Parliament to be able to investigate not only the decisions of the government, but also the internal decision-making processes, yet it is just such processes that may be protected under the practice of

[10] See *Attorney-General v Jonathan Cape* [1976] QB 752.

confidentiality. We will examine the extent to which Parliament and its committees are currently able to embark on such investigations later in this chapter.

In considering questions of confidentiality and transparency, we are touching here on the first of the three major fault-lines that we shall identify during the course of this chapter, that run through the contemporary practice of political accountability in English public law. This first is the fault-line of openness. There is an endless struggle between government and Parliament over openness and accessibility of information. It is a struggle the outcome of which will at any given moment be a critical factor in determining the effectiveness and potency of political accountability. Parliament will always be looking for more information, and the government will always be inclined to be reluctant to give it. The more open that the government is prepared (or required) to be, the more effective will be the system of political accountability. The more closed that the government is allowed to be, the more difficult will it be for Parliament to scrutinize it. We will refer back to this theme later in the chapter as we consider the various political and legal devices that regulate the provision to Parliament of government information.

INDIVIDUAL RESPONSIBILITY

The convention of individual ministerial responsibility provides that Ministers are individually responsible to Parliament for their policies, decisions, and actions, and for the policies, decisions, and actions of their departments. 'Responsible' in this context has a rather stronger meaning than in the context of collective responsibility. In that context it amounts to little more than an obligation to defend and support government policy. In the context of individual responsibility, however, it means that, in addition to having to defend their policies, Ministers are personally liable to Parliament for the quality and success of their policies. Now, such liability is political, not legal, and as such it attracts political, rather than legal, sanctions. We are not talking here about litigation and damages, but about explanation, apology, and, in the most serious cases, resignation.

Resignation from office is the ultimate sanction that Parliament can force on a Minister who breaches the convention of individual responsibility. There has been some confusion in recent times about the relationship between resignation and responsibility, with some commentators suggesting that resignations are required in order to show that Ministers are responsible—that is, that unless there is a resignation whenever anything goes wrong, the convention of individual responsibility has somehow failed. Such analysis, however, is mistaken. Resignation and responsibility are not synonymous, and should not be treated as if they were. Of course, it will sometimes be the case that the Minister's behaviour is so gravely in error that only a resignation will suffice, but in other instances it will be perfectly possible for a Minister to accept responsibility without having to resign. A Minister who inadvertently misleads Parliament, for example, because he misremembers a statistic, and who later returns to Parliament to correct his mistake and to apologize for having made it, is unlikely to have to resign over the matter: yet in returning to Parliament to rectify his earlier error he is taking, not evading, responsibility.

In the sections that follow, which analyse various aspects of and problems with individual ministerial responsibility, we will frequently have recourse to high-profile ministerial resignations, or near resignations, in order to illustrate and augment the argument. In doing so, however, it should be remembered that taking responsibility and resigning from office are not the same thing. Resignation is the ultimate sanction, but it will not always be required for the convention of individual responsibility to function properly.

(A) RESPONSIBILITY TO WHOM?

The definition of individual ministerial responsibility we have used up to this point (namely, that Ministers are individually responsible to Parliament for their policies, decisions, and actions, and for the policies, decisions, and actions of their departments), requires clarification in two important respects. First, to whom is it that the obligation of responsibility is owed? And, secondly, what exactly is it that Ministers are responsible for? The first question is easier to answer than the second. The obligation of individual ministerial responsibility, like that of collective responsibility, is owed to Parliament. If the Minister concerned is an MP, then his or her obligation of individual responsibility will be owed to the House of Commons; if the Minister is a peer his or her responsibility will be to the House of Lords. This is, at any rate, the theory. As a matter fact, however, a number of other parties intervene, and the practical operation of individual responsibility is a less straightforward matter than the simple interaction of Minister and Parliament alone. Political parties, political leaders (and especially the Prime Minister), and the media may all, in addition to Parliament, play important roles in determining a

Minister's fate in cases of individual responsibility. If a Minister finds herself under vigorous parliamentary attack, but has strong support from the Prime Minister, from her own political party (either on the back-benches or in her own constituency), or from the media, then she may well be able to ride out the storm relatively unscathed. Conversely, a Minister may find that he has no realistic option other than to resign from office, even if Parliament is not urging him to step down (perhaps because it is in recess), where he lacks support from the Prime Minister or from his party, or where he is being constantly pilloried in the media. In recent years the resignations of Edwina Currie, Tim Yeo, David Mellor, Stephen Byers, and Estelle Morris all illustrate aspects of the complex interaction between Minister, Parliament, Prime Minister, party, and the media.

Edwina Currie was forced to resign in 1988 from her post as a junior Minister in the Department of Health, over remarks that she had made about the extent of salmonella in British-produced eggs, remarks the widespread reporting of which led to a catastrophic downturn in the British egg industry. Mrs Currie was called to give evidence before the House of Commons Agriculture Select Committee, initially refused to attend, and was effectively forced to change her mind. When she did attend, she was less than helpful to the Committee, which in its sub-sequent report was deeply critical of her behaviour. A Minister more popular on the Conservative backbenches might have withstood the con-troversy, but the frequently outspoken Mrs Currie was not widely liked, and at the crucial time she found herself with too few political friends to survive in office, and was compelled to resign.[11]

Tim Yeo was one of a considerable number of ministerial casualties of John Major's ill fated 'back to basics' campaign in 1994. This campaign involved a range of government Ministers preaching about family values. Ministers not practising what their colleagues were preaching were found out, exposed, and forced to resign. Tim Yeo was one such. The saga of his fall is interesting because it seemed for a while that he would not have to resign—by the time his affair was exposed both Parliament and the coun-try had become rather tired of the whole back to basics story—until the chairman of his local constituency party spoke against him. That seemed to swing the mood against Mr Yeo, and he resigned. This story, like Mrs Currie's, shows the importance of party considerations in this context,

---

[11] For a detailed account, see D. Woodhouse, *Ministers and Parliament* (Oxford, 1994), at 53–65.

in Mrs Currie's case the parliamentary party; in Mr Yeo's the local party.[12]

David Mellor was another casualty of back to basics. The pivotal role in his downfall, however, was played not so much by the party as by the Prime Minister. As a new Prime Minister, John Major was notoriously short of political friends, and for a considerable period David Mellor was one of his closest. Indeed, the two men were so close that the Prime Minister created a new job for the football- and arts-loving Mr Mellor, who became the Secretary of State for National Heritage. In 1992 it was reported that Mr Mellor had had an extra-marital affair with an actress who had previously appeared in a soft porn video. The reporting descended into considerable detail, and Mellor became a figure of fun (as well as Minister of Fun, as he was unofficially known). For a considerable time, notwithstanding the almost constant media frenzy, he did not resign, and appeared to owe his continued political life to his friend the Prime Minister. Stories about Mr Mellor, his affair, and his associates would not go away, however, and eventually—more than two months after the story had first broken—he resigned from the Cabinet. Unpopular with both backbenchers and the media, David Mellor was able tenaciously to hang on to office for so long only because of his personal closeness to the Prime Minister.[13]

Finally, the resignation in October 2002 of Estelle Morris from her position as Secretary of State for Education illustrates the role played by the media, and particularly the press, in determining ministerial futures. Estelle Morris was not under particular pressure within Parliament to resign: neither her party nor her Prime Minister seemed to think that her resignation was required or even desirable, yet she felt that the high media profile given to a series of failings and difficulties in her department meant that the most honourable course was for her to step down. Part of the explanation for this unusual political act may be found in the fact that, as Secretary for State for Education, Ms Morris was under peculiar pressure to 'deliver': since first coming into office the New Labour government generally, and the Prime Minister in particular,

[12] See, further, R. Brazier, 'It *is* a Constitutional Issue: Fitness for Ministerial Office in the 1990s' [1994] *Public Law* 431.

[13] See further, Woodhouse, n. 11 above, at 77–86. Stephen Byers' resignation in 2002 is another illustration of the same theme: that is, of a Minister being almost constantly criticized in the press, being less than popular in Westminster, but managing for months to resist mounting pressure to resign at least in part due to the Minister's closeness to the Prime Minister. For a detailed account of the decline and fall of Mr Byers: see http://politics.guardian.co.uk/byers.

stressed that they intended to make 'education, education, education' a major priority; it has been a characteristic of the Blair government's second term in office that there has been a sharp focus on 'delivery' of public sector reform—which includes education; and it seems to have proven much more difficult than the government expected to transform state education in the way it would have liked.[14]

These stories are all illustrative of the complex interplay between Minister, Parliament, party, and press that forms the broad context within which individual responsibility operates. The core, constitutional, requirement is that the Minister is responsible to Parliament, but determining precisely what action that obligation of responsibility will in any given set of circumstances entail (and, in particular, whether it will require a resignation) is a matter that will be influenced by a number of variables.

(B) RESPONSIBILITY FOR WHAT?

The second respect in which our basic definition of individual responsibility requires further clarification concerns what it is, exactly, that Ministers are constitutionally responsible for. Perhaps the best approach to this problem is to divide the issues for which Ministers may be constitutionally responsible into three categories: first, the Minister's own policies and political decisions and actions; secondly, the Minister's private life and personal conduct; and, thirdly, the actions of, and the decisions taken within, the Minister's department. To start with the first category, which is the easiest, Ministers are clearly individually responsible for their own policies and for their own political decisions and actions. Of the resignations considered in the previous section, for example, those of Edwina Currie and Estelle Morris fall into this category. Currie resigned as a result of her comments on salmonella in eggs and over her evident reluctance subsequently to explain or defend her comments in Parliament. Morris resigned over her self-perceived failures concerning the strategic management of the Department for Education.

The second category is slightly more troublesome: to what extent are Ministers constitutionally responsible to Parliament in respect of their private behaviour, as opposed to their public policy-making? Should a Minister who finds himself embroiled in a sex or financial scandal resign?

[14] For a valuable interview with Estelle Morris, in which she reflected on her resignation, on the reasons for it, and more generally on the relationship between politics and the media: see the *Guardian*, 9 January 2003.

A frequent pattern in this context is for Ministers initially to resist calls for resignation, but for such resistance sooner or later to prove futile. This pattern can be seen to have occurred in the following cases: Cecil Parkinson (sex), David Mellor (sex), Tim Yeo (sex), Neil Hamilton (financial), and Peter Mandelson (financial), among others. One exception is the resignation of Ron Davies as Secretary of State for Wales in 1998, which was much more sudden, following a somewhat mysterious nocturnal encounter on Clapham Common. It is sometimes argued that Ministers' personal conduct should have no bearing on their public accountability, and that a distinction should be drawn between the political issues, with respect to which Ministers are responsible to Parliament, and more personal issues, with respect to which they are not. However, current practice does not appear to reflect this view, fitness for office being seen as a public and constitutional issue which can be affected by Ministers' personal conduct as well as by their public policy-making.[15]

The category that has proved most difficult is the third: namely, political errors which are the fault of the Minister's department, but not of the Minister him- or herself. Are Ministers individually responsible to Parliament for *everything* that happens in their departments? There was considerable controversy about this issue in the 1950s and again in the 1990s, and it requires careful consideration.

The controversy in the 1950s is known as the Crichel Down affair. In 1938 the government purchased a large area of chalk downland in Dorset for military use. The land was bought from three separate owners, all of whom were paid for the land, and two of whom were also paid compensation. In 1950 the land was transferred to the Ministry of Agriculture, and the Labour Minister, Thomas Williams, placed it under the management of the Agricultural Land Commission (ALC), an independent statutory body. The ALC decided to maintain the land as a single farming block and not to split it up into smaller units. Commander Marten, whose family had until 1938 owned one part of the land, wanted it back, and accordingly challenged the ALC's decision. In 1952 Sir Thomas Dugdale, the new Conservative Minister of Agriculture in Churchill's government, revisited the ALC's decision, but he concluded that it was satisfactory. Dugdale decided that the land should not be sold back to Commander Marten as there continued to be in 1952 a serious national food shortage. Dugdale therefore preferred to keep the land in state

---

[15] For a cogent and valuable discussion, see R. Brazier, 'It *is* a Constitutional Issue: Fitness for Ministerial Office in the 1990s' [1994] *Public Law* 431.

control, and it was accordingly sold on to the Commissioners of Crown Lands. The difficulty with this decision was that in the process, promises which had previously been made by officials at the ALC and elsewhere to potential purchasers of the land (such as Commander Marten) were ignored, causing a serious political controversy, with repeated allegations of wrong-doing and double standards (to say the least) in the Ministry of Agriculture and at the ALC. Sir Thomas Dugdale appointed an independent inquiry to investigate the allegations and to report back. The inquiry reported that 'there was no trace . . . of anything in the nature of bribery, corruption or personal dishonesty'[16] in the sale or management of Crichel Down, and when Dugdale subsequently went to the House of Commons he claimed that the affair was all over and although 'errors of judgment' had been made, 'no further action' was necessary.[17]

This attitude was treated with some shock, not to say anger, especially among backbench Conservative MPs from farming constituencies. There was no time, however, for Parliament to press the matter, and the House of Commons had to wait a further month before a full debate on Crichel Down could be held. This debate was opened by Dugdale himself, who, rather to everybody's surprise, announced at the end of his speech that he would resign as Minister for Agriculture. During the course of his speech Dugdale had given no indication that he was about to announce his resignation, and there is therefore little in his speech to which we can turn to elucidate exactly why he resigned. During his speech he stated that 'I, as Minister, must accept full responsibility to Parliament for any mistakes and inefficiency of officials in my department, just as, when my officials bring off any successes, I take full credit for them'. He continued, 'any departure from this long-established rule is bound to bring the civil service right into the political arena, and that we should all, on both sides of the House, deprecate most vigorously'.[18] He concluded his speech by stating that the government's policy had changed to the effect that, as food supplies had begun to grow, agricultural lands would be sold off wherever practicable. He then announced his resignation.

For more than thirty years Dugdale's resignation was frequently cited by commentators as the perfect example of a Minister honourably accepting individual responsibility for political misjudgements that were made,

---

[16] *Report of the Public Inquiry ordered by the Minister of Agriculture into the Disposal of Land at Crichel Down*, Cmd. 9176 (London, June 1954).

[17] Statement of Sir Thomas Dugdale, HC Debs., vol. 528, col. 1745 (15 June 1954).

[18] HC Debs., vol. 530, col. 1186 (20 July 1954).

without his personal knowledge, by civil servants working in his department. It was not Dugdale himself who decided that Commander Marten would not be able to purchase the land that his family had formerly owned: it was officials at the ALC and in the Ministry of Agriculture. Since the government's records of the Crichel Down affair became available in the mid 1980s, however, this interpretation—dominant as it was—has been exposed as myth.[19] Dugdale did not sacrifice himself on the altar of constitutional convention: he resigned because the (socialist) policy of keeping farms under state control that he had inherited from the Labour government of 1945–1951, and that he had sought to continue, was hated by Conservative backbench MPs to such an extent that Dugdale eventually lost support in Cabinet, which is why he had to announce the change in policy just before he resigned. It was because of his unwillingness to support the new policy that he resigned: that is, he resigned due to the obligations of collective, not individual, ministerial responsibility.

At the time of Crichel Down there was much political concern, particularly in the Conservative party, about the exponential growth in the size (and power?) of the civil service. Spurred on by two world wars and by the advent of larger, more interventionist socialist government, the fear was that the civil service had become a force unto itself, and, moreover, was one which Parliament could not effectively hold to account. As it was put during parliamentary debates on the Crichel Down affair, 'there has been criticism that the principle [of ministerial responsibility] operates so as to oblige Ministers to extend total protection to their officials and to endorse their acts, and to cause the position that civil servants cannot be called to account and are effectively responsible to no-one'.[20] Crichel Down represented a focal point for the expression of these fears: here was a situation where faceless bureaucratic officials were threatening dearly-held Tory values of private land-ownership, and who was accountable?

In an attempt to allay such fears, the Home Secretary, Sir David Maxwell-Fyfe, gave an important speech in the House of Commons in which he sought to outline the way in which the convention of individual ministerial responsibility would operate in the context of the relationship between Ministers and their civil servants. Maxwell-Fyfe distinguished

---

[19] See I. Nicolson, *The Mystery of Crichel Down* (Oxford, 1986) and J. Griffith, 'Crichel Down: The Most Famous Farm in British Constitutional History' (1987) 1 *Contemporary Record* 35.

[20] Sir David Maxwell-Fyfe, Home Secretary, HC Debs., vol. 530, col. 1285 (20 July 1954).

between four different situations. First, 'in the case where there is an
explicit order by a Minister, the Minister must protect the civil servant
who has carried out his order'. Secondly, 'equally, where the civil servant
acts properly in accordance with policy laid down by the Minister, the
Minister must protect and defend him'. Thirdly, 'where an official makes
a mistake or causes some delay, but not on an important issue of policy
and not where a claim to individual rights is seriously involved, the Minister acknowledges the mistake and he accepts the responsibility, although
he is not personally involved. He states that he will take corrective action
in the department . . . [but] he would not . . . expose the official to public
criticism'. Finally, 'where action has been taken by a civil servant of
which the Minister disapproves and has no prior knowledge, and the
conduct of the official is reprehensible, then there is no obligation on the
part of the Minister to endorse what he believes to be wrong or to defend
what are clearly shown to be errors of his officers', but even in this
situation, Maxwell-Fyfe continued, the Minister will 'of course' remain
'constitutionally responsible to Parliament for the fact that something has
gone wrong, and he alone can tell Parliament what had occurred and
render an account of his stewardship'.[21]

This is a strong and powerful reassertion of the principles of individual
ministerial responsibility, and makes it clear that Ministers will be individually responsible to Parliament not only for their own policies and
political decisions and actions, but also for those of officials working in
their departments. This is as it should be. Civil servants are not themselves accountable to Parliament, although they may under certain
limited circumstances be called to give evidence before a select committee.[22] Civil servants are accountable to their Ministers, not to Parliament,
and ministers are in turn accountable to Parliament, on the terms set out
in the Maxwell-Fyfe speech.

(C) INDIVIDUAL RESPONSIBILITY AND THE
MAJOR GOVERNMENT

Having in the previous sections set out the established rules of individual
responsibility, we can now proceed to examine the reasons these rules
have in recent years come to be regarded as being so weak. The reasons
behind this trend are closely connected to a number of events that
occurred in the mid 1990s. During this period, in three separate respects,

---

[21] Ibid., cols. 1285–1287.
[22] The powers of select committees are considered further, below.

Ministers and senior civil servants in John Major's government proposed a number of initiatives that sought significantly to undermine the tenets of individual responsibility. These initiatives require careful analysis, and each will be considered in turn.

The first of the challenges arose in 1994. The Cabinet Secretary, Sir Robin Butler, was called to give evidence to the Scott inquiry[23] and to the House of Commons Select Committee on the Treasury and Civil Service, both of which were investigating matters relating to the political account-ability of Ministers and civil servants. In his evidence, Butler argued that a distinction ought to be drawn between ministerial accountability and ministerial responsibility.[24] Ministerial *accountability* to Parliament, he argued, consisted of a Minister's ultimate duty to account to Parliament for the work of his department. This would mean that in the last resort Ministers could be challenged about any action of the civil service, since civil servants act on behalf of and are accountable to government Minis-ters, and Ministers alone are accountable to Parliament. Ministerial *responsibility*, on the other hand, arises only where a Minister is directly and personally involved in an action or decision and implies that the Minister carries personal credit or blame for that action or decision. In its report, the Treasury and Civil Service Committee criticized Butler's position, describing it as 'unconvincing'.[25] The government clarified its views in its response to the select committee's report[26] where it argued that (1) a Minister is accountable for everything that happens in his or her department in the sense that Parliament can call the Minister to account for it; (2) a Minister is responsible for the policies of his or her depart-ment, for the framework through which policies are delivered and for the resources which are allocated; and (3) a Minister is not responsible for everything in his or her department in the sense of having personal knowledge and control of every action taken and being personally blame-worthy when delegated tasks are carried out incompetently or when mistakes or errors of judgement are made at operational level.

The government argued that its position was not an original one, but was based on the constitutional precedent of Crichel Down, and in

[23] For the Scott inquiry, see below.

[24] This argument was also put to the select committee by William Waldegrave MP, the Cabinet Minister who at the time had responsibility for open government, among other matters.

[25] Treasury and Civil Service Committee, *The Role of the Civil Service*, 1993–94 HC 27, para. 132.

[26] *The Civil Service: Taking Forward Continuity and Change*, Cm. 2748, (London, January 1995), at 27–29.

particular on Maxwell-Fyfe's speech. The select committee disagreed, describing the government's position as being 'more novel than its advocates are prepared to admit'.[27] On analysis, the select committee is correct: Maxwell-Fyfe's 1954 speech is an extremely weak precedent for the position adopted forty years later by John Major's government. As we saw, the purpose of Maxwell-Fyfe's speech was to indicate that, contrary to popular fears at the time, Ministers were fully responsible to Parliament for the actions and failures of civil servants. Maxwell-Fyfe was attempting to bring the decisions and actions of civil servants *within* the framework of ministerial responsibility. The Butler distinction between responsibility and accountability, on the other hand, is a device designed to *limit* the scope of Ministers' obligations to Parliament. Nowhere in Maxwell-Fyfe's speech is there any indication that there might be a constitutionally recognized distinction between responsibility and accountability. On the contrary, the essence of his speech is that Ministers are both responsible *and* accountable to Parliament in all four of the situations he outlined: in all four examples, it will be recalled, a Minister has to 'render an account of his stewardship' and at all times Ministers remain 'of course . . . constitutionally responsible'.

The second challenge to individual responsibility that was made during John Major's time as Prime Minister was the policy/operations distinction. The architect of this challenge was Michael Howard MP, the incumbent Home Secretary. Howard argued that Ministers were individually responsible to Parliament only for their policies. In Howard's view, operational failures, as opposed to failings in policy, fell outside the scope of ministerial responsibility to Parliament. The circumstances in which this argument arose were as follows. After a series of high-profile prison escapes in 1994–1995 Michael Howard appointed Sir John Learmont to chair an independent inquiry into prison security in England and Wales. The inquiry's report was highly critical of the Prison Service (a next steps agency[28] within the Home Office) and of the entire system of prison management, from the level of prison governors and more junior staff all the way up to the chief executive of the Prison Service and to the Home Office and its ministerial team itself.[29] The report was replete with examples of how the problems in the Prison Service were not self-contained, but implicated the Home Office and,

---

[27] See n. 25 above, para. 122.
[28] Next steps agencies were considered in chapter 3, above.
[29] *Review of Prison Service Security in England and Wales and the Escape from Parkhurst Prison*, Cm. 3020 (London, October 1995).

indeed, the Home Secretary himself. Learmont stated, for example, that the structure of the senior management of the Prison Service was 'unfortunate'[30] and that 'the current management style of the Prison Service appears to owe much to an historically close involvement of the Home Office, particularly in major operational matters'.[31]

When the Learmont report was published, a political storm broke out, and the opposition called for Michael Howard's resignation. He refused to resign, however, and instead called for the resignation of Derek Lewis, the chief executive of the Prison Service. When Mr Lewis refused to resign, Mr Howard dismissed him. Why was it Mr Lewis who was held to be responsible in this way, and not the Minister? Michael Howard claimed in Parliament that he as Secretary of State was responsible only for policy matters, and the problems which had been identified in the Learmont report were operational concerns, not matters of policy. The person responsible for operational matters, both in principle and under the terms of the framework document of the Prison Service, was the chief executive, not the Secretary of State, and therefore Derek Lewis was responsible, not Michael Howard. The Secretary of State would naturally have to come to the House of Commons and explain—or give an account of—what had happened (he was in that sense constitutionally accountable to Parliament) but he was neither personally nor constitutionally responsible, in his view.

On the one hand it is nothing new for government Ministers to refuse to resign over escapes from prisons. After the break-out in 1983 from the Maze prison near Belfast the then Secretary of State for Northern Ireland and his junior Minister (James Prior and Nicholas Scott) continued in office, although the assistant governor of the prison was transferred and the governor retired. On the other hand, however, the purported distinction between policy and operations is controversial and very difficult. There are two levels of criticism: the first relates specifically to Michael Howard and his relationship with Derek Lewis, and the second is more general. As to the first, Mr Howard claimed that as a matter of fact he was not involved in operational matters concerning the Prison Service. This was a hotly disputed point, and one which, as we have seen, was not supported by the Learmont report. Contrary to Mr Howard's protestations, it was clear that the daily work of the Prison Service had been frequently and repeatedly interrupted by the Secretary of State, sometimes many times in the same day, and often this ministerial

---

[30] Ibid., para. 3.18.   [31] Ibid., para. 3.77.

involvement would relate to very specific operational matters, such as whether an individual prisoner should be searched, and so on. More significantly, however, there is a broader, more general problem with the policy/operations distinction. It is extremely difficult to know how to classify something as either policy or operational: for example, is a decision to reduce prisoners' visiting time a policy or an operational decision? What about over-crowding, or the re-introduction of slopping out, or staff shortages, or deciding to keep a set of prisoners confined in their cells for twenty-three hours per day—are these policy matters or operational matters, and how can we tell?

The final challenge that John Major's Ministers made to the doctrine of individual responsibility concerned the provision to Parliament of government information. It has always been clear—and uncontroversial—that Ministers who lie to Parliament will have to resign once their lies are revealed as such. What, however, of the situation in which a Minister misleads Parliament, but does not at the time realize that he is doing so? Do ministers have to resign whenever they mislead Parliament, or only when they knowingly mislead Parliament? If the latter, does it make any difference whether the Minister ought to have realized that he was misleading Parliament? In addressing these questions we are returning, of course, to the fault-line of openness that we identified earlier in our consideration of government confidentiality.

These questions arose out of the findings of the Scott report. Lord (formerly Sir Richard) Scott was appointed in 1992 to chair an inquiry into claims that the government had misled Parliament over its covert encouragement of British defence exporters to trade with Iraq, and had subsequently attempted to cover up its earlier deception in such a way as to risk the wrongful criminal conviction and imprisonment of a number of British exporters. The report of the Scott inquiry was published in 1996. On the core claim that a number of Ministers had misled Parliament about the content of government policy with regard to permitting defence exports to Iraq, the Scott report found that Ministers had repeatedly answered parliamentary questions in such a way as was 'inaccurate and misleading', that a variety of government statements had been 'designedly uninformative', that Ministers had 'failed to inform Parliament of the current state of government policy on . . . arms sales to Iraq', and that such failure had been 'deliberate'.[32] This may seem clear and

---

[32] *Report of the Inquiry into the Export of Defence Equipment and Dual-Use Goods to Iraq and Related Prosecutions*, 1995–96 HC 115, paras. D3.107, D4.28-D4.30, and D4.42.

unambiguous, but the matter was clouded by a further set of findings to the effect that the Ministers concerned had acted without 'duplicitous intention'.[33]

There had been a number of Ministers involved, but by the time the Scott report was published, only one remained in office: William Waldegrave MP. He argued that he had not misled Parliament. As far as Waldegrave was concerned, government policy on the circumstances in which export licences would be granted to arms dealers seeking to trade with Iraq had been announced in Parliament and the policy had not changed. The Scott report found, however, that while Waldegrave *believed* government policy not to have changed, the application of the policy certainly had changed, and moreover it had changed in such a way as to amount to a revision of the policy itself. The Scott report described any argument to the effect that the policy had not changed as being 'so plainly inapposite as to be incapable of being sustained by serious argument'.[34] Nonetheless, Ministers such as Mr Waldegrave, while they *should* have realized that their changes in the application of policy amounted to a change in the policy itself, in fact did not so realize: hence the conclusion that Ministers acted without duplicitous intent.

The 'without duplicitous intent' conclusion may be difficult to reconcile with the 'designedly uninformative' and 'deliberate failure to inform' conclusions, but it nonetheless enabled the government to present the findings of the Scott report as if the inquiry had found that to the extent that ministers had misled Parliament they had done so only unknowingly. In the government's view, while Ministers were responsible to Parliament if they knowingly misled it, they did not have to take individual responsibility where they had unknowingly misled it. Relying on this distinction, Waldegrave was rescued from having to resign: like Michael Howard before him, he was saved by the government's rewriting of the rules.

As with the Michael Howard situation, so too in the Waldegrave story there are two problems with this outcome. The first is that it is difficult to see why the distinction (between knowingly and unknowingly) should have come to Mr Waldegrave's aid, given that the Scott report had found that his answers to parliamentary questions had been designedly uninformative. But perhaps the more serious is that, as with the policy/operations distinction, the knowingly/unknowingly distinction was unheard of before the government invented it in order to save Mr Waldegrave. Indeed, in the articulation of the obligations of individual

---

[33] Ibid., para. D3.124.   [34] Ibid., para. D3.123.

responsibility in the Major government's own rule-book, there was no mention of the knowingly/unknowingly distinction. Since 1945 all Prime Ministers have issued to their Ministers a document that was until 1997 known as *Questions of Procedure for Ministers*, or QPM. Since 1997 it has become known simply as the *Ministerial Code*. John Major's version of QPM, issued following the Conservative victory in the 1992 general election, made provision for individual ministerial responsibility in paragraph 27. In full, this stated that:

Ministers are accountable to Parliament, in the sense that they have a duty to explain in Parliament the exercise of their powers and duties and to give an account to Parliament of what is done by them in their capacity as Ministers or by their departments. This includes the duty to give Parliament, including its select committees, and the public as full information as possible about the policies, decisions and actions of the government, and not to deceive or mislead Parliament and the public.

As can be seen, there is no mention in this passage—which comes from the Prime Minister himself—of any of the three distinctions that the Major government sought to introduce. Even his own version of QPM failed to provide authority for the responsibility/accountability distinction, for the policy/operations distinction, or for the knowingly/unknowingly distinction. And yet both Michael Howard and William Waldegrave managed to evade responsibility. Here we come to the second of our three fault-lines of political accountability. This is the fault-line of ownership. Government Ministers such as Howard and Waldegrave managed to evade political accountability because the government itself was able to rewrite the rules. Until 1997 the authors of the rules governing ministerial responsibility were government Ministers themselves. Maxwell-Fyfe was a government Minister (he was Home Secretary) when he gave his authoritative interpretation in 1954. So too in the 1990s were the responsibility/accountability distinction, the policy/operations distinction, and the knowingly/unknowingly distinction introduced by the government itself. Is it any wonder that commentators such as the editors of *The Changing Constitution* consider the convention of individual responsibility to be so ineffective when the government can simply move the goalposts whenever it suits them?

(D) PARLIAMENT'S RESPONSE

It is only to be expected that the opposition parties would be critical of the government's rewriting of the rule-book. But it was not only the opposition that was critical: there were many in Parliament, on all sides of the House of Commons, that considered that what the government had done was improper. In the light of the political controversy that surrounded these issues, and triggered especially by the publication of the Scott report, the Public Service Committee, an all-party select committee in the House of Commons, embarked in 1996 on a detailed inquiry into the use and abuse of the conventions of ministerial responsibility. Its report was unanimous, and constitutes a highly significant step in Parliament's response to the challenges which the Major administration had posed for it.[35]

The Committee's report was deeply critical of the responsibility/accountability distinction that Sir Robin Butler and William Waldegrave had sought to introduce in 1994. The report strongly disagreed with the approach that Butler and Waldegrave had adopted, stating that:

It is not possible absolutely to distinguish an area in which a Minister is personally responsible, and liable to take blame, from one in which he is constitutionally accountable. Ministerial responsibility is not composed of two elements with a clear break between the two. Ministers have an obligation to Parliament which consists in ensuring that government explains its actions. Ministers also have an obligation to respond to criticism made in Parliament in a way that seems likely to satisfy it—which may include, if necessary, resignation.[36]

In addition to its rejection of the responsibility/accountability distinction, the Committee also rejected Michael Howard's purported distinction between policy and operational failures. The Committee stated in its report that a broad 'pattern of incompetence' leading to a series of operational failures *is* a matter for which a Minister ought to be held individually responsible. The Committee further stated that if even a single operational failure was serious enough, and was closely connected to the Minister's responsibility for the overall organization of his department, it might well be appropriate for the Minister to resign.[37] The Committee was clear that 'what Ministers must never do is to put the blame onto civil servants for the effects of unworkable policies and their setting of unrealistic targets'.[38]

---

[35] In addition to the Scott report and to the work of the Public Service Committee, a third influence on both Parliament and government at this time was the first report of the (Nolan) Committee on Standards in Public Life: Cm. 2850 (London, May 1995).
[36] Public Service Committee, *Ministerial Accountability and Responsibility*, 1995–96 HC 313, para. 21.
[37] Ibid., para. 19.   [38] Ibid., para. 20.

Having explained what it did not consider ministerial responsibility to be, the Committee then set out what it did consider ministerial responsibility to consist of, and to require. The terms that the Committee adopted are important, and it is worth setting them out at length:

Ministers owe a fundamental duty to account to Parliament. This has, essentially, two meanings. First, that the executive is obliged to give an account—to provide full information about and explain its actions in Parliament so that they are subject to proper democratic scrutiny. This obligation is central to the proper functioning of Parliament, and therefore any Minister who has been found to have knowingly misled Parliament should resign. . . . Second, a Minister's duty to account to Parliament means that the executive is liable to be held to account: it must respond to concerns and criticism raised in Parliament about its actions because Members of Parliament are democratically-elected representatives of the people. A Minister's effective performance of his functions depends on his having the confidence of the House of Commons (or the House of Lords, for those Ministers who sit in the upper House). A Minister has to conduct himself, and direct the work of his department in a manner likely to ensure that he retains the confidence both of his own party and of the House. . . .[39]

From this passage it can be seen that the government found more support in Parliament for its insistence that ministers need not resign if they have been found to have misled Parliament unknowingly than it found for the responsibility/accountability distinction or for the policy/operations distinction. However, it should not be thought from the formulation adopted by the Public Service Committee that the Committee was entirely supportive of the government's position even on this point.

This is because, on the issue of the provision of information to Parliament, the Committee attempted to shift attention away from ministerial resignation and towards a focus on the quality of the account that Ministers would provide. In 1994 the government introduced a *Code of Practice on Access to Government Information*. This Code requires government departments to make available to Parliament and to the public a number of categories of government information.[40] As is usual in the realm of freedom of information, such duties are not absolute, but are limited by a series of exemptions, which are listed in the Code. The Public Service Committee, in its consideration of individual responsibility and Ministers' provision to Parliament of government information (whether in debate, in evidence before a select committee, or in answering a parlia-

---

[39] Ibid., para. 32.
[40] The Code remains in force, but will be replaced in 2005 when the Freedom of Information Act 2000 is due to come fully into force.

mentary question) concluded that whenever Ministers refuse to make information available to Parliament, they must explain (1) that they are doing so, (2) why they are doing so, and (3) which exemption provision of the Code they are seeking to rely on to justify the refusal to disclose.[41] Following this procedure, so the Committee felt, would significantly diminish the ability of Ministers to mislead Parliament by giving to Parliament less complete, or less accurate, information than Parliament had asked for and was entitled to receive. The government accepted the broad thrust of the Committee's recommendations, which were brought into effect through a series of amendments to the Code, and through the publication of new guidelines governing the way in which departments would in future draft answers to parliamentary questions.[42]

This outcome represents a considerable victory for the select committee, and indeed for Parliament generally. In none of the three respects in which it had sought to alter the rules of individual responsibility was the Major government ultimately successful. Both the responsibility/accountability distinction and the policy/operations distinction were unambiguously rejected by Parliament, a fact that was recognized and acknowledged by the government which, from the autumn of 1996 onwards, dropped its former insistence on them. The distinction between knowingly and unknowingly misleading Parliament was accepted by Parliament, but only in the context of ministerial resignations. As far as the routine of accountability is concerned, the effect of the reforms that followed the publication of the Scott report and of the report of the Public Service Committee was significantly to sharpen Ministers' obligations to report fully and accurately to Parliament, and to reduce the extent to which Ministers would be able to get away with half-truth and evasion. As such, these reforms constitute a determined effort to tackle the fault-line of openness that can be so damaging to the effective operation of political accountability.

Such an achievement would have marked out the work of the Public Service Committee as being of considerable constitutional significance of itself. As it was, however, this achievement was crowned by an even greater one. This is because, in addition to its work in battling against the *substance* of the Major government's attempted refinements to the rules on individual responsibility, the Public Service Committee also

---

[41] Public Service Committee, n. 36 above, para. 154.
[42] See *Guidance to Officials on Drafting Answers to Parliamentary Questions*, 1996–97 HC 67.

Public Law

agreed (again, unanimously—that is, with cross-party support) that the *means* by which the government had sought to make its refinements ought no longer to be available to it, or indeed to any future government. As we saw above, the government was able to attempt to rewrite the rules because, as the position then stood, these were rules the most authoritative articulation of which was contained in the document *Questions of Procedure for Ministers* (QPM)—a document that the government itself wrote. This problem we referred to earlier as the fault-line of ownership.

The Public Service Committee recommended, and Parliament agreed, that Parliament should take ownership of these rules, and that they should be enshrined in a way that rendered them beyond unilateral government amendment. The mechanism chosen to put this recommendation into effect was that each House of Parliament would pass a Resolution setting out the rules and expectations of individual responsibility. The purpose behind such a move was to remove the rules from the ownership of the government of the day and to place them instead in the hands of Parliament. No longer would self-serving amendment to QPM suffice to alter the rules of political accountability. Only the Houses of Parliament themselves may modify or rescind their Resolutions. The government acting alone will no longer be able to effect changes to the rules of ministerial responsibility.

The text of the Resolutions passed by the two Houses of Parliament incorporates the substance of the interpretation of individual responsibility that was offered by the Public Service Committee. The full text of the Resolution of the House of Commons is as follows:

(1) Ministers have a duty to Parliament to account, and be held to account, for the policies, decisions and actions of their departments and next steps agencies;

(2) It is of paramount importance that Ministers give accurate and truthful information to Parliament, correcting any inadvertent error at the earliest opportunity. Ministers who knowingly mislead Parliament will be expected to offer their resignation to the Prime Minister;

(3) Ministers should be as open as possible with Parliament, refusing to provide information only when disclosure would not be in the public interest, which should be decided in accordance with relevant statute and the government's Code of Practice on Access to Government Information;

(4) Similarly, Ministers should require civil servants who give evidence before parliamentary committees on their behalf and under their directions to be as helpful as possible in providing accurate, truthful and full information in accordance

with the duties and responsibilities of civil servants as set out in the Civil Service Code.[43]

The Resolutions were passed immediately before Parliament was dissolved in preparation for the 1997 general election. At that election, of course, the Conservatives were swept from office. The new Prime Minister, Tony Blair, issued to all Ministers his own version of QPM, which he re-branded the *Ministerial Code*. The provisions of Blair's Code that concern individual responsibility are significantly different from those contained in paragraph 27 of John Major's version. Under Blair's Code, ministerial responsibility is dealt with in paragraph 1.[44] The text of paragraph 1 reproduces the text of the parliamentary Resolutions, and specifically draws Ministers' attention to those Resolutions, making it clear that, as far as the government is concerned, it is Parliament that now sets the parameters of individual responsibility: the rules are no longer in the ownership of the government of the day, for the government to manipulate for its own short-term advantage. Thus, as well as reducing the dangers posed by the fault-line of openness, the fault-line of ownership has been erased from the landscape of political accountability—a fact that is significantly to Parliament's credit, and one which can only enhance the potency of politics as a vehicle of accountability.

THE MECHANISMS OF POLITICAL ACCOUNTABILITY

Having in the previous sections considered the substantive doctrines of political accountability, we turn now to the institutional structures and mechanisms by which the doctrines are put into effect. It would be all very well having rules and conventions of ministerial responsibility, but without adequate parliamentary means to apply those rules in practice, the doctrines would be useless. We saw above that during the period of the Major governments (1991–1997) there was considerable controversy surrounding the content and the meaning of the convention of individual responsibility. Under the Blair governments, ministerial responsibility seems, thus far at least, to have had a significantly smoother ride. On one account, this ought to be rather surprising. Many commentators have

---

[43] HC Debs., vol. 292, cols. 1046–1047 (19 March 1997). For the House of Lords Resolution, which is in identical substantive terms, see HL Debs., vol. 579, col. 1057 (20 March 1997).

[44] The current (2001) edition of the Ministerial Code is available on-line, at www.cabinet-office.gov.uk/central/2001/mcode/contents.htm.

assumed that when a governing party enjoys a large parliamentary majority (as has been the case since 1997, but was not the case from 1992–1997)
the House of Commons will be less able to assert itself over a government
that possesses vast numbers of loyal supporters. However, recently published research indicates that, at least with regard to the periods either
side of the 1997 election, this assumption is mistaken.[45] Such controversy
as there has been since 1997 in the arena of political accountability has
arisen in connection with the parliamentary mechanisms, rather than the
substantive content, of political accountability, particularly with regard
to select committees.

Parliament has three main ways of holding the executive to account:
debate, parliamentary questions, and select committees. Of these, debate
is probably the least penetrating. Debate is important for discussing general issues and broad principle, and big set-piece debates on topical issues
can attract significant media attention. Through debate Ministers can be
forced to come to Parliament to set out government policy and to defend
it, and opposition and backbench MPs (or peers) will have the opportunity to point out defects with, alternatives to, and inconsistencies within,
government policy, but this is about as far as debate can go. Scrutiny by
debate is painting with a broad brush. It can be a useful starting point,
but it does not generally allow Parliament to get to the detailed points that
more rigorous scrutiny will frequently need to focus on.

Parliamentary questions take two forms: oral and written. Oral questions are put during question time—there will normally be about an hour
of question time during each parliamentary day. All Ministers have to
attend a period of question time every four weeks or so, but probably the
best known aspect of question time is Prime Minister's Question Time,
which occurs weekly when Parliament is in session, and lasts for thirty
minutes each week. Oral questions are an effective means of putting
ministers on the spot, and of testing their parliamentary skills, but
whether the cut and thrust of question time really amounts to effective
political accountability is perhaps doubtful.[46]

---

[45] See D. Woodhouse, 'The Reconstruction of Constitutional Accountability' [2002]
Public Law 73. Woodhouse catalogues numerous examples from the 1997–2001 Parliament
of individual responsibility working well, over a range of domestic and foreign policy
issues, from pensions and the management of the passport office, to the controversy over
government provision of military aid to Sierra Leone.

[46] Prime Minister's question time remains the best known way in which the Prime Minister is routinely made personally to account to Parliament, but it is no longer the only way. In
a new development, the Prime Minister has since 2002 agreed that he will, every six months,
give detailed evidence on government policy to the Liaison Committee of the House of

Written questions, on the other hand, are a vital ingredient of contemporary parliamentary practice, and contribute a great deal to the system of political accountability. Answers to written questions are not delivered in the Chamber, and so they receive no air time, but they are printed in the daily parliamentary record, *Hansard*, and they constitute one of the foremost means by which MPs (and peers) may obtain information from Ministers. As we saw in the previous section, one of the central allegations investigated by the Scott inquiry was that Ministers had repeatedly misled Parliament by providing incomplete or inaccurate answers to parliamentary questions, and in particular to written questions. As a result of the findings of the Scott report on this matter, a number of reforms were made to the guidance that is issued to government departments concerning the drafting of answers to parliamentary questions. Not only were the guidelines strengthened, but so too was the monitoring of departments' compliance with the guidelines. Since 1997 the House of Commons Select Committee on Public Administration has conducted an annual inquiry into Ministers' answers to parliamentary questions. Every year the Committee publishes a report, analysing improvements that have been made and highlighting the issues with regard to which further improvement is still required. The Committee has identified good practice, and has named and shamed those departments that continue only haphazardly to abide by the guidelines. As well as valuably maintaining the high profile of this issue throughout Parliament, the Committee's work has kept up significant pressure on the government, forcing it to promise that the poorer departments improve and reform their practices.[47]

The Committee's work in this area has made a valuable contribution to Parliament's ongoing attempts to address what we have identified as the fault-line of openness in political accountability. The Committee's persistence has helped to make parliamentary questions a more reliable and more potent mechanism by which parliamentarians may force information out of government departments that would frequently prefer, if they had their way, not to have to release it. It is the constancy and tenacity of the Committee's work that is its real value—not only in providing a focal point for individual MPs dissatisfied with responses they have received

Commons. The Liaison Committee and select committees generally are considered further below.

[47] The Committee's most recent reports on parliamentary questions are published as 2001–02 HC 1086 (July 2002) and 2002–03 HC 136 (November 2002). Select committee reports are available on-line at www.publications.parliament.uk/pa/cm/cmselect.htm.

Public Law

from government departments (MPs who, if it were not for the Committee, would have no-one to turn to for assistance or advice)—but also in facilitating exactly the kind of accountability that can be attained only through political, as opposed to legal, means. Follow-up and the kind of determined, patient perseverance shown by the Committee to such good effect is a resource available only to those who scrutinize the government in the political arena.

The third mechanism Parliament has at its disposal to enable it to hold the executive to account is the select committee system. Select committees are important to both Houses, but since 1979 the departmental select committees of the House of Commons have been especially influential. These committees were restructured in 1979 so that there would be one select committee for every government department. Thus the Home Affairs Committee monitors the Home Office, and the Education Committee monitors the Department for Education, and so on. In addition, there are a number of cross-cutting committees, of which the two most important, in terms of scrutiny, are the Public Administration Committee and the Public Accounts Committee. The Standing Orders of the House of Commons provide that the role of departmental select committees is 'to examine the expenditure, administration, and policy' of government departments. In order to carry out these tasks select committees have the power to send for people, papers, and records. They have their own small staff, and they may appoint specialist advisers. Once appointed committees decide for themselves which aspects of departmental administration and policy they should investigate. Departmental select committees are the unique preserve of backbench MPs: no Ministers may serve as members. Each committee has between eleven and seventeen members, the political complexion of whom will reflect that of the Commons as a whole. Thus, if 60 per cent of MPs are from the Labour party, 60 per cent of the membership of each committee will be composed of Labour party MPs. Committees are appointed at the beginning of each Parliament (that is, following a general election) for the duration of the Parliament (that is, until the next general election).

Select committees allow small groups of MPs to develop detailed knowledge on discrete areas of policy. Under an active and enthusiastic chair, select committees are able to embark on four or five major investigations in each session (that is, each year). As well as giving otherwise generalist MPs particular areas of expertise, select committees enable the House of Commons to launch in-depth inquiries into particularly problematic or controversial aspects of government policy, allowing

Parliament to probe more systematically and more deeply into government decision-making than is possible in debates or though parliamentary questions. Complex matters that have been the subject of valuable select committee investigations in recent years include the Child Support Agency, rail privatization, arms exports, the role of the private sector in the NHS, and the Bank of England's monetary policy committee, among many others.

Which MPs will serve on, and who will chair, each committee are matters for the party managers—the whips—to resolve at the beginning of a new Parliament. This is an issue which is capable of generating considerable political controversy. Following the 2001 election, government whips sought to make a number of alterations to the membership, and chairmanship, of select committees. Most notoriously, the government sought to oust two Labour MPs, Gwyneth Dunwoody and Donald Anderson, from the chairs of the Transport and of the Foreign Affairs Committees, respectively. Further, Mr Anderson's replacement was to be the luckless Chris Smith, who in the 1997–2001 Parliament had been a member of the Cabinet. While Mr Smith was a backbencher (as the Prime Minister had reshuffled him out of the government following the 2001 election) he had been one for less than a month. Parliament—and in particular the parliamentary Labour party—revolted, and in an unusual show of defiance voted down the government's proposed membership. The whips had to think again, and Mrs Dunwoody and Mr Anderson were reinstated as the chairs of their committees.

There is nothing unusual in the government, through its whips, seeking to control membership and chairmanship of select committees. After the 1992 election the Conservative whips sought to prevent Nicholas Winterton from being reappointed to the chair of the Health Select Committee. Mr Winterton, a Conservative MP, had been the chair of the committee since 1983, and under his chairmanship the committee had published a number of reports critical of the government's programme of reforms to the NHS. Mr Winterton protested, but the whips had a defence: they argued that it was a party rule that no member would serve as chair of the same committee for more than two Parliaments. Unfortunately for the whips Sir John Wheeler had served as chair of the Home Affairs Committee for two Parliaments. Unlike Mr Winterton's committee, the Home Affairs Committee had not been especially critical of the Home Office during the 1980s, and it was not in the government's interest for him to be replaced, but the price to be paid for removing Mr Winterton was that Sir John Wheeler also had to be removed, although he (unlike Mr Winterton) was compensated through subsequent elevation to ministerial office.

Both positive and negative conclusions can be drawn from these stories. On the plus side, they suggest that select committees are sufficiently powerful, prestigious, and effective to be taken seriously by the government and its whips. If select committees were worthless, or ineffective, why go through the bother of seeking to manipulate their membership and direction? But on the minus side, of course, these committees are supposed to be rigorous and independent committees of inquiry. If the whips can so easily remove thorns from the government's flesh, will that not discourage rigour? If the whips have control over membership, does that not dilute the extent to which the committees can truly be said to be independent of government?

Here we come to the final one of our three fault-lines of political accountability. This is the fault-line of party.[48] This is the fault-line that has the potential to run deepest through the system of political accountability. We know that the government is defined as those politicians who can command majority support in the House of Commons. We know also that since the mid-nineteenth century the device that has been employed to generate and to maintain such support is the political party. Since the 1870s it has been the case that when there is a Tory majority in the Commons, there will be a Tory (or Conservative) government, and when there is a Liberal, or Labour majority, there is a Liberal, or Labour government. Thus, what we have come to mean when we say that the government is accountable to Parliament is that the government is accountable to a group of politicians the majority of whom are members of the same political party as that which forms the government.

The danger with the fault-line of party is that it blurs the distinction, which is so important to English public law, between Parliament and the Crown (remembering that it is the Crown's government that Parliament is holding to account here). There was clear separation between Parliament and government when, in the late seventeenth and early eighteenth centuries, the Crown itself was directly involved in the routine business of government. Equally, there remained clear separation between Parliament and government in the late eighteenth and early nineteenth centuries, as government moved away from royal courtiers and towards Ministers who, while they were accountable to Parliament, could not yet

---

[48] The danger that party may pose for the system of political accountability was introduced in chapter 1, above.

hope to control it. This was perhaps the golden age of genuinely *parliamentary* government: the era that followed government by the Crown but came before government by party—that is, the period between about 1830 and 1870. Indeed, in the years between the two great Reform Acts (1832 and 1867) no fewer than ten governments were forced out of power by virtue of their having lost the confidence of the House of Commons.

The function of the Reform Acts was to increase the size, and the scope, of the franchise, thus beginning the process of bringing democracy to the constitutional order. With mass democracy has come the modern, centralized organization of the political party, and with party has come the greatest single challenge that the system of political accountability has yet had to face. The challenge is formidable, but we should take care nonetheless not to exaggerate it. We have encountered already in this chapter numerous instances where party has not been the obstacle to effective political accountability that it might have been. As we have seen, several Ministers have been forced to resign from office because backbenchers from their own party have lost confidence in them. Indeed, Mrs Thatcher herself fell from office not because of opposition from the Labour party, but because she lost the support of her own party in Parliament. Just as MPs can sometimes turn against their own Ministers, so too are parliamentarians able to transcend the party divide to work together on a variety of issues that concern Parliament as a whole. We have seen several examples of this in what we have considered here: the unanimous reports of all-party committees such as that of the Public Service Committee on ministerial responsibility in 1996 or those of the Public Administration Committee on parliamentary questions since 1997 are impressive examples. Indeed, it is very much the norm, not the exception, for select committee reports to be unanimous: only rarely are they split along party lines.

Nonetheless, that the fault-line of party has the potential to disrupt the system of political accountability is amply demonstrated by the actions of the Labour whips in 2001. Potential is not always realized, however, and what was notable about the events of July 2001 was not so much that the whips tried it on, but that Parliament stood up to them, *and won*. Just as the Major government found that it was unable to secure the changes to individual responsibility that it had sought in the 1990s, so too did the Labour whips find that, even with another overwhelming majority, and even in the euphoria of a second successive election victory, Parliament was not so easy to manipulate when it came to fiddling with the ways in which it holds the government to account.

A key reason why Parliament resisted the whips in 2001 was that throughout the lifetime of the 1997–2001 Parliament concern had developed on all sides of the Commons about the continuing effectiveness of the departmental select committee system. No-one doubted the contribution the committees had made since their restructuring in 1979, but twenty years on, and faced with an unprecedented majority of MPs supportive of the governing party, there was a growing sense both in the Commons and beyond that it was time for further reform. In part this sense was simply informed by a fear that, in an era of significant constitutional reform, Parliament should not become left behind. On the one hand, with the passage of the Human Rights Act in 1998 much attention was given to the enhancements of legal accountability that that Act was thought likely to bring. On the other hand, the creation of the Scottish Parliament and of the Welsh Assembly established new sites of political accountability. Moreover, it quickly became apparent that neither of these devolved institutions would merely mimic Westminster, but that both would create their own structures and systems of political accountability, more modern in conception. With the growth of legal accountability and the challenge posed by new models of political accountability in Edinburgh and Cardiff, it is hardly surprising that the Westminster Parliament was anxious not to feel excluded from the climate of reform.

Impetus for such reform was provided by the Liaison Committee. This normally rather sleepy committee is composed of all the chairs of the departmental and other select committees in the House of Commons. In the 1987 and 1992 Parliaments it barely met and reported only cursorily at the end of each Parliament—in general terms and without great effect—on the difficulties encountered by select committees during the Parliament. However, during the 1997–2001 Parliament the Liaison Committee stirred. Its first and most important step was to publish in March 2000 a report called *Shifting the Balance: Select Committees and the Executive*.[49] This powerful (and, for a select committee, well-publicized) report sought a revision and strengthening of select committees. The Committee's goal was ambitious: it aimed to achieve for parliamentary scrutiny in the first decade of the twenty-first century what the 1979 restructuring had achieved for the 1980s and 1990s. For the Liaison Committee, the starting-point was that:

the 1979 select committee system has been a success. We have no doubt of that. At a bargain price, it has provided independent scrutiny of government . . . it has

---

[49] 1999–2000 HC 300.

exposed mistaken and short-sighted policies and, from time to time, wrong-doing both in high places and low. It has been a source of unbiased information, rational debate, and constructive ideas. It has made the political process less remote, and more accessible to the citizen who is affected by that process—and who pays the bill. Its very existence has been a constant reminder to Ministers and officials, and many others in positions of power and influence, of the spotlight that may swing their way when least welcome.[50]

However, despite the fact that the committee system had 'shown the House of Commons at its best' the Committee acknowledged that the performance of select committees had 'not been consistent' and that their success had not been 'unalloyed'.[51] The purpose of the Committee's report was to find ways of making parliamentary scrutiny of the government more effective, by reinforcing the select committee system. Among the Committee's recommendations were that: appointment and nomination ought to be taken out of the hands of the whips; committee chairs ought to be remunerated so as to create a career structure within Parliament that is independent of ministerial preferment; committees ought to devote more energy to following up their recommendations and to monitoring government compliance; and committees ought to be granted greater resources.

Rather depressingly, the government initially rejected these proposals, but after continued pressure from the Liaison Committee, and with considerable further support for the Committee's package of reforms coming from a weighty report published by the all-party Hansard Society,[52] the government reversed its earlier opposition. In part this was facilitated by a change in government personnel. In the post-election 2001 reshuffle, Robin Cook became the new Leader of the House of Commons. Mr Cook quickly showed himself to be considerably more receptive to the proposals from the Liaison Committee and the Hansard Society than his predecessor had been. Within a few months of taking up his new position Mr Cook brought forward to Parliament a series of proposals, closely based on those first advanced by the Liaison Committee, to strengthen the select committee system.[53] When the House of Commons voted on the proposals in May 2002, it rather surprisingly rejected any change to

[50] Ibid., para. 4.
[51] Ibid., paras. 5–6.
[52] See Hansard Society, *The Challenge for Parliament: Making Government Accountable* (London, 2001).
[53] The proposals were contained in a report of the Modernisation Committee, which the Leader of the House chairs: see 2001–02 HC 224.

the whips' powers of appointment and nomination, but otherwise approved the reforms, which have now come into effect.[54]

CONCLUSIONS

The lesson to be learnt from these events is positive for advocates of the system of political accountability. Through the dedicated work of a number of key select committees (Liaison, Public Administration, and others) Parliament has been made fully aware of the importance and centrality of its tasks with regard to holding the executive to account. Moreover, Parliament has shown that it is both able and willing to resist attempts by the government to weaken political accountability, and to resist such attempts so successfully that the result is actually to strengthen political accountability. This was as true of Parliament under John Major as it has been of Parliament under Tony Blair.

This is not to say that the system of political accountability is perfect. On the contrary, during the course of this chapter we have identified and discussed three fault-lines that have threatened to undermine it. One of the fault-lines (that of ownership) has, for the time being at least, been eradicated as a threat, and this will continue to be the case for as long as the parliamentary Resolutions of March 1997 remain in force. The other fault-lines, of openness and of party, are impossible to eradicate: while there is democracy there will continue to be party, and no government in the world has ever been entirely open. What these fault-lines require is vigilance, not removal. As for openness, Parliament must continue to work hard to ensure that under the new regime of freedom of information (under the Freedom of Information Act 2000, which is due to come fully into force in 2005) the government provides to Parliament accurate and truthful information. This will always be a struggle: no Parliament—and no court either, for that matter—can guarantee that government will be as fully open as its critics would like it to be.

As for party, one of the great successes of select committees is that they have provided a forum in which parliamentarians feel, and are, able to co-operate across the party divide, rather than routinely and unthinkingly to divide along party lines. Parliament desperately needs MPs who, while they may belong to political parties, can nevertheless see beyond the limited horizons of short-term party advantage and political point-scoring, and who can understand that it is by working together that those

[54] See HC Debs., vol. 385, cols. 648–727 (14 May 2002).

on the backbenches can have the most influence over, and can most effectively scrutinize, those in office. Fortunately, the political system seems to be reasonably good at producing such MPs: real parliamentarians, rather than eager-to-please Ministers in waiting. The likes of Nicholas Winterton, Gwyneth Dunwoody, Tony Wright, Robert Sheldon, Chris Mullen, Archy Kirkwood, and Edward Leigh: these are the stars of political accountability. They are not household names, perhaps, but then, how many Court of Appeal judges are?

There is, inevitably, much more that could be said about political accountability than we have covered here. The way in which the Parliamentary Ombudsman supplements the role of MPs in holding the government to account; the special powers entrusted to the House of Commons with regard to the scrutiny of the finances of government; and the variety of contributions made by regulators and auditors to the economic and financial accountability of government: all of these are important aspects of political accountability that we have not been able to consider here. But we have seen that, notwithstanding it being unfashionable to say so, Parliament and its committees continue to make an outstanding contribution to the central constitutional task of holding the Crown's government to account. Even if it is largely unloved and neglected in the legal academy, the political constitution is alive and well.

6

Legal Accountability

Like the previous chapter, this one is similarly concerned with questions of executive accountability. Here our concern is with the ways in which the courts may hold the government to account. The principal means by which this may occur is through a claim for judicial review, and the bulk of this chapter is taken up with an analysis of the strengths and limitations of the modern law of judicial review. In a claim for judicial review, the claimant asks the court to review the legality of some particular executive action. As we shall see, there are numerous grounds on which claimants may base such cases: these include arguments of illegality, irrationality, procedural impropriety, proportionality, and breach of human rights. Access to the judicial review courts is restricted, and there are rules both on the matter of who may seek judicial review and on the question of whom judicial review may be sought against. All of these issues are considered in the pages that follow. Before we proceed, one further word of introduction is required. Judicial review is exactly that: it is a review, not an appeal. In a claim for judicial review, the claimant is not appealing against the merits of what the administration has decided, but is rather seeking a review of the legality of what has been done, or is proposed to be done. The importance of this distinction, between appeal and review, will become apparent as the chapter proceeds.

THE DEVELOPMENT OF MODERN JUDICIAL REVIEW LAW

We saw in chapter 3 above that the core idea of the rule of law in English public law constitutes only a rather weak principle of legality. It provides that the executive may do nothing without clear legal authority first permitting its actions. This is a rule that an executive which has effective control over the legislative agenda of Parliament will not find to be excessively burdensome. If the government wishes to (let us suppose) intercept my telephone calls, but finds that it has no legal authority to do so, all it has to do to meet the requirements of the core idea of the rule of law is to present a Bill to Parliament which, when enacted, will grant to the executive the authority it seeks. As Parliament almost always enacts what the executive wills into law, this core idea of the rule of law need not detain the government for long.

Despite the weakness of the core idea, however, the courts have in recent years fashioned a range of legal techniques which, taken together, now comprise an altogether more potent scheme of legal accountability. This we call the law of judicial review. The first thing to understand about judicial review law is that, in its present form, it is very new. Whereas in previous chapters we have considered aspects of English public law that date back over eight centuries, in this chapter we are concerned with an area of law that is not even forty years old. This is not to say that there was no legal accountability in English public law before the mid-1960s: indeed, today's judicial review law uses remedies that date from medieval times, and adopts rules of natural justice that had already become established by the sixteenth century. But such judicial review as there was before the 1960s was, in the words of the leading commentator of the time, 'superficial' and 'little more than perfunctory'.[1]

During the 1960s what had been little more than an 'asymmetrical hotchpotch'—a bits and pieces, occasional, approach to legal accountability—started to be transformed into something closer to a series of 'coherent principles' of judicial review.[2] The figure at the forefront of the legal transformation was Lord Reid who, in a string of revisionist judgments, led the House of Lords in its task of modernizing judicial review. First the law of procedural fairness was reformed;[3] then substantive review[4] and aspects of the relationship between the law and the Crown[5] were reformulated and strengthened. Finally the arcane but important area of jurisdictional review was revisited.[6] In each case Lord Reid approached the task of reform in the same basic way: his mission was to sweep away what he saw as the unnecessary and out-moded restrictions and technicalities of the past, and to replace them not with a detailed series of rules, but rather with wide-ranging judicial discretion so that the law could be further developed and clarified on a case-by-case basis in the

---

[1] See S. de Smith, *Judicial Review of Administrative Action* (3rd edn., London, 1973), at 28.

[2] Ibid., at 4.

[3] See *Ridge v Baldwin* [1964] AC 40. The law of procedural fairness is considered below.

[4] See *Padfield v Minister of Agriculture, Fisheries, and Food* [1968] AC 997. The law of substantive review is considered below.

[5] See *Conway v Rimmer* [1968] AC 910.

[6] See *Anisminic v Foreign Compensation Commission* [1969] 2 AC 147.

future. Thus, a significant characteristic of modern judicial review law is
that it possesses a remarkable degree of judicial discretion. One of the
purposes of this chapter will be to assess how subsequent generations of
judges have used the discretion that Lord Reid bequeathed to them. The
advantage of discretion is that it can facilitate valuable flexibility in the
law. But if overdone such flexibility can easily descend into uncertainty,
unpredictability, and even arbitrariness, or at least the appearance of arbitrariness. An issue we shall have to consider in the pages that follow is the
extent to which the courts have been able to manage their discretionary
powers successfully.

By 1984 the courts had developed the law of judicial review to such a
point that Lord Diplock was able to synthesize it, giving it a new and
authoritative framework for analysis. In his seminal judgment in the
GCHQ case of that year, Lord Diplock stated that there were three
'heads' or 'grounds' of judicial review, which he labelled 'illegality',
'irrationality', and 'procedural impropriety'.[7] We shall use Lord
Diplock's terminology to structure our account.

(A) PROCEDURAL REVIEW: PROCEDURAL IMPROPRIETY

Let us start with what Lord Diplock called procedural impropriety. This
area of law is also known as natural justice. There are two established
rules of natural justice: the rule against bias and the duty to hear the other
side.[8] These are among the oldest aspects of judicial review law, although
the rules of natural justice have not always been applied as widely as they
are now. Both aspects of natural justice are extremely interesting, and
simultaneously illustrate both the potential strengths and the limitations
of legal accountability. The rules of natural justice represent a certain
vision of procedural fairness. It is immediately apparent, however, that
the vision of fairness that they represent is not the only tenable understanding of what fair procedures might look like. Equally, it may well be
the case that the aspects of procedural fairness that the rules of natural
justice prioritize (that is, not being biased and hearing the other side) may
not always be the ones that are most important: what makes a procedure
fair may depend on the context, or on the subject-matter.

---

[7] *Council of Civil Service Unions v Minister for the Civil Service* [1985] AC 374, at 410.

[8] As well as the two established rules, there are some cases in which it has been suggested
that a duty to give reasons might constitute an additional procedural requirement. As the
law currently stands, however, such a duty is specific to certain forms of decision-making,
and is not a general requirement: see *R v Secretary of State for the Home Department, ex
parte Doody* [1994] 1 AC 531.

What is deemed to make a procedure fair or unfair may also depend on ideology. We saw above in chapter 3 that over the course of the past twenty years aspects of the organization and structure of government have undergone significant reform. The driving principle behind such reform was the desire to maximize efficiency in the public sector, and to recreate the public sector in the image of the private. To this end values of 'new public management', that is to say of economy, effectiveness, and efficiency, were prioritized, sometimes (as we saw) at the expense of more traditional values of public service. In a sense, the values of new public management constitute a rival vision of fairness to that represented by the rules of natural justice. For the advocate of new public management, public administration is fair when it is efficient, when it does not waste its financial and human resources, when it is low-cost, and when it is speedy. Such an understanding of fairness is clearly at odds with that preferred by the rules of natural justice. Giving fair hearings, or giving reasons for decisions, is both time-consuming and inefficient. It may make for better administration from the point of view of the aggrieved individual, but it does not necessarily make for better administration from the point of view of the taxpayer.

This clash of values—this disagreement about what constitutes a fair procedure—does not mean that one side is necessarily wrong, or per-petuating an unfairness. That the rules of natural justice are not always compatible with new public management does not mean that the rules of natural justice are necessarily misguided any more than it means that new public management is. The contrast between the two illustrates only that there are many accounts of what makes a procedure fair, and the law's preferred account is not the only one, and may not always be the most appropriate one.

It is unsurprising that the law has chosen to focus on bias and fair hearings as the two facets of procedural fairness that it promotes most, as it is these facets of fairness that feature most prominently in the sort of procedure that the law knows best: namely, the adversarial trial. If you were to think of the situations in which it would be most important to you that the decision-maker is not biased, and that you are given the opportunity to put your case—that the decision-maker is obliged to hear you—then the situation in which this would probably be most critical would be that of the criminal trial. It is central to criminal procedure that the jury or magistrate that determines your guilt or innocence does so on the basis of the evidence laid before the court, and not on the basis of its prejudice, and that you and your legal representatives have the opportunity freely to cross-examine that evidence before it is relied on by the decision-maker (i.e., by the jury or magistrate).

It is easy to see where the ideas underpinning the rules of natural justice come from—they come from the judges' own experience. But it is rather less easy to apply these rules to the variety of decision-making procedures that public administrators and executive officials employ. Think, for example, of the decision by a local authority whether or not to grant planning permission for the construction of a new building. The councillors who make up the local authority are all directly elected politicians. They may have been elected by the local people on the basis, among other things, of their views on planning and development. The council may, for example, have a significant number of Green party councillors, who vigorously oppose development particularly on the green belt. Alternatively, the council may have been elected on a platform of trying to attract investment into the community in order to reduce local unemployment, one way of doing this being to encourage construction projects which generate both employment and economic development. In other words, the decision-maker (the local authority) may well have— indeed, is expected to have—a stated policy on the issue of planning. Is having a policy not akin to prejudging the issue? That is to say, is a decision-maker who implements a pre-stated policy not a biased decision-maker? In a series of cases, the courts have struggled to adapt the rules of natural justice to fit decision-making contexts such as those involving local planning authorities.[9] It has not been an easy accommodation: on the one hand the courts are surely right to insist that decision-makers should in principle not be biased. But on the other hand it is equally important that those who have the power to make decisions on issues as contentious as planning are accountable to the local community, so that the local community can ensure (through local elections) that its decision-makers are responsive to the preferences of the community. Such a process necessarily requires that those who stand for office first declare their hand: once in office, what will their policy be?

The determination of planning applications constitutes just one area of public administration where the rules of natural justice may not appear to be the most appropriate criteria against which the fairness of decision-making procedures can be judged. In the context of planning decisions

---

[9] See e.g. *R v Secretary of State for the Environment, ex parte Kirkstall Valley Campaign* [1996] 3 All ER 304. See also *Franklin v Minister of Town and Country Planning* [1948] AC 87.

made by local authorities it is the rule against bias that has proved difficult to apply. Putting the second rule of natural justice—the duty to hear the other side—into practice has also been less than straightforward. One technique of modern government in which the duty to hear the other side has proven to be particularly problematic is the public inquiry. Public inquiries are frequently established by the government as a response when something goes wrong. Often chaired by judges or other senior lawyers, inquiries are asked to gather evidence, to draw up an official report, and to make recommendations. Recent examples include the Scott inquiry into arms-to-Iraq, the Phillips inquiry into BSE, and the Saville inquiry into Bloody Sunday. Where, as in all three of these examples, there are literally hundreds of witnesses and other interested parties, how should the duty to hear the other side be put into operation? Does that duty include the right of all witnesses and interested parties to cross-examine the evidence of all other witnesses? Does it include the right of all parties to be legally represented? Both the Scott inquiry and the Bloody Sunday inquiry generated heated and impassioned debate on these issues, with serious disagreements being expressed about which sorts of procedures are fair and which unfair.

We need not here recount the detail.[10] The point for us is simply to note that the apparent simplicity and straightforwardness of the rules of natural justice are deceptive. Indeed, as the controversies over procedure at recent public inquiries demonstrate, it can often be extremely difficult to know how the rules of natural justice should be applied in practice. Sometimes natural justice will require that the decision-maker provide those affected by her decision the opportunity of making oral as well as written representations, and at other times it will not.[11] Sometimes natural justice will require that at an oral hearing those affected are legally represented, and at other times it will not.[12] Sometimes there will be a right to cross-examine others, and other times there will not.[13] Sometimes the decision-maker will be required to give reasons for her decision, and at other times not.[14] And so forth. As Lord Bridge expressed it in *Lloyd v McMahon*, 'The so-called rules of natural justice are not engraved on

---

[10] For the controversy over the procedures at the Scott inquiry, see Sir Richard Scott, 'Procedures at Inquiries: The Duty to be Fair' (1995) 111 *Law Quarterly Review* 596 and Lord Howe, 'Procedure at the Scott Inquiry' [1996] *Public Law* 445. For the Bloody Sunday inquiry, see *R v Lord Saville, ex parte A* [2000] 1 WLR 1855.

[11] See *Lloyd v McMahon* [1987] AC 625.

[12] See *R v Board of Visitors of the Maze Prison, ex parte Hone* [1988] AC 379.

[13] See *Bushell v Secretary of State for the Environment* [1981] AC 75.

[14] See n. 8 above.

tablets of stone. To use the phrase which better expresses the underlying concept, what the requirements of fairness demand when any body, domestic, administrative, or judicial, has to make a decision which will affect the rights of individuals depends on the character of the decision-making body, the kind of decision it has to make and the statutory or other framework in which it operates'.[15]

With such a degree of elasticity the courts have to walk a fine line here. If they are overly rigid in their insistence on the observation of the rules of natural justice they will stand accused of inappropriately imposing their own trial-based conception of procedural fairness on a range of administrative procedures that on a proper analysis require different procedures from those used in criminal courts. On the other hand, however, if the courts are overly flexible in reviewing the compatibility of administrative procedures with the requirements of natural justice, then they risk diluting the protection which the law can afford to the individual. The courts have perhaps fallen into this second trap more than they have the first. Thus, in *Lloyd v McMahon* the House of Lords held that a district auditor was not required to afford councillors an oral hearing before identifying them as having failed to discharge their duty as members of the council (a finding which exposed the councillors concerned to substantial personal financial liability). Similarly, in *ex parte Hone* the House of Lords ruled that a prison board of visitors was not required to allow a prisoner on a disciplinary charge to be legally represented even where the facts of the offence constituted a crime.[16] And in a string of much criticized deportation cases courts have held that the requirements of natural justice must give way when the executive deems it necessary in the interests of national security.[17]

(B) SUBSTANTIVE REVIEW: ILLEGALITY AND IRRATIONALITY

The rules of natural justice or, as Lord Diplock preferred, procedural impropriety concern questions of fairness of procedure. Judicial review has also developed grounds on which aggrieved individuals may challenge

---

[15] See n. 11 above, at 702.   [16] N. 12 above.

[17] See *R v Secretary of State for Home Affairs, ex parte Hosenball* [1977] 1 WLR 766 and *R v Secretary of State for the Home Department, ex parte Cheblak* [1991] 1 WLR 890. The ECtHR found aspects of English procedure in this context to be in violation of the ECHR: see *Chahal v United Kingdom* (1996) 23 EHRR 413. The ruling in *Chahal* led to a number of procedural changes, brought about by the Special Immigration Appeals Commission Act 1997.

the acts and decisions of public administrators on the basis of their substance. Some commentators favour the view that there is only one ground of substantive review: namely that the decision-maker has acted beyond her powers (or *ultra vires*, in Latin). Lord Diplock, however, divided the law of *ultra vires* into two separate, although clearly closely related, categories. These he labelled illegality and irrationality. The first of these he defined as meaning that the 'decision-maker must understand correctly the law that regulates his decision-making power and must give effect to it'.[18] Suppose that a statute empowers the Secretary of State to issue directions to broadcasters regulating the times at which various grades of obscene material may be broadcast on terrestrial television. Suppose further that the Secretary of State relies on this power to issue directions to broadcasters regulating the content of political speech. This would be an example of what Lord Diplock called illegality. The decision-maker (here the Secretary of State) has applied a power (to regulate the broadcasting of obscene material) in a context that is not covered by the power he has purportedly relied on. The decision-maker has failed to understand correctly the law that regulates his decision-making power. The decision is therefore illegal, and in a judicial review action the court could grant a remedy quashing the Secretary of State's decision.

Irrationality is Lord Diplock's name for what is also known as *Wednesbury* unreasonableness. *Wednesbury* was a case decided in 1947 in which Lord Greene MR stated that while the courts could not intervene to quash a decision solely because they considered it to be unreasonable, they could so intervene if the decision was 'so unreasonable that no reasonable authority could ever have come to it'.[19] Lord Diplock refined this somewhat tautological test, stating that an irrational decision was one which is 'so outrageous in its defiance of logic or of accepted moral standards that no sensible person who had applied his mind to the question to be decided could have arrived at it'.[20] To illustrate the difference between this idea and that of illegality let us return to our hypothetical. The Secretary of State is empowered by statute to issue directions to broadcasters regulating the times at which various grades of obscene material may be broadcast on terrestrial television. Suppose this time that the Secretary of State exercises this power to issue directions to the broadcasters to the effect that images of the naked human body may be

---

[18] N. 7 above, at 410.
[19] *Associated Provincial Picture Houses v Wednesbury Corporation* [1948] 1 KB 223, at 230.
[20] N. 7 above, at 410.

broadcast on terrestrial television only between the hours of midnight and 6.00 a.m., regardless of the nature of the programme. The direction therefore applies equally to pornography, to movies, and to factual, educational, and other documentaries. Whereas in our first example the Secretary of State was seeking to exercise a power he did not have (he had a power to regulate obscenity but not to regulate political speech), in this second example the Secretary of State is seeking to exercise a power he does have, but he is exercising it in such an extreme manner that the court might be invited to intervene to quash the decision on the ground that it is irrational: it is outrageous in its defiance of accepted moral standards.

The application of *Wednesbury* unreasonableness, or irrationality, has been exceptionally controversial. The idea is, as we have seen, that the courts are not able to intervene solely where they find that a decision-maker has acted unreasonably. Before the courts can intervene, so the theory runs, the decision-maker must have acted so unreasonably that no reasonable decision-maker could possibly have acted in this way. Lord Greene MR stated in his judgment in the *Wednesbury* case that 'to prove a case of that kind would require something overwhelming'.[21] The test of *Wednesbury* unreasonableness has proved easier to state than it has been for the courts to apply in practice, and a good deal of the controversy surrounding this area of the law has been caused by the courts intervening, and not intervening, in ways which appear to cross and re-cross the line in disturbingly unprincipled ways.

Two cases that illustrate this are *Tameside*[22] and *Bromley v GLC*.[23] In *Tameside* the House of Lords held that it was unlawful for the (Labour) government to order a (Conservative) local education authority to change a school from a selective grammar into a comprehensive. Part of the reason given by the court was that the local education authority had been democratically elected on a manifesto commitment that pledged support for grammar schools. In *Bromley v GLC* the House of Lords held that the (Labour-controlled) Greater London Council acted unlawfully in cutting fares on the London underground and in paying for the cuts through the rates (that is, through the system of local government finance that was in place at the time) despite the fact that the Labour GLC had been democratically elected on a manifesto commitment to do just that. Thus it appears that the court in one case allowed a party to defend itself by

---

[21] N. 19 above, at 230.
[22] *Secretary of State for Education v Tameside MBC* [1977] AC 1014.
[23] *Bromley London Borough Council v Greater London Council* [1983] 1 AC 768.

arguing that it was only doing what it had been elected to do, whereas in the other case this argument was held to be irrelevant. It will not have gone unnoticed that in both cases the result was that the Conservatives won and that Labour lost the legal argument. Could it be that the courts were misusing their discretionary powers of review to promote certain political interests over others? Or is there a more benign explanation: to the effect that manifesto commitments may allow a party to act irrationally (*Tameside*) but not illegally (*Bromley v GLC*)?

Wheeler v Leicester City Council[24] is another case illustrative of the sorts of controversies that can be generated in this area of public law. Here Leicester Rugby Club had been using a recreation ground owned by the (Labour-controlled) local authority for training purposes. Several members of the club participated in an unofficial England tour of South Africa—this during the depths of apartheid, when much sport in South Africa was internationally boycotted. Leicester is a city with a significant ethnic minority population, and there was considerable controversy in the city about the fact that some of Leicester's players were participating in the tour. As a result the council decided to withdraw from the rugby club its permission to use the recreation ground. The House of Lords held that this action was unlawful. There are two ways in which this case generated controversy. The first, echoing *Tameside* and *Bromley v GLC*, concerned the politics of the judiciary: why did the courts reject the council's legal argument that its decision was justified—even required— by the statutory duty it was under to promote good race relations?[25] But it is the second debate about the case that has probably had the deeper impact on the way in which judicial review law has developed since the mid 1980s, when this case was decided.

Reading the case, it is remarkably difficult to pinpoint why the court held that the council's action was unlawful. It is difficult even to know on which of the three established grounds of judicial review the court's decision is based. Between the Court of Appeal and the House of Lords there were five substantial judgments. The Court of Appeal held by a two to one majority that the council had not acted unlawfully. The House of Lords unanimously allowed the rugby club's appeal. The majority of the Court of Appeal, holding for the council, reasoned their judgments along lines of *Wednesbury* unreasonableness, Ackner LJ and Sir George Waller concluded that, given the statutory duty on the council to promote good race relations, given the ethnic mix of the local population, and given the

---

[24] [1985] AC 1054. [25] See Race Relations Act 1976, s. 71.

council's long-standing policy with regard to race relations in general and apartheid in particular, its decision could not be described as being so unreasonable that no reasonable authority would have come to it. Browne-Wilkinson LJ dissented, holding that the council's decision was unlawful on the ground that it breached what he described as the fundamental, though unwritten, constitutional right to freedom of speech and conscience. Browne-Wilkinson LJ was unable to cite authority in support of his notion that such a right is known to English common law, and his view was not supported in the House of Lords.

In the House of Lords there were two speeches, given by Lords Roskill and Templeman, with which the remaining law lords agreed. Lord Roskill gave an extremely curious and cryptic speech in which he held that the council had acted unlawfully on grounds of procedural impropriety—an argument that was not even put to the court by the claimant's legal team! Lord Roskill also stated that, even though he did not need to come to a view on this issue given his conclusion on the procedural impropriety point, that he would have held that the council's action was *Wednesbury* unreasonable. Lord Roskill offered not a single reason why he would so have held. This omission is particularly surprising, given that his Lordship had accepted the council's argument on the point concerning the statutory duty to promote good race relations. Why was Lord Roskill prepared to hold that the council had acted irrationally when all it had been doing was seeking to promote good race relations in its area? It would have been nice to know. Lord Templeman did not even mention the statutory duty point, an omission even more stark than Lord Roskill's. Lord Templeman held that the council must have acted unlawfully as it had punished the rugby club, yet the rugby club had done nothing wrong: after all, it was not the club that had toured South Africa. It was an England tour, albeit one which had included three players who played for Leicester. Despite the fact that Lord Diplock's careful speech in the *Council of Civil Service Unions* case had been delivered only eight months before the House of Lords handed down its judgment in *Wheeler v Leicester*, Lord Templeman did not condescend to articulate which ground of judicial review he thought he was relying on when he held that Leicester City Council had acted unlawfully. If ever you are looking for a poorly reasoned case in English public law, *Wheeler v Leicester* provides a notable example.

Two things happened as a result of cases such as this. The first was that the courts themselves began to fear that they might have overstepped the mark. Two House of Lords cases that followed soon after *Wheeler v*

Leicester restated the law of irrationality in significantly narrower terms than had been favoured in the earlier cases. In *Nottinghamshire County Council v Secretary of State for the Environment* two local authorities argued that the Secretary of State had sought unreasonably to cap their budgets. The House of Lords held for the Secretary of State, Lord Scarman ruling that an argument on grounds of irrationality could be successful only if the local authorities could have shown that the Secretary of State had acted in a way that was 'so absurd that he must have taken leave of his senses'.[26] In *Puhlhofer* a husband and wife with two young children who were living together in a single room in a guest house applied to their local authority for housing under the Housing (Homeless Persons) Act 1977. Their application was refused on the ground that the family was not homeless: it had the room in the guest house. The family sought judicial review arguing that the decision of the local authority was unreasonable. The House of Lords unanimously held for the local authority, Lord Brightman ruling that for such an argument to have succeeded the family would have had to have shown that the local authority had acted 'perversely'.[27]

Insisting that for an argument based on *Wednesbury* unreasonableness or irrationality to succeed a claimant must show that the decision-maker has acted absurdly or perversely constitutes a significant tightening of the law after the expansionism of *Tameside*, *Bromley*, and *Wheeler v Leicester*. It may well be thought that the account of the law offered in the *Notts CC* case and in *Puhlhofer* is one that is closer to the intentions of Lord Greene in *Wednesbury* and Lord Diplock in the *CCSU* case. It is nonetheless interesting to observe who it was that lost out by the re-tightening of the law after *Wheeler*: Labour-controlled local authorities trying to free themselves from the constraints imposed on them by a Conservative Secretary of State, and a family of four crammed into a single bed-and-breakfast room with no laundry or cooking facilities, and no meal provided other than breakfast. Is it mere coincidence that it is when Labour local authorities and the under-privileged in our society go to court for protection that the court chooses to rein in the law?

Whether we should attribute this to nothing more sinister than bad luck or bad timing on the part of the litigants concerned, cases such as those considered in the previous paragraphs caused grave concern not just to the judges' critics, who might be expected to start jumping up and

---

[26] [1986] AC 240, at 247.
[27] *Puhlhofer v Hillingdon London Borough Council* [1986] AC 484, at 518.

down,[28] but also to more establishment figures. Thus, the second development that ensued as a result of these cases was a concerted and remarkable effort on the part of those who were leading advocates *in favour* of the potential and of the benefits of greater judicial involvement in public law and legal accountability to try to find ways of giving substantive judicial review law a more solid and respectable structure, so that at the least the judges could start giving some reasons for their decisions. Perhaps the most notable contribution to this debate was an article published in 1987 written by Jowell and Lester.[29] Their argument was that the *Wednesbury* test, even as refined by Lord Diplock in the *CCSU* case, constituted an inadequate basis as a justification for substantive review: 'intellectual honesty requires a further and better explanation of *why* the act is [or is not] unreasonable', they insisted.[30] To supplement *Wednesbury* and to give structure to it, Jowell and Lester argued that four 'substantive principles' of judicial review should be adopted: the principles of proportionality, legal certainty, consistency, and respect for fundamental human rights. Many of these principles, they suggested, were already lurking in the existing law, albeit only semi-visibly under the *Wednesbury* 'camouflage'.

JUDICIAL REVIEW AND RIGHTS: ARGUMENT AND REFORM

Jowell and Lester had fired the opening salvo in what was to prove a long campaign. For a full decade public law scholarship became overtaken by a series of arguments between lawyers and judges about how the constitutional system of legal accountability needed to be reformed and improved. For all the development of modern judicial review since the 1960s, it was clear to practically everyone that what had occurred was but the first step. What should the next step be? There were two levels to the debate. First there was what might be termed the internal argument, which focused on how the judges themselves might further develop the grounds of judicial review. Secondly, and closely related to the first, there was a broader and more overtly political debate about

---

[28] See e.g. J. Griffith, 'Judicial Decision-Making in Public Law' [1985] *Public Law* 564.

[29] J. Jowell and A. Lester, 'Beyond *Wednesbury*: Substantive Principles of Administrative Law' [1987] *Public Law* 368.

[30] Ibid., at 371, emphasis in original. Tellingly, they added: 'the reluctance to articulate a principled justification naturally encourages suspicion that prejudice or policy considerations may be hiding underneath *Wednesbury*'s ample cloak'.

constitutional reform, and in particular about whether the United Kingdom should incorporate the terms of the European Convention on Human Rights into its domestic law. Let us consider this broader theme first.

There had been some debate since the early 1970s to the effect that the United Kingdom needed a bill of rights, but it was not until the early 1990s that the argument started to rage. The debate had from the beginning been staged principally for the benefit of the Labour party. No bill of rights, whether modelled on the ECHR or not, could be incorporated without government support, and the principal political goal of the proponents of a British bill of rights was to persuade the Labour party of the justice of their cause. The Liberals/SDP–Liberal Alliance/Liberal Democrats had always been in favour, but as they were unlikely to be voted into power, their support was as much a hindrance as a blessing. The Conservatives of course were in power for the whole of the period we are now considering, and were unlikely to drop their long-standing opposition to incorporation. The Labour party was in the 1970s as deeply opposed to the idea of a bill of rights as were the Conservatives, although for different reasons. The old left was deeply scarred by what it considered to be an appalling judicial record in the fields of trade union and employment law. The judges had shown themselves time and again to be no friends of socialism or of collectivism, and the old left was extremely reluctant to grant to the privileged classes of the judiciary the further powers that incorporation of the ECHR would entail.

It is important to remember that this deep fear (and indeed loathing) of the judiciary continued to inform Labour party policy until well into the 1990s. It was not until John Smith replaced Neil Kinnock as leader of the party in 1992 that it began to subside, and it was not until Tony Blair replaced the suddenly and prematurely dead John Smith in 1994 that it began to be appreciated that the change was more than cosmetic and was likely to be permanent. Early into Blair's tenure as Labour leader, it became clear that unless something extraordinary happened Labour was going to win the coming general election, and the long period of Conservative government (and hence governmental opposition to a bill of rights) was about to come to an end. One result of these changes—from old to new Labour, and from Labour opposition to Labour government-in-waiting—was that the arguments over public law and constitutional reform took on a new intensity. Whereas before 1992 the argument had been carried out principally by academics, think-tanks, and pressure groups,[31] after this date the judges too started to weigh in.[32]

The argument about public law reform was not confined to a debate about whether or how to incorporate a new bill of rights. If Lord Reid had transformed judicial review law in the 1960s without recourse to external reforms such as a bill of rights, could not the judges of the 1990s follow suit and further develop the common law principles of judicial review, regardless of whatever the political outcome of the bill of rights debate would be? In a series of public lectures, written up into articles in journals such as *Public Law*, a number of prominent judges advocated various reforms that might be made to the existing law of judicial review. While there were variations of detail among the proposals contained in these lectures, they were all pushing in broadly the same direction: the rule of law should be strengthened; the courts should be seen as the guardians not only of the rule of law but also of rights and even of democracy itself; notions of subjecting the executive to the rule of law should be extended also to subjecting Parliament to the rule of law; and the courts should be ever bolder in intervening to right the wrongs of the polity, regardless of subject-matter.[33]

Unsurprisingly, it was not long before the sorts of ideas the judges were talking about on the public lecture circuit began to percolate through into the case law itself. Over the course of the mid 1990s two lines of authority developed: one concerning how rights-based arguments could be used to deepen judicial scrutiny of executive acts under the head of illegality in judicial review law and the other concerning how rights-based arguments could be employed to strengthen the doctrine of irrationality in judicial review. Let us now consider each of these in turn. The first case to consider is *R v Secretary of State for the Home Department, ex parte Leech*.[34] This case concerned a challenge to the prison rules. Section 47 of the Prison Act 1952 provided that 'the Secretary of State may make rules for the regulation and management of prisons . . . and for

---

[31] See e.g. D. Oliver, *Government in the United Kingdom* (Buckingham, 1991), the Institute for Public Policy Research, *The Constitution of the United Kingdom* (London, 1991), and Liberty, *A People's Charter* (London, 1991).

[32] See e.g. Lord Browne-Wilkinson, 'The Infiltration of a Bill of Rights' [1992] *Public Law* 397 and Sir Thomas Bingham, 'The ECHR—Time to Incorporate' (1993) 109 *Law Quarterly Review* 390.

[33] See, among many examples, Lord Woolf, 'Droit Public—English Style' [1995] *Public Law* 57, Sir John Laws, 'Law and Democracy' [1995] *Public Law* 72, and Sir Stephen Sedley, 'Human Rights—A 21st Century Agenda' [1995] *Public Law* 386.

[34] [1994] QB 198.

the . . . control of persons detained therein'. Under rule 33(3) of the Prison Rules 1964 a prison governor could read any letter to or from a prisoner and could stop any such letter which was objectionable. Rule 37A provided for an exception to this general rule and stated that 'a prisoner who is a party to any legal proceedings may correspond with his legal adviser in connection with the proceedings'. The applicant Leech, who was a prisoner, sought a declaration that rule 33(3) was *ultra vires* the 1952 Act in so far as it purported to enable a governor to read and stop correspondence between prisoners and their lawyers where no legal proceedings were pending. At first instance the application was unsuccessful, but the Court of Appeal unanimously allowed Leech's appeal.

The reasoning of the court's judgment was based on an analysis that centred upon prisoners' rights. The starting point was the decision in the House of Lords in *Raymond v Honey* and the dictum in that case in which Lord Wilberforce had ruled that a convicted prisoner, in spite of his imprisonment, retains all civil rights which are not taken away expressly or by necessary implication.[35] In *Leech*, Steyn LJ held that these 'civil rights' include the 'principle of our law that every citizen has a right of unimpeded access to a court . . . [which] even in our unwritten constitution . . . must rank as a constitutional right'.[36] Steyn LJ ruled that nothing in the Prison Act conferred on the Secretary of State a power to interfere with or to hinder the exercise of this right to unimpeded access to the court and that, on the facts, rule 33(3) did create a substantial impediment to the exercise of the right as access to a solicitor was a part of the right of access to the court. The Court of Appeal therefore allowed the appeal and granted a declaration that rule 33(3) was *ultra vires*. No authority was cited in support of the assertion that English law recognizes a judicially enforceable right of unimpeded access to a court. This was a new development, and was emblematic of precisely what judges such as Laws, Sedley, and Woolf had been arguing for in their lectures: namely, that the courts should use the law of judicial review to develop a jurisprudence of constitutional rights, which can then be employed to strengthen the position of the judiciary as against the government, just as Steyn LJ did in *Leech*.

The approach of the court in *Leech* was adopted and modified in *R v Lord Chancellor, ex parte Witham*.[37] The Supreme Court Act 1981, section 130 provided that the Lord Chancellor 'may by order . . . prescribe the fees to be taken in the Supreme Court'. Exercising this power the Lord

[35] [1983] 1 AC 1, at 10.   [36] [1994] QB 198, at 210.   [37] [1998] QB 575.

Chancellor made the Supreme Court Fees (Amendment) Order 1996, article 3 of which repealed an earlier provision under which litigants in person in receipt of income support were relieved from having to pay certain court fees. Witham, who was on income support, wished to bring proceedings in defamation, but found that he could not do so as he could not afford to pay the required court fee (a sum of £120). Witham sought judicial review of the legality of article 3 of the 1996 Order, arguing that it was *ultra vires* section 130 of the Supreme Court Act. The court accepted the argument and held for Witham. Laws J followed *Leech* in finding that the common law recognized a constitutional right of unimpeded access to the court, and ruled that the right 'cannot be abrogated by the State save by specific provision in an Act of Parliament'. General words, such as those found in section 130 of the Supreme Court Act, 'will not suffice'.[38] In *R v Secretary of State for the Home Department, ex parte Simms* the House of Lords gave its general endorsement to this rule, Lord Hoffmann stating that: 'Fundamental rights cannot be overridden by general or ambiguous words. . . . In the absence of express language or necessary implication to the contrary, the courts . . . presume that even the most general words were intended to be subject to the basic rights of the individual'.[39]

These cases were all decided before the Human Rights Act came into force. Their effect is significantly to strengthen the illegality doctrine in judicial review law where 'constitutional rights' are at stake. Constitutional rights, according to these cases, are common law rights that executive action may not interfere with, even where that executive action is apparently authorized by statute, unless the statute expressly states[40] otherwise. The difficulty with this rule lies in knowing in advance what the court is likely to hold to be a constitutional right. *Leech* and *Witham* concerned the constitutional right of unimpeded access to the court, and *Simms* concerned the constitutional right of freedom of expression. Before these cases were decided, while there was considerable authority behind the view that the common law recognized some form of right to freedom of expression, there was at best only scant authority in support

---

[38] Ibid., at 581.

[39] [2000] 2 AC 115, at 131. It is to be noted that, whereas in *Witham* Laws J had expanded the scope of the rule such that it would apply in all circumstances other than where statute *expressly* abrogated a constitutional right, in *Simms* Lord Hoffmann stated that the rule would apply other than where statute *either* expressly abrogated a constitutional right *or* did so by necessary implication.

[40] Or states by necessary implication.

of the view that prisoners and others enjoyed a right of unimpeded access to the court, and there was no authority at all for the view that this right ranked as a constitutional right that was capable of bearing the weight that *Leech* and *Witham* placed on it.

The second line of authority that developed in the mid 1990s concerned irrationality. The first hint that the courts might seek to adapt the doctrine of irrationality so as to strengthen it in cases involving constitutional rights came in a first instance decision of Laws J in 1995. The case, *R v Cambridge Health Authority, ex parte B*, was brought by the father of a seriously ill young girl against a health authority that had, in part on financial grounds, refused to sanction an expensive and experimental course of treatment for the girl that had been given only a slim chance of success. Laws J held that the health authority had acted irrationally, apparently on the ground that 'where a public body enjoyed a discretion whose exercise might infringe a fundamental human right, such as the right to life, it should not be permitted to perpetrate any such infringement unless it could show substantial objective justification for doing so on public interest grounds'.[41] The Court of Appeal unanimously allowed the health authority's appeal. There is no mention of fundamental human rights such as the right to life in the judgments of the Court of Appeal, which held that it was for the health authority, and not for the court, to allocate the limited resources of the health service.[42]

The approach that had been taken by Laws J at first instance in the *B* case was subsequently adopted in *R v Ministry of Defence, ex parte Smith*.[43] This case concerned four former members of the armed services who had been administratively discharged, in each case on the sole ground that they were homosexual. In seeking judicial review of the decisions to discharge them, they argued that the policy under which the decisions had been taken was irrational. In the Court of Appeal their counsel, David Pannick QC, proposed that the following test with regard to irrationality should be adopted:

The court may not interfere with the exercise of an administrative discretion on substantive grounds save where the court is satisfied that the decision is unreasonable in the sense that it is beyond the range of responses open to a reasonable decision-maker. But in judging whether the decision-maker has

---

[41] See R. James and D. Longley, 'Judicial Review and Tragic Choices: *Ex parte B*' [1995] *Public Law* 367, at 368.

[42] The decision of the Court of Appeal is reported at [1995] 1 WLR 898.

[43] [1996] QB 517.

exceeded the margin of appreciation the human rights context is important. The more substantial the interference with human rights, the more the court will require by way of justification.[44]

All three judges in the Court of Appeal accepted this formulation as an accurate distillation of the law: that is they ruled, as Laws J had at first instance in the *B* case, that irrationality is an elastic concept, which can be applied more or less tightly as the particular circumstances of the case require. In cases concerned with or touching on constitutional or human rights, as here, the courts will apply the irrationality concept so as to provide an unusually intense scrutiny of the government's decision-making.

In applying this test of irrationality the Court of Appeal unanimously concluded, as the Divisional Court before it had done, that the Ministry of Defence had not acted irrationally. Even under the intensified approach that is to be adopted in human rights cases such as this, the 'threshold of irrationality is a high one' that was 'not crossed in this case'.[45] The judgment of the Court of Appeal in this case was subsequently found by the European Court of Human Rights to be in violation of a number of provisions of the European Convention on Human Rights.[46] This was a verdict with substantial implications for public law, which we shall consider later in this chapter.

THE IMPACT OF THE HUMAN RIGHTS ACT 1998

It is clear from the cases considered in the previous section that constitutional or human rights were beginning to play a greater role in judicial review and legal accountability even before the Human Rights Act. Now that the Human Rights Act has come fully into force, what has been its impact on the law of judicial review? We examined in chapter 4 above the impact of the Human Rights Act on the legislative supremacy of Parliament. Here we are concerned with its impact on issues of legal accountability. Whereas in chapter 4 our focus was on sections 3 and 4 of the Act, here our focus is principally on section 6. Section 6(1) provides that 'It is unlawful for a public authority to act in a way which is incompatible with a Convention right'. There are a number of ways in which this provision alters the principles of judicial review law that we have been considering. First, the section reforms the general relationship between judicial review

---

[44] Ibid., at 554.   [45] *Per* Sir Thomas Bingham MR: ibid., at 558.
[46] See *Smith and Grady v United Kingdom* (2000) 29 EHRR 493.

and human rights. But more than this, it can also be seen to affect the sorts of ways in which rights-based arguments may be made under each of the existing heads of judicial review: illegality, irrationality, and procedural impropriety. Each of these will now be examined in turn.

Consideration of the first issue—the general relationship between judicial review and human rights—requires us to rewind a little, to the *Brind* case.[47] Brind was a journalist who sought judicial review of the government's decision taken in 1988 in the wake of a series of terrorist outrages in Northern Ireland to impose restrictions on the broadcasting of spokespeople for political parties that were associated with terrorist groups. Brind argued that the government's decision was irrational and also that it unlawfully violated Article 10 of the European Convention on Human Rights.[48] Brind lost the case, with both the Court of Appeal and the House of Lords unanimously holding that the government's decision was lawful.[49] What concerns us about the case is the treatment given to the ECHR argument. Both the Court of Appeal and the House of Lords ruled that, as the law then stood, the Convention could not be used in judicial review cases to show that the government had acted unlawfully. While the United Kingdom was bound by the Convention as a matter of international law, such international law was for the European Commission and Court of Human Rights, in Strasbourg, to enforce, and was not a matter for the domestic courts. This did not mean that the Convention had no role to play in English public law before the Human Rights Act, but it did mean that such a role as it could play was strictly limited. The Convention could be used as an aid to interpret ambiguous statutes[50] but it could not be used as a device against which the lawfulness of government decision-making could be assessed: the terms of the Convention had no role to play in judicial review. Clearly this rule does not survive section 6(1) of the Human Rights Act. Under the Act if a public authority acts in way that is incompatible with a Convention right, such action is

[47] *R v Secretary of State for the Home Department, ex parte Brind* [1991] 1 AC 696.

[48] Art. 10 is the provision of the Convention that concerns freedom of expression.

[49] Brind subsequently took his case to the European Commission of Human Rights, but he was equally unsuccessful there, the Commission holding that his case was manifestly ill-founded on the ground that the interference with freedom of expression was not disproportionate: see Application No. 18714/91, decision of 9 May 1994.

[50] As we saw in chapter 4 above, it is a principle of statutory construction that Parliament does not lightly intend to legislate so as to be in breach of the Crown's international treaty obligations. If Parliament does so intend, it will make its intention clear. Where legislation is clearly in breach of international law the courts will give effect to the statute, but where the statute is unclear or ambiguous the courts will endeavour to construe it so that it complies with, rather than is in conflict with, the Crown's international treaty obligations.

prima facie unlawful, and in a claim for judicial review the court could quash it.

We saw in the previous section of this chapter how the courts had developed, under the doctrine of illegality in judicial review, a new jurisprudence of constitutional rights (the *Leech*, *Witham*, and *Simms* line of authority). What is the impact of the Human Rights Act on this case law? All of these cases concerned subordinate rule-making (such as delegated legislation): an Act empowered the Minister to make rules; the Minister's rules were found to interfere with a common law constitutional right; the court held that the rules were unlawful. Even though the statute empowered the Minister to make rules, the statute was to be construed as allowing the Minister to make only such rules as would not interfere with constitutional rights. Where his rules did interfere with a constitutional right, the statute could not save him, unless the statute expressly (or by necessary implication) authorized him to make rules that interfered with constitutional rights. This is the common law position, as developed in cases such as *Witham* and *Simms*. The position under section 6 of the Human Rights Act is in similar terms. Section 6(1) provides, as we have seen, that it is *prima facie* unlawful for a public authority to act in a way which is incompatible with a Convention right. This provision embraces delegated rule-making by Ministers. However, two exceptions are provided for in section 6(2): the first is that it will not be unlawful for a public authority to act in a way which is incompatible with a Convention right if, as the result of a provision of primary legislation, the authority could not have acted differently. Thus, if an Act *requires* a public authority (such as a Minister or a prison governor) to act in a way which is incompatible with a Convention right, such executive action is not unlawful.[51]

The second exception provided for under section 6(2) is that it will not be unlawful for a public authority to act in a way which is incompatible with a Convention right if the authority was acting so as to give effect to or to enforce a provision of primary legislation which itself cannot be read or given effect to in a way which is compatible with Convention rights. The wording here refers back to sections 3 and 4 of the Act. These are the provisions, of course, that govern the relationship between human rights and legislative supremacy. It will be recalled from chapter 4 that under section 3 courts are under a duty, so far as it is possible for them to do so,

---

[51] The executive action is not unlawful, but the provision of primary legislation could of course be challenged under ss. 3 and 4 of the Human Rights Act.

to read and to give effect to primary legislation in such a way as to make it compatible with Convention rights. If such a reading is impossible, the courts may grant a declaration of incompatibility. It is an essential feature of the scheme of the Act, however, that even where such a declaration is granted, the validity, continuing operation and enforcement of the legislation remain unaffected. The second exception provided for by section 6(2) means that it will not be unlawful for a public authority to give effect to or to enforce statutory provisions that are incompatible with Convention rights.

Probably the most substantial difference between these provisions and the doctrine of illegality as the courts had developed it in the *Leech*, *Witham*, and *Simms* cases is the replacement of the concept of common law 'constitutional rights' with the statutory concept of 'Convention rights'. Whereas there was considerable difficulty in identifying in advance what the rights were that the common law would recognize as 'constitutional' for the purposes of the illegality doctrine in judicial review, the identification of 'Convention rights' is much more straight-forward, as these are specified in a closed list in section 1 of the Human Rights Act. In this sense, as Sandra Fredman has argued in an important essay, the Human Rights Act may be seen as a curtailment of certain aspects of the judicial adventurism that we saw in cases such as *Leech* and its progeny.[52] Under both the Act and the common law it is for the courts to enforce the rights, but whereas under the common law the courts could for themselves identify what the rights were that they could enforce, under the Act this task is removed from the discretion of the courts, as the Act itself lists what the Convention rights are, and the courts have no power to add to the list.

This is an attractive argument, but there may be a flaw in it. It is not clear from the Act that the statutory concept of Convention rights has *replaced* the earlier common law concept of constitutional rights. The common law concept may still be with us, awaiting further development. It is easy to imagine circumstances that somehow affect 'rights' but which do not affect 'Convention rights'. After all, the catalogue of 'Convention rights' is not a complete list of all rights known to modern legal systems: compare it for example to the more far-reaching list of rights contained in the European Union Charter of Fundamental Freedoms. Neither are all of the rights contained in the list of Convention rights always

---

[52] S. Fredman, 'Judging Democracy: The Role of the Judiciary under the Human Rights Act' (2000) 53 *Current Legal Problems* 99.

particularly well protected—some are more flexible than others, and some are relatively easily interfered with on grounds of the extensive exceptions that are written into the European Convention. In such circumstances, there is nothing in the Human Rights Act to prevent the courts from resurrecting the woollier common law concept of constitutional rights.[53] Fredman's desire that the Act will curtail certain aspects of judicial activism may prove overly optimistic.

While the Human Rights Act makes relatively little difference to the doctrine of illegality in judicial review, its impact has been rather greater in the context of irrationality. We saw above that the courts had accepted (in *ex parte Smith*) that the doctrine of irrationality could be modified such that it could provide a more intense degree of scrutiny in cases where rights were at issue. In the *Smith* case, the Court of Appeal found that even under the intensified version of irrationality, the threshold of irrationality remained a high one, such that on the facts of the particular case the administrative discharge of the four homosexual service personnel was found not to have been unlawful. As was mentioned above, after this ruling the applicants took their case to the European Court of Human Rights, where they were successful. It is because of this ruling, coupled with sections 1 and 2 of the Human Rights Act, that the doctrine of irrationality has undergone significant change. The legal position here is somewhat complex. Let us start with the decision of the European Court of Human Rights: *Smith and Grady v United Kingdom*.[54]

The Court held that the Convention had been breached in two separate respects: first, both the investigations by the Ministry of Defence into the applicants' sexuality and their subsequent discharge from the armed forces breached Article 8 of the Convention; and secondly the decision of the Court of Appeal in *ex parte Smith* constituted a violation of Article 13 of the Convention. For reasons that will become obvious, it is essential to keep these two aspects of the Court's decision separate: the Article 8 point on the one hand and the Article 13 point on the other. Let us consider the Article 8 point first. It is as well to set out Article 8 in its entirety. It provides:

---

[53] Canada adopted a bill of rights in 1982, but this has not stopped the Canadian Supreme Court from continuing to discover previously unheard of unwritten rights in Canadian constitutional law: see most notoriously its remarkable decision in the *Quebec Secession Reference* case: (1998) 161 DLR (4th) 385. In England, Laws LJ has continued to decide cases based on rights that he considers to be immanent common law rights, as well as statutory Convention rights: see e.g. *R (Prolife Alliance) v British Broadcasting Corporation* [2002] 2 WLR 1080.

[54] (2000) 29 EHRR 493.

(1) Everyone has the right to respect for his private and his family life, his home and his correspondence.

(2) There shall be no interference by a public authority with the exercise of this right except such as is in accordance with the law and is necessary in a democratic society in the interests of national security, public safety or the economic well-being of the country, for the prevention of disorder or crime, for the protection of health or morals, or for the protection of the rights and freedoms of others.

The structure of Article 8 is extremely important, and is typical of the Convention rights. Like almost all of the rights in the European Convention, the right to privacy in Article 8 is qualified, and not absolute. There are a small number of absolute rights in the Convention (Article 3, prohibiting torture, is one such right) but most of the Convention rights are structured similarly to Article 8.[55] The first paragraph of the Article contains the right, and the second provides for the circumstances in which it will be lawful for the State to interfere with the right. From Article 8(2) it can be seen that three conditions must be met before an interference with privacy will be lawful. First, the interference must be 'in accordance with the law'; secondly it must be 'necessary in a democratic society'; and thirdly the interference must be made in the interests of one of the legitimate aims listed (national security, public safety, economic well-being, etc.). Only interferences with privacy that satisfy all three of these tests will be lawful under the terms of Article 8.

In *Smith and Grady* the Court held that the first and third of these tests were satisfied on the facts of the case. The interference with privacy was in accordance with the law,[56] and was in the interests of a listed legitimate aim—in this case, national security and the prevention of disorder.[57] The argument in the case centred upon the 'necessary in a democratic society' test. There is extensive case law from the European Court of Human Rights on the meaning of this test. Essentially, it is a proportionality test. The Court has held that in order for it to be met the State must satisfy the Court that there is a 'pressing social need' requiring the State to act in such a way as to interfere with fundamental rights. While the European

[55] This is true of Art. 5 (the right to liberty), Art. 9 (freedom of thought, conscience, and religion), Art. 10 (freedom of expression), and Art. 11 (freedom of peaceful assembly and association).

[56] See para. 73 of the Court's judgment. This point was not disputed by the parties to the case: the government's policy on homosexuals in the military was given statutory recognition in both the Sexual Offences Act 1967 and the Criminal Justice and Public Order Act 1994.

[57] See para. 74 of the Court's judgment.

Court of Human Rights, being an international court, grants to the States which are parties to the Convention a generous discretion (known in the jargon of the case law as the 'margin of appreciation') as regards what measures are 'necessary' in a democratic society, this margin of appreciation is not so generous as to denude judicial review of all content. This is the first aspect of the test. It will be noted, however, that the test is not a simple necessity test: the terms of the Convention are that the interference must be not merely necessary, but necessary in a democratic society. A 'democratic society', the Court has repeatedly held, is one that exhibits values of 'pluralism, tolerance, and broadmindedness'.[58]

Applying these standards to the facts of the *Smith and Grady* case, the Court found that neither the necessity element of the test, nor the democratic society element of the test, was satisfied. As regards the former, the Court found that less intrusive means could have been adopted to meet the policy objectives that the Ministry of Defence had set out. The government's concern was that homosexual service personnel compromised operational effectiveness and reduced fighting power. Even if this were true, the Court held, any behavioural issues arising out of homosexual misconduct (or, for that matter, heterosexual misconduct) could be adequately dealt with by codes of conduct and disciplinary procedures. As to the latter, the Court found that the evidence on which the government's policy was based was itself based on little more than the prejudices of heterosexual service personnel towards homosexuals. Taking these findings together the Court concluded that neither the investigations into the applicants' homosexuality, nor their subsequent discharge, were justified under Article 8(2), and that Article 8 was therefore breached.[59]

Article 13 of the Convention provides that 'Everyone whose rights and freedoms as set forth in this Convention are violated shall have an effective remedy before a national authority'. Smith and Grady argued that the doctrine of irrationality in domestic judicial review law failed to satisfy the requirements of Article 13. This was because, in their view, judicial review law precluded the domestic courts from considering the merits of the applicants' individual complaints, and did not allow the courts to consider whether a fair balance had been struck between the general interest and the applicants' rights. The Court agreed, holding that 'the threshold at which the High Court and the Court of Appeal could find the Ministry of Defence policy irrational was placed so high that it effectively excluded any consideration by the domestic courts of the question

---

[58] Ibid., para. 87.   [59] Ibid., paras. 90–112.

of whether the interference with the applicants' rights answered a pressing social need or was proportionate to the national security and public order aims pursued'.[60]

What are the implications of the Court's decision in *Smith and Grady* for domestic judicial review and human rights law? Here again, the position is somewhat complex: the domestic consequences of the Court's ruling on the Article 8 point are different from the immediate consequences as regards Article 13. This is because Article 8 has been domestically incorporated under section 1 of the Human Rights Act, whereas Article 13 has not. Even after the Human Rights Act Article 13 continues not to form part of domestic English law. However, it may be that despite the (deliberate) omission of Article 13 from the scheme of the Act, the domestic courts might nonetheless have adjusted the law so as effectively to comply with the European Court's ruling on Article 13. The key issue as regards both the Article 8 and the Article 13 point is the doctrine of proportionality. Following *Smith and Grady* and the Human Rights Act, to what extent must the domestic courts now incorporate European understandings of proportionality into the irrationality doctrine in judicial review law? We have seen already the view of the European Court of Human Rights. What does the Human Rights Act say about the doctrine of proportionality?

Section 1 of the Act lists the Convention rights that are incorporated into domestic law. This list includes rights such as privacy and freedom of expression, in the interpretation and application of which, as we have seen, proportionality figures prominently in European human rights law. But it is the text of the Convention Articles that is incorporated under section 1, not the entirety of the European Court's case law interpreting the text. The concept of proportionality is not expressly mentioned in the text of the Convention: rather, as we have seen, it is a device that the European Court has employed in order to interpret the notion of necessity in a democratic society. Thus, while section 1 incorporates the text of the Convention right to privacy under Article 8 into domestic law, in so doing it does not incorporate the European Court's case law on proportionality as that doctrine applies to the permissible restrictions on privacy set out in Article 8(2). This does not mean, however, that concepts (such as that of proportionality) developed in the case law of the European Court are excluded from the scheme of the Human Rights Act, but they are dealt with in section 2 of the Act, not in section 1. This is

---

[60] Ibid., para. 138.

important because the form and extent of domestic incorporation under section 2 are significantly different from those under section 1. Section 2 provides that domestic courts determining questions that concern Convention rights 'must take into account' the relevant case law of the European Court. This is an interesting verbal formulation: must take into account. It means that the domestic court is obliged to consider the relevant jurisprudence of the Strasbourg court—there is no discretion here—but that having considered it the domestic court does not have to follow it—the instruction is merely to take it into account. It is this curious construction that now governs the role of proportionality in English judicial review and human rights law. In relevant cases, that is to say where Convention rights are at issue, domestic courts must take account of the case law of the European Court of Human Rights concerning the doctrine of proportionality, but they are not obliged by statute to follow it.

Even in the relatively short period that the Human Rights Act has been in force, the House of Lords has already shown some inconsistency in how section 2 should be interpreted. In the *Alconbury*[61] case, which will be considered in more detail below, two of the five law lords giving speeches made reference to section 2. Lord Slynn stated that 'In the absence of some special circumstances it seems to me that the court should follow any clear and constant jurisprudence of the European Court of Human Rights'.[62] This seems to give considerably less latitude to domestic courts than Parliament legislated for in section 2. However, Lord Hoffmann offered an interpretation of section 2 that was somewhat closer, perhaps, to what Parliament intended. He stated that 'The House is not bound by the decisions of the European Court, and if . . . they compelled a conclusion fundamentally at odds with the distribution of powers under the British constitution, I would have considerable doubt as to whether they should be followed'.[63]

From this rather lengthy account of the *Smith and Grady* decision and of the relevant provisions of the Human Rights Act, it can be seen that neither of these legal sources compels the courts to incorporate the doctrine of proportionality into domestic judicial review law. This is for two reasons. On the one hand the Human Rights Act specifically excludes Article 13 (the right to an effective remedy) from the scheme of the Act. On the other hand the Act relegates judicially-created interpretative

---

[61] *R (Alconbury) v Secretary of State for the Environment* [2001] 2 WLR 1389.
[62] Ibid., para. 26.   [63] Ibid., para. 76.

devices such as proportionality and the margin of appreciation to a far weaker form of incorporation (under section 2) than is enjoyed by the text of the Convention Articles (under sections 1, 3, 4, and 6).

Despite this, however, the House of Lords has now moved to embrace a doctrine of proportionality in English judicial review law. It is important to appreciate that it did so not because European human rights law compelled it, nor because Parliament mandated it, but of its own volition.[64] The leading case is *Daly*.[65] This case concerned a challenge to the standard prison policy in place at the time to the effect that prisoners were not to be present when their cells were searched. This policy had been introduced in the mid 1990s as a response to a problem which had arisen whereby prisoners would intimidate the prison officers conducting cell searches, and would learn their search techniques. Daly argued that the policy was disproportionate, in that it automatically excluded all prisoners from being present, even where there had been no pattern of intimidation, and it applied irrespective of what was being searched (in particular Daly objected to the application of the policy to the searching of legally privileged correspondence between a prisoner and his solicitor). The Court of Appeal dismissed Daly's claim for judicial review, but the House of Lords unanimously allowed his appeal. Both the law lords who gave substantive speeches (Lords Bingham and Steyn) based their decisions on proportionality.[66]

Lord Bingham held that the facts of the case constituted an interference by the prison authorities with Daly's common law right that the confidentiality of his privileged legal correspondence be maintained, and that it was therefore necessary to ask whether such interference could 'be justified as a necessary and proper response to the acknowledged need to maintain security, order and discipline'. Lord Bingham answered this question in the negative. He stated that 'Any prisoner who attempts to intimidate or disrupt a search of his cell, or whose past conduct shows that he is likely to do so, may properly be excluded even while his privileged correspondence is examined . . . but no justification is shown for routinely excluding all prisoners, whether intimidatory or disruptive or not, while that part of the search is

---

[64] Clearly the House of Lords was strongly *influenced* by both the European Court's decision in *Smith and Grady* and the Human Rights Act, but there is a difference between being influenced by something and being required to do something.

[65] *R (Daly) v Secretary of State for the Home Department* [2001] 2 AC 532.

[66] The other three (Lords Cooke, Hutton, and Scott) stated that they agreed with both the substantive speeches, expressly so on the proportionality point.

conducted'.[67] Lord Bingham made it clear that he reached this conclusion on what he described as an 'orthodox application of common law principles', and not on the basis of the European Convention or of the Human Rights Act.[68]

Lord Steyn ruled in similar terms. He explained that when applying the principle of proportionality the court should ask itself whether '(i) the legislative objective is sufficiently important to justify limiting a fundamental right; (ii) the measures designed to meet the legislative objective are rationally connected to it; and (iii) the means used to impair the right or freedom are not more than is necessary to accomplish the objective'. His lordship went on to state that 'the intensity of review is somewhat greater under the proportionality approach' than it is under *Wednesbury* unreasonableness or irrationality, such that it may 'sometimes yield different results':

First the doctrine of proportionality may require the reviewing court to assess the balance which the decision maker has struck, not merely whether it is within the range of reasonable or rational decisions. Secondly, the proportionality test may go further than the traditional grounds of review inasmuch as it may require attention to be directed to the relative weight accorded to interests and considerations. Thirdly, even the heightened scrutiny test developed in *ex parte Smith* is not necessarily appropriate to the protection of human rights.[69]

Daly can be seen as the conclusion to a fifteen-year argument about the inadequacy of *Wednesbury* unreasonableness as a ground of judicial review. Just as Jowell and Lester advocated, *Wednesbury* unreasonableness has not been abandoned—it remains as a residual category—but it is no longer at the forefront of substantive judicial review. At least as far as cases relating to fundamental or constitutional rights are concerned, it is the doctrine of proportionality that is now key, not that of *Wednesbury* unreasonableness. One issue left open by *Daly* is the extent to which English law will make use of proportionality in judicial review cases that are not concerned with rights. Given that the courts have embraced proportionality not because Parliament required them to do so under the Human Rights Act, nor because they were forced into it by the European Court of Human Rights, but because they chose for themselves to

[67] Ibid., paras. 18–19.

[68] Ibid., para. 23. We may question the extent to which Lord Bingham was being 'orthodox', proportionality not previously having been so unambiguously recognized in the common law, but the important point is that this was a common law decision, not one based on European human rights law.

[69] Ibid., paras. 27–28.

develop the common law in that direction, there is no reason to assume that the doctrine of proportionality will be confined to the context of Convention rights in the long term.

As Lord Steyn's speech in *Daly* makes clear, the shift from *Wednesbury* unreasonableness to proportionality is more than a mere change of nomenclature. The new proportionality is not the old irrationality in fresh Euro-friendly garb. Rather, it is a device which enables the judiciary to probe more deeply into government decision-making, but which also requires the courts to make clear the precise grounds on which they do so. Proportionality may therefore lead to greater transparency in judicial decision-making. But it may also signal the abandonment of, or at least a substantial adjustment to, the distinction, which has been central to the law of judicial review for forty years, between appeal and review. A decade before *Daly* the Court of Appeal and House of Lords had been invited in the *Brind* case to consider the introduction into English law of pro-portionality as a new ground of judicial review. Both courts refused the invitation. Lord Donaldson MR stated in the Court of Appeal that

> it must never be forgotten that [judicial review] is a *supervisory* and not an *appellate* jurisdiction. . . . Acceptance of 'proportionality' as a separate ground for seeking judicial review . . . could easily and speedily lead to courts forgetting the supervisory nature of their jurisdiction and substituting their view of what was appropriate for that of the authority whose duty it was to reach that decision.[70]

In the House of Lords Lord Ackner spoke in similar terms, ruling that use of a proportionality test would inevitably require the court to make 'an inquiry into and a decision upon the merits' of the matter and would as such amount to a 'wrongful usurpation of power'.[71] Whether the change in the law brought about by *Daly* should be categorized as being a 'wrongful usurpation' or not, what is clear is that in embracing pro-portionality, the courts have significantly altered the law of judicial review, and have further shifted the relationship between the executive and the judiciary at the expense of the former and to the advantage of the latter.

Before leaving the Human Rights Act and its impact on judicial review and legal accountability as a theme of public law, there is one further issue to be addressed. This concerns the impact of rights on procedural

---

[70] *R v Secretary of State for the Home Department, ex parte Brind* [1991] 1 AC 696, at 722, emphasis in the original.
[71] Ibid., at 762.

review—on the rules of natural justice. Article 6 of the European Convention on Human Rights provides that 'In the determination of his
civil rights and obligations . . . everyone is entitled to a fair and public
hearing . . . by an independent and impartial tribunal'. An issue which
has been heavily litigated since the Human Rights Act came into force
concerns the extent to which this provision applies to a variety of
administrative decision-making processes and procedures. As we saw
above in our consideration of the rules of natural justice, not all administrative decision-making procedures resemble criminal trials, and legal
notions of fairness, notions on which Article 6 is based, are not always
easy to apply in contexts of public administration.

The leading case on Article 6 and judicial review law is *Alconbury*.[72]
This case concerned a series of challenges to aspects of planning procedure. A feature of planning procedure is that in certain circumstances
the Secretary of State may 'call in' or 'recover' planning applications after
they have been considered by a planning inspector. Inspectors hold public
planning inquiries, and report to the Secretary of State. The Secretary of
State is not obliged to follow the recommendations of the inspector
(although in practice such recommendations are followed in about 95 per
cent of cases). Thus, there are cases in which the final decision-maker is
not the inspector, but is instead the Secretary of State. The challenge
posed by *Alconbury* was that under the terms of Article 6 the Secretary of
State is not an 'independent and impartial tribunal': rather, he is a politician elected to pursue certain policies. The Divisional Court accepted
this argument and granted a declaration under section 4 of the Human
Rights Act that certain provisions of the town and country planning
legislation were incompatible with Article 6. The House of Lords unanimously overturned this verdict, however, holding that as the Secretary of
State was acting administratively rather than judicially, and that as his
administrative discretion under the planning legislation was subject to
judicial supervision (through the ordinary law of judicial review) the
terms of Article 6 were not breached.

This decision is surely to be welcomed. Imposing an overly rigid interpretation of Article 6 on all species of public decision-making would lead
to an undesirable judicialization of the administrative system. As was
discussed above, sometimes it will be essential that what might be termed
the judicial values of fairness take pride of place (the criminal trial was
cited as an example of where not being biased and hearing the other side

---

[72] *R (Alconbury) v Secretary of State for the Environment* [2001] 2 WLR 1389.

are of critical importance to the overall fairness of the procedure). But the House of Lords in *Alconbury* was surely right to recognize that such judicial values of fairness are not the only values of fairness, and are not always going to be the most important values of fairness. In the context of major planning decisions, such as whether to build a new motorway or a new airport terminal, what is important is that the full spectrum of views can be aired and heard in a forum which is able to make sense of those views and to place them sensibly in an overall context of coherent transport strategy and planning. It is also important that whoever it is who makes the final decision on such delicate and hotly controversial issues is someone who can be held meaningfully to account for the considerable expenditure of public revenue that will ensue (motorways and airports being cheap neither to build nor to maintain), and is someone who can effectively weigh up all the competing considerations—any decision to commit millions of pounds of taxpayers' money to this project will necessarily mean that there is less for that project, and so forth. Such deliberative processes are the essence of democratic politics, and the House of Lords (in contrast to the judgment of the lower court) is to be commended for recognizing that even in the context of fundamental rights such as Article 6, there needs to be a degree of controlled flexibility in the way the courts apply the basic requirements of fair procedures. After all, Article 6 is called the right to a fair *trial*, and developers are hardly on trial when they are submitting their proposals to the democratic and professional scrutiny of the planning process.

THE REACH OF LEGAL ACCOUNTABILITY

In the preceding sections we have surveyed the content of the doctrines that the courts have used to develop a system of legal accountability in English public law, but we have not said anything about their reach or scope. Who may access these doctrines, and to whom do they apply? These are questions of central importance to public law. It is all very well having a more or less developed system of rules of legal accountability, but if only a select few can get into court to argue that the State has acted unlawfully, this will clearly act as a major constraint on the utility and effectiveness of the doctrines that the courts have taken such trouble to develop. It is equally important to know to whom the doctrines of legal accountability apply. The rules we have been considering are rules of public law, that apply to the government: that is, to public administration. But what qualifies now as 'public'? Modern life is characterized by a series of trends which seem designed to blur old certainties between public and private. In chapter 3 above we saw how the Conservative governments of the 1980s and 1990s sought to apply principles of privatization to the governmental sector as much as they did to the regulation and ownership of formerly public utilities. Even Labour governments now embrace and indeed positively encourage private finance initiatives and public/private partnerships (think of prison management, road-building, Wembley stadium, financing hospitals, the London underground, and so forth). Where do developments such as these leave the rules of legal accountability? Is it only the traditional executive (Ministers and local government officers) that is captured by the rules of legal accountability, or do government contractors, housing associations, hived-off agencies, and semi-autonomous self-governing regulators also fall within the scope of 'public' law? These are the sorts of questions that are addressed in this section.

Let us start with access. Who has standing to seek judicial review? Statute provides that only those with a 'sufficient interest' in the matter have standing to seek judicial review.[73] Of itself this test does not get us very far. The more telling issue is not what the test is but how the courts have applied it in practice. The courts enjoy much discretion here: indeed the entire procedure governing claims for judicial review is governed by extensive—some would say excessive—judicial discretion. This is true for questions not only of standing, but also of leave, and even of the granting of remedies. On the whole, the courts seem to have exercised their discretion as to who has 'sufficient interest' to bring proceedings reasonably generously.[74] We have already encountered a number of cases in which the courts could quite easily have held that the claimants did not have standing. Under a strict rule of standing, it is arguable that, for example, neither the *Fire Brigades Union* case nor the *Brind* case would have been allowed to proceed.

It is sometimes observed that the courts have been more generous with regard to individual claimants than they have been to groups. The *Rose Theatre Trust* case is often cited as an example of this: here a group of actors and other activists concerned with the preservation of the site of a Shakespearean theatre were refused judicial review of the decision of the

---

[73] Supreme Court Act 1981, s. 31(3).

[74] Indeed, sometimes perhaps even unreasonably generously: for a remarkable case of individual standing, in which a well known Euro-sceptic journalist was granted standing to seek judicial review of the government's decision to ratify the Maastricht Treaty, see *R v Secretary of State for Foreign Affairs, ex parte Rees-Mogg* [1994] QB 552.

Secretary of State for the Environment to allow an office building to be developed on the site, on the basis that the group lacked sufficient interest.[75] However, more recent cases granting standing to pressure groups such as Greenpeace and the World Development Movement, among others, have suggested that the *Rose Theatre Trust* case, rather than laying down any general rule, should be confined to its own facts.[76] As long as the group concerned has a well established and genuine interest in the issue, the courts will grant standing to seek judicial review to groups as well as to individuals.

There is a danger in extending standing too far, of course. Unrestricted access to the courts is not necessarily a good thing. It is important when considering the law of standing to remember what the courts are for. Courts are not a substitute for political processes. It may be that Parliament would be a more appropriate forum to hear some of these complaints: if a pressure group such as the World Development Movement dislikes the way in which government aid is being given to a developing country, why should it be in the court-room, rather than in Parliament, that the government is challenged? It has been a recurrent theme of this book that over recent years many questions that would formerly have been perceived as being political in character are now being transferred into the legal arena. The rules of standing in judicial review have played their part in this ongoing process of what might be called the judicialization of constitutional politics. These are not arcane rules of procedural technicality, but constitute the very place where the political is demarcated from the legal.[77]

Here again the Human Rights Act is likely to have a considerable impact, although not in the way that might at first be expected. Thus far in this chapter we have seen the Human Rights Act as being an instrument that gives sustenance to the further growth of judicial review. In the context of standing, however, it may be that the Act works more as a brake than as an accelerator. This is because the Act provides that arguments based on Convention rights may be brought only by such persons as are the 'victims' of the alleged breach of the right.[78] The victim concept is

---

[75] See *R v Secretary of State for the Environment, ex parte Rose Theatre Trust* [1990] 1 QB 504.

[76] See *R v Inspectorate of Pollution, ex parte Greenpeace (No 2)* [1994] 4 All ER 329 and *R v Secretary of State for Foreign Affairs, ex parte World Development Movement* [1995] 1 WLR 386.

[77] See C. Harlow, 'Public Law and Popular Justice' (2002) 65 *Modern Law Review* 1.

[78] Human Rights Act 1998, s. 7(1).

drawn directly from the European Convention, and case law from Strasbourg on the meaning of the victim test is markedly less liberal than
domestic English law on sufficient interest in judicial review. The extent
to which domestic courts will in practice allow the European case law to
narrow the rules of standing in public law is unclear. Once again, it will
depend on how the courts interpret section 2 of the Act: under this
section the European case law on the victim test must be taken into
account, but does not necessarily have to be followed.

If the courts have been reasonably flexible and progressive with regard
to questions of standing, the same cannot be said for their attitude to the
issue of whom judicial review may be sought against. Indeed it is the
cases that concern this question that probably illustrate the judicial
review courts at their antediluvian worst. Judicial review procedure was
reformed in 1977. Before 1977 different procedural rules applied depending on what remedy, or combination of remedies, was sought by the
claimant. In 1977 a new Order 53 of the Rules of the Supreme Court
replaced the old rules with a new, unified procedure, with a single rule of
standing (irrespective of remedy sought), and a greatly simplified process.[79] Almost immediately, however, the courts re-complicated the issue,
by reading into the new Order 53 a rule of 'procedural exclusivity', a rule
which was to dog judicial review law for a full decade, until the House of
Lords finally extricated itself from its stymieing effects in the early 1990s.
The rule of procedural exclusivity, introduced into the law by the Court
of Appeal and the House of Lords in *O'Reilly v Mackman*[80] provided that
irrespective of the remedy that the claimant sought, if the remedy was
sought against a public authority, the claimant would have to proceed by
way of judicial review under Order 53.

This was not what Order 53 was designed to do: on the contrary, the
purpose behind Order 53 was to give claimants a choice, albeit only a
limited choice. While claimants seeking certiorari, mandamus, or prohibition[81] would have to proceed by way of judicial review, those seeking an
injunction or a declaration would be able to proceed either by way of
judicial review under Order 53 or by ordinary writ procedure. In *O'Reilly
v Mackman* the House of Lords ruled that even this degree of choice
would not be available to claimants. The Lords ruled that irrespective of

---

[79] O. 53 was replaced by Part 54 of the Civil Procedure Rules with effect from October
2000.

[80] [1983] 2 AC 237.

[81] Since 2000 the remedies of certiorari, mandamus, and prohibition have been renamed
quashing order, mandatory order, and prohibiting order.

the remedy sought, all claimants taking legal action against public authorities would have to proceed by way of judicial review under Order 53. This ruling was important for two reasons. First, Order 53 procedure contains considerable procedural hurdles over which claimants have to jump if they are to be successful. Claims for judicial review must, for example, be brought within three months (in contrast to the six-year limitation period for breach of contract actions); claimants for judicial review must obtain the leave or permission of the court before proceeding—there is no right to sue; all evidence in judicial review cases is written—there is no cross-examination; and remedies are discretionary— even if the claimant wins her case on the merits, she will not necessarily receive the remedy she wanted.

More importantly, however, the ruling in *O'Reilly v Mackman* meant that it became imperative for claimants to be able to tell in advance whether their anticipated legal proceedings were against a 'public authority' or not. The consequences if a claimant got this wrong were fatal: a case brought in the wrong procedure would be thrown out for being in abuse of the process of court, regardless of its merits (such indeed was O'Reilly's fate). Yet it is not always obvious whether a body is a public authority or not. While Ministers and local government officers are clearly public authorities, there are very many bodies that fit neatly into neither of the categories 'public' or 'private'. The British Broadcasting Corporation, the Football Association, the Jockey Club, the City Panel on Takeovers and Mergers, and the Chief Rabbi are all examples of bodies or institutions that are neither clearly public nor clearly private. In the decade following *O'Reilly v Mackman* there was an enormity of litigation, which often went all the way to the House of Lords, on this preliminary procedural issue. Eventually the Court of Appeal and the House of Lords were able to formulate tests that seemed to work,[82] so that a degree of certainty and predictability returned to this area of law, and in two cases in the early 1990s the House of Lords relaxed some of the harsher consequences of the rule in *O'Reilly*, such that more exceptions to the doctrine of procedural exclusivity were allowed for. In addition, some actions that were commenced in the 'wrong' way could be transferred into the 'right' court.[83]

As with the law on standing, the Human Rights Act has an impact on

---

[82] See *R v City Panel on Takeovers and Mergers, ex parte Datafin* [1987] QB 815 and *R v Disciplinary Committee of the Jockey Club, ex parte Aga Khan* [1993] 1 WLR 909.

[83] See *Roy v Kensington and Chelsea Family Practitioner Committee* [1992] 1 AC 624 and *Mercury Communications v Director-General of Telecommunications* [1996] 1 WLR 48.

the question of who can be judicially reviewed. Recall that section 6 of the Act provides that it is unlawful for a public authority to act in a way which is incompatible with a Convention right. What is a public authority for the purposes of this section? Following on from the liberalization of the rule of procedural exclusivity in the early 1990s the courts had begun to approach the question of what is a public authority for the purposes of judicial review law in a more flexible, even fluid, manner. Will section 6 of the Human Rights Act draw the courts once again into the treacherous territory of having to draw bright lines between the public and the private, between those who are bound by the Human Rights Act and those who are not? It is already clear that the answer to this question is yes. The issue has arisen in the context of housing: is the provision of public housing by a private or voluntary sector housing association a private or a public activity for the purposes of section 6? Case law suggests that sometimes it will be public, and sometimes not, depending on a host of subtle factual distinctions.[84]

CONCLUSIONS: THE LIMITATIONS OF LEGAL ACCOUNTABILITY

The point here is not to go into vast detail about the various ways in which the courts have struggled to distinguish the public from the private, either for the purposes of judicial review law or in the context of human rights law. Rather, the point is simply that even when the substantive principles of legal accountability are extended, their effectiveness may be significantly curtailed by the limited reach of public law. In the previous chapter we identified a number of 'fault-lines' of political accountability. Is legal accountability also possessed of a number of fault-lines and, if so, what are they? Three fault-lines may be discerned from our analysis thus far: these we shall call the fault-lines of capacity, of potency, and of democracy.

The fault-line of capacity relates to areas of government that, for whatever reason, legal accountability fails to reach. The reach of legal accountability is constrained not only by such matters as the rules of standing and the public/private divide, but also, and more profoundly, by virtue of the fact that there remain several aspects of government that the courts prefer not to penetrate. For all the expansion of judicial review

---

[84] See *Poplar Housing Association v Donoghue* [2002] QB 48 and *R (Heather) v Leonard Cheshire Foundation* [2002] ACD 43.

over the past forty years or so, it is still the case that the courts maintain no-go areas that, largely by self-denying ordinance, they continue to keep out of. Commercial decisions by government, national security, and aspects of the royal prerogative are all good examples.

The courts have always been reluctant to extend judicial review to commercial and contractual disputes. Contract is regarded as being a private law matter—indeed, the law of contract is one of the cornerstones of English private law. When contractual disputes come to court they should therefore be governed by private law remedies and procedures, and not by the public law of judicial review. Now, as we saw in chapter 3, since the 1980s the government has tried to associate itself more closely with models derived from the private sector. Privatization, next steps agencies in the civil service, compulsory competitive tendering in local government and in the NHS and the trend towards government by contract, are all prominent features of this reform. The law has found it difficult to keep pace with this reform. As government has made greater use of methods of contractualization, so a gap has opened in the legal accountability of government, as the courts have struggled to lose their presumption that matters of contract are for private law, not public. Thus, when a firm of shorthand reporters challenged the way in which the Lord Chancellor's Department had conducted the tendering process in respect of the (highly lucrative) contract for court reporting, the Divisional Court, on an application for judicial review, held that it lacked jurisdiction to hear the case, on the ground that it was a mere contractual dispute and not a matter for public law. This, despite the fact that the claimant had no alternative remedy in private law.[85] Similar gaps have been made apparent in judicial review cases concerning issues as diverse (but as important) as the allocation of television franchises and rail privatization.

Decision-making in matters of national security is a second area of government from which the courts generally prefer to keep away. Lord Diplock stated in 1984 that national security is 'par excellence a non-justiciable' issue,[86] and in 2001 the House of Lords reconfirmed this view, ruling that the determination by a government Minister of what was necessary for the State to do (or not to do) in the interests of national security was not a question that could be judicially reviewed, but was rather a matter of judgement and policy for the executive alone.[87] Thus, if

---

[85] *R v Lord Chancellor's Department, ex parte Hibbit and Saunders* [1993] COD 326.
[86] *Council of Civil Service Unions v Minister for the Civil Service* [1985] AC 374, at 412.
[87] *Secretary of State for the Home Department v Rehman* [2001] 3 WLR 877.

the government decides that it is appropriate in the interests of national security for trade union membership to be prohibited within a certain branch of the civil service, or if the government decides that a certain individual should in the interests of national security be deported, there is very little that the courts can do about it—even after the Human Rights Act. This is true in the national security context whether the government's decision-making is based on statutory or prerogative powers. But there is a more general point about prerogative powers that constitutes a third respect in which the fault-line of capacity may be seen as limiting the efficacy of legal accountability. This point we encountered above (in chapters 2 and 3) in our consideration of the Crown and of its relationship to the rule of law, where we saw that, despite some advances, the law continues to suffer from a number of significant limitations when it comes to the question of holding the Crown to account.[88]

The fault-line of potency relates primarily to the issue of remedies. Even where the courts, through a judicial review case, do find (1) that the claimant has standing, and (2) that the respondent falls within the scope of judicial review, and (3) that the issue is justiciable, and (4) that the claimant's argument that the government has acted unlawfully is correct, and (5) that a remedy ought to be granted to the claimant—in other words, even in a case in which the claimant is successful at every stage of the argument, what can the court do to protect the claimant and to reverse the illegality of what the government has done? Damages are only very rarely awarded in judicial review, and even if they were more widely available it is far from clear that they could constitute an effective deterrent against a body with the resources of the State.[89] The court may quash government decisions, may order the government to fulfil its duties, and may prohibit the government from acting unlawfully. While the grant of any of these remedies may cause immediate inconvenience to the government, how difficult will it really be for the government reasonably shortly to be able to overcome their inconvenience? Suppose that a court quashes a decision on the ground that it has been made in a procedurally defective way. The court's remedy does not mean that the government may not make exactly the same decision again, albeit this time round using a different procedure. Equally, if a decision is quashed

---

[88] See above, at 51–60 and 81–9.

[89] Both European Community law and human rights law have recently brought about an increase in the extent to which damages and compensation may play a role in public law. These changes have been the subject of a variety of assessments: for a sample, see the bibliographical essay.

on substantive, rather than procedural, grounds, the government may well be able simply to remake the same decision, but on alternative grounds, or relying on an alternative source of authority. If this course of action turns out not to be open to the government, there is nothing to prevent it from going to Parliament to seek further authority, as we have seen repeatedly above.

Now, the government behaving in this way may well not have been what the court granting the remedy had intended, but this is beside the point. The courts can do nothing to ensure that the remedies they grant are executed in the manner in which either they or the claimants who brought the action would ideally wish. Here the system of legal accountability stands in stark contrast to that of political accountability. We saw in the previous chapter that one of the most important advantages enjoyed by the select committees of the House of Commons is their ability to follow up on their recommendations, to hound the government, maintaining the profile within Parliament of the issue that is of concern, simultaneously keeping the pressure on the government to address the issue properly. Courts can do none of these things. This is not to say, of course, that the grant of a court order against the government will never be effective, but it is to say that considerable care should be taken to avoid making the rather lazy assumption that the mere award of a court order will necessarily mean that the government has lost, and the claimants have won, the argument.

The third fault-line of legal accountability is democracy. Why should it be to the unrepresentative and—still—overwhelmingly old, white, male, upper-middle class judges that we turn when we desire to hold the democratically elected government to account? Why should it be for the judges (and not for the people of Leicester) to decide whether or not Leicester City Council acted appropriately in taking action against rugby players who had toured in apartheid South Africa? Why should it be for the judges (and not for Parliament) to decide whether homosexual men and women should be allowed to serve in the armed forces? And why should it be for the judges (and not for the electorate) to decide whether republican political voices should be broadcast or silenced in response to political violence in Northern Ireland? These are not rhetorical questions: they are not posed here as if they have no answers. On the contrary, it is clear that many would find the task of answering these questions relatively straightforward. The answer would be roughly the same in each case: namely, that it was the constitutional role of the courts to ensure that the minority was not being treated unreasonably by the majority.

On one account, it is undemocratic to have unrepresentative and un-elected State officials (judges) deciding constitutional questions such as these. But on another account, it is an essential feature of democracy that, while the majority should govern, it should not be permitted to govern in such a way as to trample upon the rights or interests of minorities. Politics in a democracy is the vehicle through which the will of the majority is identified and given authority. But as majoritarian politics will always find it difficult to accommodate and to protect the interests of minorities, particularly those minorities that the majority finds distasteful or disturbing, such protection as minorities are going to receive may well have to come from sources not under the immediate control of the majority—sources such as the courts of law. Further interpretations of democracy focus neither so much on representation nor on minority rights, but more on values of participation, of deliberation, or of openness. Here, the relationship between democracy and legal accountability will depend on access to justice (both in terms of the rules of standing and in terms of the affordability of litigation), on third-party interventions and the courts' ability and willingness to hear a plurality of viewpoints, and on the extent to which the courts can mediate, rather than merely adjudicate on, disputes.

All of these are matters of considerable subtlety and complexity, which here we can do no more than merely introduce. The point is simply this: that in assessing the extent to which a fault-line of democracy runs through, or undermines, any system of legal accountability, a great deal of thought will first have to be given to what is meant by, and what import-ance attached to, the values of democracy. It is not good enough merely to condemn the judges simply because nobody voted for them or because they tend to come from a limited socio-economic class. But equally, we all, and lawyers especially, must guard against complacency. It is unsafe to assume that greater judicial power, even greater judicial power that is ostensibly confined to the enforcement of human rights, is either a good or a democratic thing. And lawyers do tend to make exactly these assump-tions: that no constitutional problem is solved unless or until it is judi-cially solved, and that there is no constitutional problem that cannot be successfully solved by the judiciary. These assumptions dangerously underplay the significant role that political accountability, notwithstand-ing its imperfections, can and should continue to play, while simul-taneously they exaggerate the contribution that it is reasonable to expect the law to be able to make. As the struggle between constitutional politics and public law goes on, and as the relationship between political and legal institutions and methods of accountability continues to be renegotiated, let us just remember this. There are serious fault-lines running through legal accountability—fault-lines of capacity, of potency, and also, on some accounts at least, of democracy—and to overlook them or to pretend that they do not exist is to ask more of the law than it is able to deliver. And if we do that, it will in the end be the law itself that suffers most.

Bibliographical Essay

CHAPTER 1: ON CONSTITUTIONS

There is now a considerable literature on the scope and nature of public law, and on its relation to the State. General discussions are offered by M. Loughlin in his *Public Law and Political Theory* (Oxford, 1992), chapters 1–3 and *The Idea of Public Law* (Oxford, 2003), and by J. Allison in *A Continental Distinction in the Common Law: A Historical Perspective on English Public Law* (Oxford, rev. edn., 2000), chapter 5. For public law analysis of the State, see C. Himsworth, 'In a State no Longer: the End of Constitutionalism?' [1996] *Public Law* 639; N. Walker, 'Beyond the Unitary Conception of the United Kingdom Constitution' [2000] *Public Law* 384 and 'The Idea of Constitutional Pluralism' (2002) 65 *Modern Law Review* 317; and N. MacCormick, 'Beyond the Sovereign State' (1993) 56 *Modern Law Review* 1 and *Questioning Sovereignty: Law, State, and Nation in the European Commonwealth* (Oxford, 1999). On devolution, see generally N. Burrows, *Devolution* (London, 2000), and A. Tomkins (ed.), *Devolution and the British Constitution* (London, 1998).

Among the classics of Enlightenment constitutional thought are J. Locke, *Two Treatises of Government* [1690] (ed. P. Laslett, Cambridge, 1960); J.-J. Rousseau, *The Social Contract* [1762] (ed. M. Cranston, Harmondsworth, 1968); A. Hamilton, J. Madison, and J. Jay, *The Federalist* [1788] (ed. I. Kramnick, Harmondsworth, 1987); and T. Paine, *Rights of Man* [1792] (ed. G. Claeys, Indianapolis, Ind., 1992).

For analysis of the English constitutional order, the following are generally regarded as the three major classics: W. Bagehot, *The English Constitution* [1867] (ed. P. Smith, Cambridge, 2001), on which see A. Tomkins, 'The Republican Monarchy Revisited' (2003) 20 *Constitutional Commentary*, forthcoming; A. Dicey, *Introduction to the Study of the Law of the Constitution* [1885] (10th edn., ed. E. Wade, London, 1959), on which see the special issue of *Public Law* commemorating the book's centenary: [1985] *Public Law* 587–723; and Sir Ivor Jennings, *The Law and the Constitution* [1933] (5th edn., London, 1959). However, as Loughlin has powerfully argued, to imagine that English constitutional scholarship dates only from the mid-nineteenth century is not only mistaken but would also be to overlook an earlier, and arguably much more promising, approach to constitutional scholarship, more sociological and less scientific in method, that is exemplified, in Loughlin's view, by the work of John Millar. See J. Millar, *An Historical View of the English Government* [1787], (Glasgow, rev. edn., 1803) and M. Loughlin, *Public Law and Political Theory* (Oxford, 1992), chapter 1.

Contemporary accounts of constitutional law include the following: for major textbooks, see A. Bradley and K. Ewing, *Constitutional and Administrative Law* (13th edn., London, 2003), S. de Smith and R. Brazier, *Constitutional and Administrative Law* (8th edn., Harmondsworth, 1998), O. Hood Phillips and P. Jackson, *Constitutional and Administrative Law* (8th edn., by P. Jackson and P. Leopold, London, 2001), J. McEldowney, *Public Law* (3rd edn., London, 2002), and I. Loveland, *Constitutional Law: A Critical Introduction* (2nd edn., London, 2000). For edited collections of cases and materials, with commentary, see C. Turpin, *British Government and the Constitution* (5th edn., London, 2002) and M. Allen and B. Thompson, *Cases and Materials on Constitutional and Administrative Law* (7th edn., Oxford, 2002). For collections of essays, see C. Munro, *Studies in Constitutional Law* (2nd edn., London, 1999) and J. Jowell and D. Oliver (eds.), *The Changing Constitution* (4th edn., Oxford, 2000). Finally, for a fascinating attempt to tell the story of public law through a series of case-studies, see A. Le Sueur and M. Sunkin, *Public Law* (London, 1997).

For argument about the unwritten constitution and on constitutional reform, see D. Oliver, *Government in the United Kingdom: the Search for Accountability, Effectiveness, and Citizenship* (Milton Keynes, 1991). Further argument on constitutional reform may be found in: M. Foley, *The Politics of the British Constitution* (Manchester, 1999), R. Brazier, *Constitutional Reform: Reshaping the British Political System* (2nd edn., Oxford, 1998), R. Blackburn and R. Plant (eds.), *Constitutional Reform: the Labour Government's Constitutional Reform Agenda* (London, 1999), and R. Hazell (ed.), *Constitutional Futures: A History of the Next Ten Years* (Oxford, 1999).

On the political model of constitutionalism, the seminal contribution is J. Griffith, 'The Political Constitution' (1979) 42 *Modern Law Review* 1. Long associated with scholars at the London School of Economics, the model of the political constitution owes a considerable intellectual debt to Laski and to Robson: see for example H. Laski, *A Grammar of Politics* (London, 1925) and *Parliamentary Government in England: A Commentary* (London, 1938), and W. Robson, *Justice and Administrative Law* (London, 1928). See also Jennings, *The Law and the Constitution* (5th edn., London, 1959). Aspects of the political constitution model have been developed by Harlow and Rawlings: see C. Harlow and R. Rawlings, *Law and Administration* (2nd edn., London, 1997), chapter 3, and analysed by Loughlin: see M. Loughlin, *Public Law and Political Theory* (Oxford, 1992), chapters 6–8. On the relationship between politics and law, see M. Loughlin, *Sword and Scales: An Examination of the Relationship between Law and Politics* (Oxford, 2000), and A. Tomkins, 'In Defence of the Political Constitution' (2002) 22 *Oxford Journal of Legal Studies* 157.

On legal approaches to constitutionalism, see T. Allan, *Law, Liberty, and Justice: The Legal Foundations of British Constitutionalism* (Oxford, 1993) and *Constitutional Justice: A Liberal Theory of the Rule of Law* (Oxford, 2001). The work of Paul Craig and of Jeffrey Jowell has also been significant in advancing an understanding of legal constitutionalism: see, for example, P. Craig, 'Prerogative, Precedent, and Power', in C. Forsyth and I. Hare (eds.), *The Golden Metwand and the Crooked Cord* (Oxford, 1998), and J. Jowell, 'Beyond the Rule of Law: Towards Constitutional Judicial Review' [2000] *Public Law* 671. For an extreme position, see J. Laws, 'Law and Democracy' [1995] *Public Law* 72. Much of the work on legal constitutionalism owes an intellectual debt to the work of Ronald Dworkin: see, for example, R. Dworkin, *Taking Rights Seriously* (London, 1977) and *Law's Empire* (London, 1986).

CHAPTER 2: THE SEPARATION OF POWER

From the vast literature of contemporary political philosophy, the following are perhaps of special relevance to public law: J. Rawls, *A Theory of Justice* (Oxford, 1971) and *Political Liberalism* (New York, 1993), J. Habermas, *Between Facts and Norms* (Cambridge, Mass., 1996), J. Tully, *Strange Multiplicity: Constitutionalism in an Age of Diversity* (Cambridge, 1995), and P. Pettit, *Republicanism: A Theory of Freedom and Government* (Oxford, 1997). For an introductory text, see W. Kymlicka, *Contemporary Political Philosophy: An Introduction* (2nd edn., Oxford, 2001). A valuable introductory collection of essays is R. Goodin and P. Pettit (eds.), *Contemporary Political Philosophy: An Anthology* (Oxford, 1997).

For works on public law and constitutional history, see F. Maitland, *The Constitutional History of England* (Cambridge, 1908), Erskine May, *The Constitutional History of England 1760–1860* (London, 1861), W. Anson, *The Law and Custom of the Constitution* (Oxford, 1886),

D. Keir, *The Constitutional History of Modern Britain 1485–1937* (London, 1938), and K. Wheare, *Modern Constitutions* (Oxford, 1951).

On the eighteenth century idea of the separation of powers, the classic texts are Montesquieu, *The Spirit of the Laws* [1748] (ed. A. Cohler, B. Miller, and H. Stone, Cambridge, 1989), especially Book 11, chapter 6, and A. Hamilton, J. Madison, and J. Jay, *The Federalist* [1788] (ed. I. Kramnick, Harmondsworth, 1987), especially Nos. 10, 47, and 51. For commentary, see M. Vile, *Constitutionalism and the Separation of Powers* (2nd edn., Indianapolis, Ind., 1998), E. Barendt, 'Separation of Powers and Constitutional Government' [1995] *Public Law* 599, and N. Barber, 'Prelude to the Separation of Powers' (2001) 60 *Cambridge Law Journal* 59. For an account of the history of the separation of powers, see W. Gwyn, *The Meaning of the Separation of Powers* (The Hague, 1965). For two diverse and fascinating pleas for re-assessment, see J. Braithwaite, 'On Speaking Softly and Carrying Big Sticks: Neglected Dimensions of a Republican Separation of Powers' (1997) 47 *University of Toronto Law Journal* 305 and B. Ackerman, 'The New Separation of Powers' (2000) 113 *Harvard Law Review* 633, and for a stimulating economic analysis, see G. Brennan and A. Hamlin, *Democratic Devices and Desires* (Cambridge, 2000), chapter 11.

On English law and politics in the seventeenth century, there is an extraordinarily rich literature. What follows can be nothing more than the barest minimum sketch. To start with primary materials, the following collections are invaluable: G. Prothero, *Select Statutes and Constitutional Documents 1558–1625* (Oxford, 1894), S. Gardiner, *The Constitutional Documents of the Puritan Revolution 1625–1660* (Oxford, 1889), and J. Kenyon, *The Stuart Constitution: Documents and Commentary* (2nd edn., Cambridge, 1986). For a classic (Whiggish) interpretation, see J. Tanner, *English Constitutional Conflicts of the Seventeenth Century 1603–1689* (Cambridge, 1928). For more recent re-interpretation, see M. Kishlansky, *A Monarchy Transformed: Britain 1603–1714* (London, 1996) and J. Scott, *England's Troubles: Seventeenth Century English Political Instability in European Context* (Cambridge, 2000). On the earlier part of the century particularly valuable are M. Judson, *The Crisis of the Constitution: An Essay in Constitutional and Political Thought in England 1603–1645* (New Brunswick, NJ, 1949), W. Jones, *Politics and the Bench: the Judges and the Origins of the English Civil War* (London, 1971), and G. Burgess, *The Politics of the Ancient Constitution: An Introduction to English Political Thought 1603–1642* (Philadelphia, Penn.: 1992). On mid-century, P. Zagorin, *A History of Political Thought in the English*

Revolution (Bristol, 1997) is an accessible overview, and C. Hill, *Intellectual Origins of the English Revolution Revisited* (Oxford, 1997) remains a towering achievement: see in particular the chapter on Coke (chapter 5). On the later part of the seventeenth century, R. Hutton, *The Restoration: A Political and Religious History of England and Wales 1658–1667* (Oxford, 1985) and J. Western, *Monarchy and Revolution: the English State in the 1680s* (London, 1972) contain numerous valuable insights.

Works on the other topics considered in chapter 2 (i.e., the sovereignty of Parliament, ministerial responsibility, and the law and the Crown) are listed below, under chapters 4, 5, and 3, respectively.

CHAPTER 3: THE CROWN

The two most valuable constitutional analyses of the Crown are V. Bogdanor, *The Monarchy and the Constitution* (Oxford, 1995) and M. Sunkin and S. Payne (eds.), *The Nature of the Crown: A Legal and Political Analysis* (Oxford, 1999). Bogdanor focuses on the Crown-as-monarch, and is written from the perspective of a political scientist and historian. The essays in Sunkin and Payne are, despite the book's subtitle, all written by lawyers, and most focus on aspects of the Crown-as-executive rather than on the monarchy itself. Of particular importance are the essays by Wade and Loughlin (chapters 2–3). Also notable are the following, by J. Jacob: 'The Debates behind an Act: Crown Proceedings Reform, 1920–1947' [1992] *Public Law* 452, 'From Privileged Crown to Interested Public' [1993] *Public Law* 121, and *The Republican Crown: Lawyers and the Making of the State in Twentieth Century Britain* (Aldershot, 1996). J. Chitty, *The Prerogatives of the Crown* (London, 1820) and P. Hogg and P. Monahan, *Liability of the Crown* (3rd edn., Toronto, 1999) offer authoritative works of reference.

On the present Queen, the best biography is B. Pimlott, *The Queen: Elizabeth II and the Monarchy* (2nd edn., London, 2002). On financing the monarchy, see P. Hall, *Royal Fortune: Tax, Money, and the Monarchy* (London, 1992). On the constitutional crisis of 1909–1911, see G. Dangerfield, *The Strange Death of Liberal England* (New York, 1935), P. Magnus, *King Edward VII* (London, 1964), H. Nicolson, *King George V: His Life and Reign* (London, 1952), R. Jenkins, *Asquith* (London, 1964), chapters 14–15, and Bogdanor (above), chapter 5.

For legal analysis of central government, see R. Brazier, *Ministers of the Crown* (Oxford, 1997) and T. Daintith and A. Page, *The Executive in the Constitution: Structure, Autonomy, and Internal Control* (Oxford, 1999).

For argument that public lawyers should consider techniques of govern-ance rather than institutions of government, see J. Morison, 'The Case Against Constitutional Reform' (1998) 25 *Journal of Law and Society* 510. For analysis by political scientists, a classic statement is J. Mackintosh, *The British Cabinet* (London, 1961). For more recent contributions, see R. Rhodes and P. Dunleavy (eds.), *Prime Minister, Cabinet, and Core Executive* (London, 1995), and two works by Peter Hennessy: *Whitehall* (London, 1989) and *The Prime Minister: the Office and its Holders since 1945* (London, 2000). On the civil service and its reform since 1979, see C. Foster and F. Plowden, *The State under Stress: Can the Hollow State be Good Government?* (Buckingham, 1996), W. Plowden, *Ministers and Man-darins* (London, 1994), and C. Campbell and G. Wilson, *The End of Whitehall: Death of a Paradigm?* (Oxford, 1995). For acute legal analysis of civil service reform, see M. Freedland 'The Rule against Delegation and the *Carltona* Doctrine in an Agency Context' [1996] *Public Law* 19, and 'The Crown and the Changing Nature of Government', in Sunkin and Payne (above), chapter 5.

Issues of monarchism and republicanism are not widely written about by English public lawyers, although for a notable (pro-monarchic) excep-tion, see R. Brazier, 'A British Republic' (2002) 61 *Cambridge Law Journal* 351. There is by contrast a lengthy tradition of writing about law and republicanism in the USA: see for example, F. Michelman, 'Law's Republic' (1988) 97 *Yale Law Journal* 1493, C. Sunstein, 'Beyond the Republican Revival' (1988) 97 *Yale Law Journal* 1539, and C. Sunstein, *The Partial Constitution* (Cambridge, Mass., 1993). There is a rich, and rapidly growing, literature on republicanism in political thought: see for example J. Pocock, *The Machiavellian Moment: Florentine Political Thought and the Atlantic Republican Tradition* (Princeton, NJ, 1975), P. Rahe, *Republics Ancient and Modern* (Chapel Hill, NC, 1992), P. Pettit, *Republicanism: A Theory of Freedom and Government* (Oxford, 1997), Q. Skinner, *Liberty before Liberalism* (Cambridge, 1998), R. Bellamy, *Liberalism and Pluralism: Towards a Politics of Compromise* (London, 1999), and M. van Gelderen and Q. Skinner (eds.), *Republicanism: A Shared European Heritage* (Cambridge, 2002), 2 volumes. Little of this work seems (yet) to have penetrated the English legal academy, although for a notable exception, see R. Bellamy, 'Constitutive Citizenship versus Constitutional Rights: Republican Reflections on the EU Charter and the Human Rights Act', in T. Campbell, K. Ewing, and A. Tomkins (eds.), *Sceptical Essays on Human Rights* (Oxford, 2001), chapter 2. For the popu-lar case against monarchy, see J. Freedland, *Bring Home the Revolution:*

the Case for a British Republic (London, 1999) and T. Nairn, *The Enchanted Glass: Britain and its Monarchy* (London, 1988). For a (pro-monarchic) history of popular republicanism in Britain, see F. Prochaska, *The Republic of Britain 1760–2000* (London, 2000), and for an account more sympathetic to republicanism, see A. Taylor, *'Down with the Crown': British Anti-Monarchism and Debates about Royalty since 1790* (London, 1999).

A referendum was held in Australia in 1999 on whether it should remain a monarchy or become a republic. The referendum and the constitutional convention that preceded it spawned a considerable academic literature: see, for example, G. Winterton, *Monarchy to Republic: Australian Republican Government* (rev. edn., Melbourne, 1994), G. Williams, 'A Republican Tradition for Australia?' (1995) 23 *Federal Law Review* 133 (and the reply by A. Fraser at (1995) 23 *Federal Law Review* 362), and the special issue on republicanism at (1993) 28 *Australian Journal of Political Science 1*. For a note on the result of the referendum, see C. Munro, 'More Daylight, Less Magic' [2000] *Public Law* 3.

CHAPTER 4: PARLIAMENT

The leading texts on Parliament are the practitioner-oriented Erskine May's *Parliamentary Practice* (22nd edn., London, 1998) and the rather more student-friendly J. Griffith and M. Ryle's *Parliament: Functions, Practice, and Procedures* (2nd edn., by A. Kennon and R. Blackburn, London 2003). Still valuable is Bagehot's account of Parliament: *The English Constitution* [1867] (ed. P. Smith, Cambridge, 2001), chapters 5–6. A good overview is B. Winetrobe, 'The Autonomy of Parliament', in D. Oliver and G. Drewry (eds.), *The Law and Parliament* (London, 1998), chapter 2.

Questions of parliamentary reform are well considered in all the literature on constitutional reform (see above, under chapter 1): see especially D. Oliver, *Government in the United Kingdom*, chapters 3 and 8; R. Brazier, *Constitutional Reform*, chapters 4–5; and Blackburn and Plant (eds.), *Constitutional Reform*, chapters 1–5. A good summary is provided by D. Oliver, 'The Reform of the United Kingdom Parliament', in J. Jowell and D. Oliver (eds.), *The Changing Constitution* (4th edn., Oxford, 2000), chapter 10.

On the sovereignty of Parliament, for the Diceyan view, see A. Dicey, *Introduction to the Study of the Law of the Constitution* [1885] (10th edn., ed. E. Wade, London, 1959), chapters 1–3, and H.W.R. Wade, 'The Basis

of Legal Sovereignty' (1955) 14 *Cambridge Law Journal* 172. For challenges to this view, see Sir Ivor Jennings, *The Law and the Constitution*
(5th edn., London, 1959), chapter 4, R.F.V. Heuston, *Essays in Constitutional Law* (2nd edn., London, 1964), chapter 1, and G. Marshall,
Constitutional Theory (Oxford, 1971), chapter 1. For a valuable overview
of the arguments of these authors, see P. Craig, 'Sovereignty of the
United Kingdom Parliament after *Factortame*' (1991) 11 *Yearbook of
European Law* 221, at 222–233, and C. Munro, *Studies in Constitutional
Law* (2nd edn., London, 1999), chapter 5. For a scholarly account of
the sovereignty of Parliament in English constitutional history, see
J. Goldsworthy, *The Sovereignty of Parliament: History and Philosophy*
(Oxford, 1999).

For analysis of the relationship between parliamentary sovereignty and
European Community law, see P. Craig, 'Sovereignty of the United
Kingdom Parliament after *Factortame*' (above), H.W.R. Wade, 'Sovereignty—Revolution or Evolution?' (1996) 112 *Law Quarterly Review* 568,
and T.R.S. Allan, 'Parliamentary Sovereignty: Law, Politics, and Revolution' (1997) 113 *Law Quarterly Review* 443. Much of the literature on
public law and the State (cited above under chapter 1) includes analysis of
this issue: see especially N. MacCormick, *Questioning Sovereignty: Law,
State, and Nation in the European Commonwealth* (Oxford, 1999), chapter
6. On sovereignty and the Human Rights Act, see K. Ewing, 'The
Human Rights Act and Parliamentary Democracy' (1999) 62 *Modern
Law Review* 79, and T. Campbell, K. Ewing and A. Tomkins (eds.),
Sceptical Essays on Human Rights (Oxford, 2001), especially the essays by
Loughlin, Goldsworthy, Campbell, and Ewing (chapters 3–6).

On parliamentary privilege, see the following, all by P. Leopold: 'The
Parliamentary Papers Act 1840 and its Application today' [1990] *Public
Law* 183, 'Free Speech in Parliament and the Courts' (1995) 15 *Legal
Studies* 204, and 'Report of the Joint Committee on Parliamentary Privil-
ege' [1999] *Public Law* 604. See also C. Munro, *Studies in Constitutional
Law* (2nd edn., London, 1999), chapter 7.

CHAPTER 5: POLITICAL ACCOUNTABILITY

General works on constitutional accountability are few and far between:
most of the literature, especially that written by lawyers, focuses on the
accountability of specific bodies. There is nothing in English public law to
compare with the general assessment of accountability at the EU level
that is offered by C. Harlow, *Accountability in the European Union*

(Oxford, 2002). The classic overview of government accountability in Britain is A. Birch, *Representative and Responsible Government* (London, 1964). A more recent study is D. Woodhouse, *Ministers and Parliament: Accountability in Theory and Practice* (Oxford, 1994). For a valuable historical approach, see A. Beattie, 'Ministerial Responsibility and the Theory of the British State', in R. Rhodes and P. Dunleavy (eds.), *Prime Minister, Cabinet, and Core Executive* (London, 1995), chapter 8, and for a discussion of the relationship between political and legal accountability, see M. Radford, 'Mitigating the Democratic Deficit? Judicial Review and Ministerial Accountability', in P. Leyland and T. Woods (eds.), *Administrative Law Facing the Future: Old Constraints and New Horizons* (London, 1997), chapter 2. On accountability in local government, see M. Loughlin, *Legality and Locality: The Role of Law in Central-Local Relations* (Oxford, 1996), chapter 2, and I. Leigh, *Law, Politics, and Local Democracy* (Oxford, 2000), chapters 3–5. On the accountability of the police, see G. Marshall and B. Loveday, 'The Police: Independence and Accountability', in J. Jowell and D. Oliver (eds.), *The Changing Constitution* (3rd edn., Oxford, 1994), chapter 11, and S. Bailey, D. Harris and B. Jones, *Civil Liberties: Cases and Materials* (5th edn., by S. Bailey, D. Harris, and D. Ormorod, London, 2001), chapter 2. The leading work on the accountability of the security and secret intelligence services is L. Lustgarten and I. Leigh, *In From the Cold: National Security and Parliamentary Democracy* (Oxford, 1994).

On collective ministerial responsibility, as well as Birch's *Representative and Responsible Government* (above) among the more valuable general accounts are R. Brazier, *Constitutional Practice: The Foundations of British Government* (3rd edn., Oxford, 1999), chapter 7, and G. Marshall, *Constitutional Conventions: The Rules and Forms of Political Accountability* (Oxford, 1984), chapter 4. On the fall of Margaret Thatcher, see G. Marshall, 'The End of Prime Ministerial Government?' [1991] *Public Law* 1, and R. Brazier, 'The Downfall of Margaret Thatcher' (1991) 54 *Modern Law Review* 471. On the historical importance attached to collective responsibility, see S. Low, *The Governance of England* (London, 1904), chapter 8, and I. Jennings, *Cabinet Government* (Cambridge, 1936), chapter 14.

There is a far greater literature on individual ministerial responsibility than there is on modern collective responsibility. The classic statement is S. Finer, 'The Individual Responsibility of Ministers' (1956) 34 *Public Administration* 377. The leading modern monograph is Woodhouse, *Ministers and Parliament* (above), although this book now needs to be considered in the light of subsequent developments, on which see D. Woodhouse, 'Ministerial Responsibility: Something Old, Something New' [1997] *Public Law* 262, and 'The Reconstruction of Constitutional Accountability' [2002] *Public Law* 73. Rodney Brazier has considered aspects of individual responsibility in many of his publications, including 'It *is* a Constitutional Issue: Fitness for Ministerial Office in the 1990s' [1994] *Public Law* 431, and *Ministers of the Crown* (Oxford, 1997), chapter 15. For my own account of individual responsibility, focusing in particular on the Scott report, see A. Tomkins, *The Constitution after Scott: Government Unwrapped* (Oxford, 1998), chapters 1–3. Further valuable contributions on the Scott report and individual responsibility are to be found in the special issues of *Public Law* and *Parliamentary Affairs* that were devoted to the Scott inquiry: see [1996] *Public Law* 357–527 (especially the article by Scott himself, at 410), and (1997) 50 *Parliamentary Affairs* 1–189 (especially the article by V. Bogdanor, at 71). This latter collection was also published in book form, as B. Thompson and F. Ridley (eds.), *Under the Scott-light: British Government seen through the Scott Report* (Oxford, 1997). On the relationship between individual responsibility and freedom of information, see A. Tomkins, 'A Right to Mislead Parliament?' (1996) 16 *Legal Studies* 63.

Detailed studies of aspects of parliamentary procedure relevant to political accountability include M. Franklin and P. Norton (eds.), *Parliamentary Questions* (Oxford, 1993) and the now severely dated, but nonetheless informative, G. Drewry (ed.), *The New Select Committees* (2nd edn., Oxford, 1989). For commentary on the post-2000 reforms to select committees, see D. Oliver, 'The Challenge for Parliament' [2001] *Public Law* 666, and A. Tomkins, 'What is Parliament for?', in N. Bamforth and P. Leyland (eds.), *Public Law in a Multi-Layered Constitution* (Oxford, 2003), chapter 3. For analysis of the value that the Parliamentary Ombudsman adds to political accountability through Parliament, see C. Harlow and R. Rawlings, *Law and Administration* (2nd edn., London, 1997), chapters 12–13, and M. Seneviratne, *Ombudsmen: Public Services and Administrative Justice* (London, 2002), chapter 4. On audit and financial accountability, see F. White and K. Hollingsworth, *Audit, Accountability, and Government* (Oxford, 1999), and, more sceptically, M. Power, *The Audit Society: Rituals of Verification* (Oxford, 1997). For a fascinating case-study of how various forms of political accountability come together, see C. Harlow, 'Accountability, New Public Management, and the Problems of the Child Support Agency' (1999) 26 *Journal of Law and Society* 150.

CHAPTER 6: LEGAL ACCOUNTABILITY

The first major treatises on judicial review in English law were S. de Smith, *Judicial Review of Administrative Action*, first published in 1959 (now in its fifth edition (London, 1995) with Lord Woolf and Professors J. Jowell and A. Le Sueur as editors), and H.W.R. Wade, *Administrative Law*, first published in 1961 (now in its eighth edition (Oxford, 2000) by Wade and C. Forsyth). In addition to these works, P. Craig, *Administrative Law* (4th edn., London, 1999) offers a further now well-established account.

For criticism of the ways in which the courts have used or misused the doctrines of judicial review, see J. Griffith, *The Politics of the Judiciary* (5th edn., London, 1997), chapter 4, and *Judicial Politics Since 1920: A Chronicle* (Oxford, 1993), chapters 4–6; G. Peiris, '*Wednesbury* Unreasonableness: the Expanding Canvas' (1987) 46 *Cambridge Law Journal* 53; and J. Dignan, 'Policy-Making, Local Authorities, and the Courts: the "GLC Fares" Case' (1983) 99 *Law Quarterly Review* 605.

On the relationship between judicial review and human or constitutional rights, as well as the seminal essays cited in the text (at notes 32–33 of chapter 6), see also J. Laws, 'Is the High Court the Guardian of Fundamental Rights?' [1993] *Public Law* 59, 'The Constitution: Morals and Rights' [1996] *Public Law* 622, and 'The Limitations of Human Rights' [1998] *Public Law* 254; and Lord Irvine, 'Judges and Decision-Makers: The Theory and Practice of *Wednesbury* Review' [1996] *Public Law* 59 and 'The Development of Human Rights in Britain' [1998] *Public Law* 221. Much of the legal analysis of the impact of the Human Rights Act 1998 on judicial review law has been either technical (for an example see M. Supperstone and J. Coppel, 'Judicial Review after the Human Rights Act' [1999] *European Human Rights Law Review* 301) or focused on the rather narrow issue of the extent to which the Act will bind private parties as well as public bodies (on which point the preferred analysis appears to be M. Hunt, 'The Horizontal Effect of the Human Rights Act' [1998] *Public Law* 423). For commentary on the early cases under the Act, see R. Edwards, 'Judicial Deference under the Human Rights Act' (2002) 65 *Modern Law Review* 859, and P. Craig, 'The Courts, the Human Rights Act, and Judicial Review' (2001) 117 *Law Quarterly Review* 589 and 'Contracting Out, the Human Rights Act, and the Scope of Judicial Review' (2002) 118 *Law Quarterly Review* 551.

On standing and access to judicial review, see K. Schiemann, 'Locus

Standi' [1990] *Public Law* 342, P. Cane, 'Standing up for the Public' [1995] *Public Law* 276, C. Himsworth, 'No Standing Still on Standing', in P. Leyland and T. Woods (eds.), *Administrative Law Facing the Future: Old Constraints and New Horizons* (London, 1997), chapter 9, and C. Harlow, 'Public Law and Popular Justice' (2002) 54 *Modern Law Review* 1. Following the decision of the House of Lords in *O'Reilly v Mackman*, the law reviews published an enormous volume of articles on the reach of judicial review and the public/private split, most of which is now showing its age. Two notable pieces from this period are H.W.R. Wade, 'Procedure and Prerogative in Public Law' (1985) 101 *Law Quarterly Review* 180, and H. Woolf, 'Public Law—Private Law: Why the Divide? A Personal View' [1986] *Public Law* 220. A valuable international and comparative collection of essays on the topic is M. Taggart (ed.), *The Province of Administrative Law* (Oxford, 1997). The most sustained scholarly account is J. Allison, *A Continental Distinction in the Common Law: A Historical and Comparative Perspective on English Public Law* (rev. edn., Oxford, 2000).

For analysis of the difficulties posed for legal accountability by the growth of government by contract, see C. Harlow and R. Rawlings, *Law and Administration* (2nd edn., London, 1997), chapters 8–9, M. Freedland, 'Government by Contract and Public Law' [1994] *Public Law* 86, and A. Davies, *Accountability: A Public Law Analysis of Government by Contract* (Oxford, 2001).

On remedies, see C. Lewis, *Judicial Remedies in Public Law* (2nd edn., London, 2000), I. Zamir and H. Woolf's *The Declaratory Judgment* (3rd edn. by H. Woolf and J. Woolf, London, 2001), and M. Amos, 'Extending the Liability of the State in Damages' (2001) 21 *Legal Studies* 1. For a sceptical approach that focuses on remedies in EC public law but contains numerous insights of general applicability, see C. Harlow, '*Francovich* and the Problem of the Disobedient State' (1996) 2 *European Law Journal* 199.

On the relationship between judicial review and democracy, the classic critique remains J. Griffith, *The Politics of the Judiciary* (above), chapters 8–9. For a defence of judicial review as the protection of minority rights, see R. Dworkin, *Taking Rights Seriously* (London, 1977) and T. Allan, *Law, Liberty, and Justice: The Legal Foundations of British Constitutionalism* (Oxford, 1993). There is a huge American literature on judicial review and democracy. For a survey, see P. Craig, *Public Law and Democracy in the United Kingdom and the United States of America* (Oxford, 1990). Among the leading contributions to the American debate are A. Bickel,

The Least Dangerous Branch: The Supreme Court at the Bar of Politics (Indianapolis, Ind., 1962), and J. Ely, *Democracy and Distrust: A Theory of Judicial Review* (Cambridge, Mass., 1980). More critical perspectives are offered by M. Glendon, *Rights Talk: The Impoverishment of Political Discourse* (New York, 1991), and M. Tushnet, *Taking the Constitution away from the Courts* (Princeton, NJ, 1999). On deliberative and participatory democracy, see J. Elster (ed.), *Deliberative Democracy* (Cambridge, 1998), J. Dryzek, *Deliberative Democracy and Beyond: Liberals, Critics, Contestations* (Oxford, 2000), and S. Benhabib (ed.), *Democracy and Difference: Contesting the Boundaries of the Political* (Princeton, NJ, 1996).

Index